AF248547

PRACTICAL TRUTHS
FROM THE
PASTORAL EPISTLES

by
Eugene Stock

PRACTICAL TRUTHS
FROM THE
PASTORAL EPISTLES

by
Eugene Stock

KREGEL PUBLICATIONS
Grand Rapids, Michigan 49501

Library of Congress Cataloging in Publication Data

Stock, Eugene, 1836-1928.
  Practical Truths from the Pastoral Epistles.

  Reprint. Originally published: Plain Talks on the
Pastoral Epistles. London : R. Scott, 1914.
  Includes indexes.
  1. Bible. N.T. Pastoral Epistles — Criticism,
interpretation, etc. I. Title.
BS2735.S75   1983   227'.8306   83-6113
ISBN 0-8254-3746-6

Printed in the United States of America

CONTENTS

Foreword . . . . *vii*
Preface . . . . *ix*

PART 1 GENERAL INTRODUCTION

1. Three Letters: The Writer and the Occasions 1
2. Who was Titus? 6
3. Who was Timothy? 12
4. The Environment at Ephesus and Crete 19
5. Counsels to Timothy: Flee, Follow, Fight 27
6. Paul on Himself: The Lord's Servant 34
7. Paul on Himself: The Apostle 41
8. Paul's Retrospect and His Charge to Timothy . . . 47
9. Five Faithful Sayings 54
10. Three Hymn Stanzas 60

PART 2 DOCTRINAL TEACHING

11. Doctrinal Teaching: The Gospel, The Faith 66
12. Doctrinal Teaching: The Truth 73
13. Doctrine of God 79
14. God, the Savior 85
15. Doctrine of Christ 91
16. Christ's Second Advent 98
17. The Holy Spirit 105
18. The Holy Scriptures: Meaning 112
19. The Holy Scriptures: Practical Teachings 119
20. The Grace of God 125
21. Doctrine of Salvation: What and How 131
22. Doctrine of Salvation: Five Metaphors 138
23. Doctrine of Salvation: Life and Faith 144
24. Doctrine of Baptism 150

vi   Contents

25. The Church: Meaning 157
26. The Church: Visible 163
27. The Church: Worship 169
28. The Church's Ministry: Leadership 176
29. The Church's Ministry: Bishops 183
30. The Church's Ministry: Elders 190
31. The Church's Ministry: Deacons 196
32. Women in the Church 202
33. Care and Service of Widows 210

PART 3 FALSE TEACHING

34. Heterodox (False) Teachers: Introduction 217
35. False Teachers: 1 Tim. Chapters 1 and 4 224
36. False Teachers: 1 Tim. 6:3-10; Titus 1:10-16 230
37. False Teachers: 2 Tim. 3:1-13 234
38. Dealing with Heretics: 1 Tim. 1:19-20; 4:6-12 . . .242
39. Dealing with Heretics: 2 Tim. 2:22-26 248

PART 4 ETHICAL TEACHING

40. Ethical Teaching of the Epistles: Good Works . .254
41. Ethical Teaching: Godly, Righteous and Sober .261
42. Ethical Teaching: Love and Purity 269
43. Ethical Teaching: Passive Graces 275
44. Ethical Teaching: Active Graces 282
45. Ethical Teaching: Christian Servants 289
46. Other Ethical Teachings 296

CONCLUSION

47. The Last Letter 304
48. Seventeen Names 310
49. Paul's Trial and Imprisonment 317
50. Paul's Last Days and Continuous Influence 325
Index of Topics, Biblical Names,
Writers, Works, and Greek Words 333
Bibliography 341

FOREWORD

When I was teaching Pastoral Theology to seminary students, I often wished that *Plain Talks On The Pastoral Epistles* had been available as a text. Now that it is available, I am no longer teaching! But at least this valuable book is now back in print, and I commend Kregel Publications for making this possible. Why am I enthusiastic? Because I know of no book on pastoral theology, based on the Pastoral Epistles, that contains more solid scholarship, more practical application, and is more of a delight to read. It is a perfect, companion volume to W.E. Chadwick's *The Pastoral Teaching of St. Paul* which, I trust, will also soon be reprinted.*

To begin with, this book is not cluttered with a lot of verbiage or scholarly apparatus. The scholarship is there! Dr. Stock's purpose, however, is not to impress the reader but to express the truth as he sees it. His disarming style has both clarity and beauty. The book is a joy to read.

The remarkable thing is this: Eugene Stock did not enter the ministry until he was thirty-seven years old! Born February 26, 1836, Eugene Stock was educated in private schools and then entered the business world and became quite successful. He became involved in the Church of England Sunday School Institute in 1867, and in 1873 was named Editor of the Church Missionary Society's Publications, a position he held until 1902. He was Diocesan Lay Reader for London, Rochester, and

---

*Retitled *Pastoral Teaching of Paul* , Kregel Publications, Grand Rapids, 1984.

Winchester. In 1908, the University of Durham honored him with the degree, Doctor of Canon Law.

Dr. Stock travelled a good deal for the Church Missionary Society, visiting the Colonies in 1892 and 1895, India in 1892-93, and the United States in 1900. He also did a good deal of writing. He contributed the "English Teachers' Notes" to the American *Sunday School Journal* (1873-81), wrote a number of study books and books about missions, and published his autobiography, *My Recollections,* in 1909. His most monumental work is the four-volume *History of the Church Missionary Society.*

However, I think that *Plain Talks On The Pastoral Epistles* (now published as *Practical Truths from the Pastoral Epistles*) is the best and most useful book of all that he wrote. You need not agree with all of his interpretations and conclusions to benefit from his studies. When I was writing my book *Be Faithful,* on the Pastoral Epistles, I turned to Stock's book more than to any other single volume in my library. In his modest Preface, Dr. Stock disclaims any homiletical purpose behind this book; and yet the astute preacher will find dozens of "sermon nuggets" in these chapters.

Dr. Stock published *Plain Talks On The Pastoral Epistles* in 1914, after a long and full life of Christian ministry. He gives to us the mature fruit of study, meditation, and service, and we are the grateful benefactors. He died September 7, 1928, at the age of ninety-two.

This is a book to read and to re-read, and to share with others who are in the ministry and who believe in the importance of the local church.

WARREN W. WIERSBE

PREFACE

The Pastoral Epistles seem to be a comparatively neglected part of the New Testament. No doubt some people who read the Bible chapter by chapter come to them in due course and do not pass them over. But when a particular chapter is to be chosen for reading, whether it is in private, in the family, or a prayer meeting, seldom is it taken from these Epistles, in comparison with the frequent selection from the Epistles to the Romans or the Ephesians or the Hebrews—to say nothing of the Four Gospels.

It is true that the Pastoral Epistles contain a good many of the more familiar individual texts, such as "Christ Jesus came into the world to save sinners," "The love of money is the root of all evil" (A.V.), "I know whom I have believed," etc., "All Scripture is given by inspiration of God," "Instant in season, out of season," "Unto the pure all things are pure." But I am not sure how many persons who quote these texts so glibly know their Bible references. One thing about these Epistles everybody knows, viz., that St. Paul advises Timothy to take a little wine for his stomach's sake. Also many seem to believe that there is little in them but rules about bishops, deacons, widows, subjection of women, and dark descriptions of rising heresies. How many have any idea of the mass of important teaching, both doctrinal and ethical, contained in these three Letters?

To correct this false impression, and to draw out the impressive teaching of the three Letters, is the object of this work. I do not write for scholars, but for the plain men and women who are glad to be helped in their simple Bible studies. I desire to repel no one from my pages by the use, in the text, of Greek characters. I frequently mention Greek words, with the express purpose of showing the extreme interest attaching to them, an interest which any intelligent reader can share, even if he knows nothing of the language; but I print such words, in the text, in roman letters. Greek characters are, however, not excluded from the occasional footnotes. The initials, A.V., R.V., O.T., N.T. etc., are sufficiently familiar for use; also the symbol LXX for the Septuagint Greek translation of the Old Testament.

The book is not a commentary. It does not take the Epistles chapter by chapter, nor comment on them verse by verse. The treatment is topical. After some introductory remarks, I take up the various doctrinal, ecclesiastical, and ethical topics to which the Epistles refer, however incidentally. So far as I am aware, this method of treatment has at least the merit of novelty.

The book is not primarily homiletical. It is not directly hortatory or devotional in character. Nevertheless, it does frequently suggest spiritual applications, and it is written with the earnest desire that its readers develop a practical Christian life.

1
THREE LETTERS:
THE WRITER AND THE OCCASIONS

THAT the three Pastoral Epistles were written by St. Paul was never questioned until the nineteenth century, except by Marcion and other heretical writers in early times. Although other Epistles were not universally accepted as canonical Scripture for two or three hundred years, these were generally received in the Church, and they are quoted from by several of the Fathers in the second century. It was reserved for modern German critics to raise the question.

The grounds upon which St. Paul's authorship is disputed are four :—

1. It is urged that they cannot be fitted into the history of his travels as recorded in the Acts. This is quite true in itself. There have been attempts to find a place for them within that period, but none are satisfactory, not even the latest, by Professor

Vernon Bartlet. The generally accepted view, however, is that after the " two years " of Acts xxviii. 30, St. Paul was released by the Roman authorities and resumed his work and his journeys ; that the First Epistle to Timothy and that to Titus were written during that period, and the Second to Timothy during a second imprisonment at Rome which ended in his execution. This view, held by almost all the recognised commentators, has lately been freshly and cogently set forth by Professor Ramsay.

2. It is urged that the particular heresies referred to in the Epistles belong to the second century, and not to the first. It is needless to particularise here, but one point may be mentioned. The objectors do not seem to notice that while Greek speculations were no doubt rife at Ephesus in the first century, the teachings denounced in these Epistles are mostly of Jewish origin. It was Jewish scribes who professed to be " teachers of the law " (I. i. 7), but built up strange doctrines on " fables and endless genealogies " (I. i. 4, Tit. i. 14, iii. 9). These certainly belonged to the first century.

3. It is urged that these Epistles reveal a more developed ecclesiastical organization than we find in the rest of the New Testament. Certainly this indicates that they were written later than St. Paul's other Epistles ; but critics who would date them in the second century forget that quite early in that century the organisation was more advanced than we find here. The Episcopate, in particular, had by that time passed from the transition state, in which it emerged from apostolic times, to the settled

arrangement which became permanent. At least, it was so in the East, although, no doubt, the West was slower in this development ; and it was to Churches in the East that these Epistles were written.

4. The only serious difficulty in the way of accepting the Pauline authorship is an internal one. The language used differs in many ways from that of St. Paul's other writings. Several of his characteristic expressions do not appear : for instance, the Greek words which we render " boasting " or "glorying," which he uses sixty times in the other Epistles and not once here ; and the words for " reveal " and " revelation," which we find twenty-seven times elsewhere and not once here. Even in smaller matters we are puzzled ; for instance, why should he never in these Letters use the common word for " with " (*sun*), which he largely uses elsewhere, but always here puts another word (*meta*) instead ? Moreover, there are in the three Letters about 170 words not used by him elsewhere, and some of these are remarkable ; for instance, the word rendered " godliness " (*eusebeia*), which we find ten times here, and which he nowhere else uses. Also there are words which, though to be seen elsewhere, are found here far more frequently ; for instance, one of the two words for " good " (*kalos*) occurs twice as often as in all the other Epistles put together ; and the word for " Saviour " (*sotēr*) is used ten times here and only twice elsewhere. He calls God the Father " Saviour " six times here, and never elsewhere. He is fond of words beginning with *philo* (lover or loving), and uses seventeen such words in his Epistles generally (two being the originals of our " philanthropy " and

" philosophy "), and ten of these are only found in the Pastorals. Many other cases will come before us in future chapters. One notable difference between the letters to Timothy and St. Paul's other Epistles is that in the salutation he adds " mercy " to the ordinary " grace and peace " ; " grace, mercy, and peace, from God the Father. . . ." Liddon quaintly suggests that " mercy " is added to Timothy because he was a bishop, and " bishops, on account of their responsibilities, especially need it " !

There is, however, another side to the question. There are many phrases in the Pastoral Epistles which are exactly like St. Paul's phrases elsewhere, and which may well balance against the differences ; for instance, the peculiar phrase about the Gospel being " intrusted " or " committed " to him. There are also favourite words of his, like " manifest " and " mystery," and words beginning with " hyper," and many words, some of them rare ones, which occur in the New Testament only in St. Paul's writings, but in both the Pastorals and others, such as " grave," " meekness," " goodness," " perdition," " heap up," " earthen," " gentle," " boaster," etc. This is a strong evidence of his authorship.

Again, if St. Paul did not write these letters, who did ? All sorts of theories have been started, every one of which is more or less futile. So we may confidently accept the Church's verdict from the beginning, and rejoice to have in these three wonderful Letters the genuine work of the great Apostle, written under the inspiration of the Holy Ghost.

We may think of St. Paul's career after the date to which the Acts brings us as follows :—

1. It was his intention to go to Spain, as he tells us in Rom. xv. 24, 28. Clement of Rome, in his Epistle to Corinth, written a few years after St. Paul's death, tells us that the apostle did " reach the farthest bound of the west," which must mean Spain or Britain [1]; and a document of about A.D. 170, known to us as " the Muratorian Canon," mentions " the departure of Paul from the city to Spain "; so it may well be that he did carry out his intention. On the other hand, Phil. ii. 24 and Philem. 22, written during his first Roman imprisonment, certainly suggest that he meant to go East.

2. On his return to the East he visited Crete and left Titus there to carry on his work (Tit. i. 5). Afterwards he was in Asia (the small Roman province) ; certainly at Ephesus (I. i. 3) ; then in Macedonia (I. i. 3) ; then in Epirus, spending the winter at Nicopolis (Tit. iii. 12) ; and probably from that city he wrote the First Epistle to Timothy, whom he had left at Ephesus, and the Epistle to Titus, whom he had left in Crete. From the former letter (iv. 13) it appears that he was expecting to go back again to Ephesus.

3. Subsequently he was at Ephesus once more (II. i. 18) ; at Miletus (II. iv. 20) ; at Troas (II. iv. 13) ; perhaps at Corinth (II. iv. 20). Then came his arrest, we know not where ; his second imprisonment at Rome ; his trial (II. iv. 16) ; his writing the Second Epistle to Timothy ; his execution.

If his release at the end of the " two years " of Acts xxviii. was in A.D. 63, three or four years would

---

[1] Some have said it meant Rome, but how could Rome be so called in a letter written at Rome ?

suffice for these journeys, and he may have been put to death in A.D. 66 or 67, or early in 68, before the death of the Emperor Nero.

2
WHO WAS TITUS?

LET us now inquire who the two men were to whom these Epistles are addressed. And we will take Titus first, as he was probably older than Timothy, and certainly was earlier a companion of St. Paul.

It is remarkable that Titus is never once named in the Acts. The R.V., following some MSS., adds the name Titus to Justus, the Greek to whose house St. Paul went at Corinth at a particular epoch in his mission there (Acts xviii. 7) ; but it is not likely that this was the Titus of the Epistle, who had been with the Apostle long before that time.

The earliest mention of him is in Gal. ii. 1, where St. Paul says, " I went up again to Jerusalem with Barnabas, taking Titus also with me." Whether this was the visit recorded in Acts xv., as generally considered, or the visit of Acts xi. 30, as Professor Ramsay urges, does not concern us here. Either way it was before St. Paul chose Timothy as a companion, as recorded in Acts xvi. 1–3.

This passage in Galatians shows that Titus was a Gentile. " Not even Titus, who was with me, being

a Greek, was compelled to be circumcised " (ver. 3).
We may confidently believe him to have been a convert of St. Paul's, as the Apostle calls him " my true
child after a common faith " (Tit. i. 4). The A.V.
has " my own son," but the Greek word is the regular
one for " child " (*teknon*). The word for " true " or
" own " has the sense of genuineness, and perhaps the
best rendering is that of Dean Spence-Jones, " my
very own child "; the words " after a common
faith " showing that spiritual and not natural parent-
age is meant. We can fancy St. Paul taking his
convert up to the Jewish Christians at Jerusalem
with joy, and vindicating the young Greek's right to
a place in the Church without by the rite of circumcision becoming a Jew.

We next find him in the Second Epistle to the
Corinthians. St. Paul had come from Ephesus to
Troas, expecting to meet him there ; see ii. 12 :
" Now, when I came to Troas for the Gospel of
Christ . . . I had no relief for my spirit because I
found not Titus my brother." Why was the Apostle
expecting to meet Titus, and why was he so sadly
disappointed ? In answering this question let me
try to sketch the position as it most probably was,
while admitting that no explanation can be quite
certain.

We must think of St. Paul as in the midst of his
" three years' " ministry at Ephesus (see Acts xx. 31).
During that time he had much anxiety about the
Church at Corinth, which he had founded three or
four years before. He wrote a letter, which has not
come down to us, but which he refers to in 1 Cor. v. 9,
and then, in consequence of a letter from the Corin-

thians and of other information (1 Cor. i. 11, vii. 1), he wrote what we call the First Epistle. This was probably taken to Corinth by Titus, who while there started the " collection for the poor saints " in Judæa (1 Cor. xvi. 1 ; see 2 Cor. viii. 6, where it is said that he had " made a beginning before "). Then he was sent again, a year later (see 2 Cor. viii. 10, " a year ago," and comp. ix. 2), partly to further the collection and partly to deal with the grave evils in the Church. This time he took a third letter from St. Paul, which again is not preserved,[1] but which is referred to in 2 Cor. ii. 1–4 and vii. 8, written " out of much affliction and anguish of heart " and " with many tears " (ii. 4)— a description not applicable to our " First Epistle." Now, the Apostle was intensely anxious to know the result of this letter and the mission of Titus ; and on leaving Ephesus for Macedonia and Greece (Acts xx. 1) he hoped to meet Titus at Troas, but was disappointed, as we have seen : " I had no relief for my spirit, because I found not Titus my brother." On he went into Macedonia, where he was " afflicted on every side ; without were fightings, within were fears " (2 Cor. vii. 5). But, to his great joy, presently Titus appeared, returning from Corinth ; and the next verse goes on, " Nevertheless, he that comforteth the lowly, even God, comforted us by the coming of Titus " ; and all the more because Titus brought good news of the " mourning " of the Corinthians over their back-

---

[1] Some commentators, notably Dr. Plummer, think that three or four chapters in our 2nd Corinthians (x.–xii. at least) are really a part of that third letter, and were misplaced by early copyists. There is much to be said for this view ; but as we are not now studying 2nd Corinthians, it is needless to discuss it further here.

slidings and failures, their true " repentance," and, adds St. Paul, their " zeal for me " (ver. 7–11). Titus himself had been " refreshed " by them (ver. 13), and had learned to love them (ver. 15). Probably it was due in part to his strong character that the result had been obtained. They had received him " with fear and trembling " (ver. 15). Timothy had been sent before (1 Cor. iv. 17, xvi. 10, 11), and (if he got there at all) had not prevailed.

Before continuing the narrative, let me here inject a reminiscence which many readers will share with me. The late George Ensor, the first English missionary in Japan, used at C.M.S. meetings to tell the story of his first convert. Open missionary work was then impossible in Japan, but an inquirer came at night who was eventually baptized and given the name of Titus ; " for God," Mr. Ensor used to say, " who comforteth the downcast, comforted me by the coming of Titus."

To resume. Apparently, St. Paul now sent Titus back again to Corinth for the third time, sending by him a fourth letter, the one we call Second Corinthians. Two other brethren went with him, that they might stimulate the collection. See 2 Cor. viii. 6, 16–24. These verses tell us something of Titus's character. He was " very earnest " (ver. 17) ; he had courageously volunteered for the difficult mission (ver. 17, " of his own accord "). He was an upright man, taking no " advantage " of his authority (xii. 18). Perhaps there had been some who asked, " Who is this fellow, taking so much on himself ? "—for St. Paul says, " Whether any inquire about Titus, he is my partner and my fellow-worker " (viii. 23). He and his colleagues are " the messengers of the churches and " the glory of Christ."

This is the man whom St. Paul, some years later, chose for the arduous post of superintending missionary in Crete. The Gospel had probably been first carried thither by the foreign Jews from the island, who are mentioned in Acts ii. as being at Jerusalem on the Day of Pentecost. St. Paul's visit was long after, subsequently to his first Roman imprisonment, as we have seen. Titus was there with him, evidently, and was left behind when the Apostle sailed away. " For this cause *left I thee* in Crete " (Tit. i. 5). The Cretans as a people had no high reputation, as we see from the Epistle ; and, although there was a numerous Church, the converts needed warnings against many serious faults and failings. They had been to some extent a prey to the influence of heretical Jewish teachers (i. 14). Titus would require all his firmness and tact to deal with them. Nevertheless, there were no doubt some qualified to be " bishops " or " elders," and Titus was to seek them out and appoint them. Two of the most beautiful doctrinal passages in the N.T. occur in this short Letter ; but Titus was not to aim only at securing orthodoxy. Again and again does St. Paul insist on " good works " as the indispensable fruits of faith in Christ.

All these points will come before us hereafter. Here let us only notice the example that Titus is to set in his personal conduct. In ii. 7, 8, St. Paul calls on him to be " an ensample," and this in two respects : first in " good works," and secondly in his " teachings," as Wiclif renders *didaskalia* in this place (" doctrine,"

A.V. and R.V.). Three desirable qualities of his teaching are enjoined, " uncorruptness, gravity, sound speech," [1] all significant words, to be further examined by and by. Meanwhile, is there not a passing lesson for us here ? To set an example, a pattern, in a sense a *type* (for the Greek word is *tupos*, whence our " type " is derived)—*that* is one duty of the Christian worker. But in fact every one of us is an example, a pattern, a type. The question is, what sort of type ? Is our example a good one ? " Uncorruptness " : transparent sincerity, especially in discussing controversial matters, when the temptation is to *twist* our opponents' words and to stretch a point in our own. " Gravity " : not heavy dullness, but an obvious sense of the seriousness of what we are doing. " Sound speech " : teaching that is healthy and health-giving. If Titus needed these three qualities for his teaching in his high office, so also do we in our humbler spheres.

Concerning Titus's ecclesiastical position we must inquire hereafter. Here it need only be said that he does not seem to have been appointed to a permanent position of authority over the Church, at least not then. St. Paul tells him (iii. 12) that Artemas or Tychicus is to be sent to Crete, and that then Titus is to come to the Apostle at Nicopolis. Whether this means that the one to be sent would be his successor, or only temporarily to take his place, we cannot say. Certainly he was sent elsewhere a little later, to Dalmatia (2 Tim. iv. 10). There are traditions that he

---

[1] In the A.V. there is a fourth, " sincerity," but this is a gloss, not in the original Epistle.

was afterwards Bishop of Crete in the fuller sense ; and there are ruined churches still to be seen which are dedicated to him.

3

WHO WAS TIMOTHY?

WHILE Titus was a Gentile, Timothy was neither a Gentile nor a Jew in the full sense. His father was a Greek and his mother a Jewess (Acts xvi. 1).   We have the names of both his mother and his grandmother in 2 Tim. i. 5, Eunice and Lois ; and the mention of these in this way suggests that his father had died early.   Although, no doubt, his Gentile paternity was the cause of his not being circumcised as a child, the mother and grandmother brought him up to know the God of the Hebrews, and he was taught the " sacred writings " of the Old Testament from infancy, as the Greek word for " child " in 2 Tim. iii. 15 indicates, meaning literally " babe." It is a beautiful picture that is thus presented to our view : the widowed " daughter of Abraham " with her one young boy, living with her old mother in the far-off heathen city of Lystra, in the heart of the great territory we now call Asia Minor ; the child denied the much-prized sign of God's covenant with Israel in deference to the father's wishes, but learning what was much better, the Book of the Covenant, daily at his mother's knee ; yet without the advantage which so many Jews in foreign cities enjoyed, of a synagogue for Sabbath worship and teaching—as we may fairly gather from Acts xiv.

Then, one day, occur the events recorded in that chapter. Two travelling Jews come to Lystra, and begin preaching, not to countrymen of their own in a synagogue as elsewhere, but to such heathen as will listen to them (verse 7). Apparently they are not much noticed until one day a startling sight rouses the whole city. Here is a well-known character, a cripple from his birth, leaping and walking, at one brief word from these strangers. The cry is raised " The gods are come down ! " " This dignified personage must be Zeus himself, the father of gods and men ; and this one, who does most of the speaking, must be his attendant Hermes ! [1] Fetch the priest ! Bring oxen and garlands ! Let sacrifices be offered ! Lystra is indeed honoured ! " Barnabas and Paul, not being acquainted (apparently) with the mother-tongue of the Lycaonians used by the populace in their excitement (though evidently Greek was also spoken), fail at first to make out what is going on. It was as if an English preacher in Wales were puzzled by the cries of the bilingual Welsh, who understand him though he does not understand them. But presently the strangers do perceive what is meant, for here is the priest about to sacrifice the ox before them ; and then we hear their indignant remonstrance, and their

---

[1] Zeus and Hermes are the names of these gods in the Greek (see R.V. margin). The A.V. adopted the more familiar Latin names, Jupiter and Mercury, and the R.V. does not alter these in the text.

appeal to the people to turn to the one Living God Who has given the rain and fruitful seasons.

Did young Timothy witness all this ? It does anyway seem that he saw the sequel, when Paul was stoned and left for dead ; for, long years after, the Apostle reminded him of his " suffering and persecutions " " at Lystra " (2 Tim. iii. 11).   And was Timothy's conversion to Christ one of the fruits of this missionary visit ? It seems so ; for he, like Titus, was spiritually a " very own child " of St. Paul's (1 Tim. i. 2).

Two or three years pass away, and St. Paul is again at Lystra (Acts xvi. 1–3). Timothy is now " a disciple," " well reported of by the brethren," not only there, but at the more important city of Iconium. Had the young Christian been evangelizing already ? There were " prophets " in the Church who marked him out and named him as a future missionary (1 Tim. i. 18).   No wonder St. Paul, who no longer had Barnabas and Mark with him, but only Silas, felt that God had raised up for him a fresh and promising companion, and " would have him to go forth with him." But there was one obstacle. The Gentile converts were not to be subjected to the Jewish rite of circumcision, but here was a young man who was half a Jew, and who was to accompany St. Paul to many cities where there were large Jewish communities. Certainly they would not tolerate one of their own race without the covenant token. So the Apostle, on his great principle of being " all things to all men," " took and circumcised " Timothy, seeing no inconsistency in this even while at that very time he was conveying to the various Churches the decrees of the Council of Jeru-

salem which exempted Gentiles from the rite (Acts
xvi. 4).

And then came the " laying on of hands." In
1 Tim. iv. 14, St. Paul writes, " Neglect not the gift that
is in thee, which was given thee by prophecy, with the
laying on of the hands of the presbytery " ; and in
2 Tim. i. 6, " Stir up the gift of God, which is in thee
through the laying on of my hands." Do these verses
refer to one occasion or to two ? Various answers to
this question are given by the commentators. I confess that I am struck by the reasonableness of the
suggestion that the second text refers to Timothy's
" confirmation " (as we should call it), when St. Paul's
hands alone were laid on him, as in Acts viii. 14–17 and
xix. 6 ; and that the first text refers to his subsequent
" ordination," when the presbyters joined in the laying on of hands. The Greek prepositions used are
different : the " gift " coming " through " (*dia*) St.
Paul's hands, but " with " (*meta*) the presbyters'
hands.[1]

The young evangelist now leaves his home and his
mother, and goes forth with Paul and Silas to preach
the Gospel. Their progress through Asia Minor is
traced in Acts xvi. 4–8, till at Troas they stand on the
seashore and look across the Ægean Sea towards
Europe ; and the vision of the " man of Macedonia "
calls them thither. They have now become a party of
four, as we find by the word " we " occurring for the
first time (verse 10), showing that they had been
joined by Luke, the beloved physician, who writes the

---

[1] I derive this suggestion from a letter in the *Record* of
Dec. 12, 1913, from the Rev. W. J. L. Sheppard. I have not
noticed it elsewhere.

narrative. But he is only with them a little while.
The " we " occurs again at Philippi (verse 16), but
after that we find " they " as before. Only Paul and
Silas are mentioned by name, but Timothy is with
them, as we find a little later (xvii. 15) ; and a passage
in the Epistle to the Philippians (ii. 19–20), written
years after, reveals Timothy's presence at Philippi
on this first occasion : " I hope . . . to send Timothy
shortly unto you. . . . Ye know the proof of him
that, as a child serveth a father, *so he served with me*
in furtherance of the Gospel." Moreover, we know
that he joined in the preaching at Thessalonica, for
both the Epistles to the Thessalonians are written in
the names of " Paul and Silvanus (*i.e.* Silas) and Timo-
theus," and the words " we " and " our," which occur
so often in those letters—thirty-five times in the first
three chapters of the First Epistle—tell us that
Timothy had his share in their labours and trials.

But when St. Paul is hurried away from the next
city, Berea, to escape his Jewish pursuers, he goes on
to Athens alone, leaving Silas and Timothy at Berea.
He sends them, however, instructions to follow him
quickly (Acts xvii. 14, 15), but the narrative only
shows them joining him later at Corinth. It is only
from the First Epistle to the Thessalonians that we
find that Timothy did follow him to Athens, but was
sent back to Macedonia to comfort and strengthen the
Church at Thessalonica. (See 1 Thess. ii. 17, 18 ;
iii. 1, 2. Ramsay explains Timothy's movements
differently, but I fail to reconcile his view with these
passages.) Then St. Paul, discouraged by his lack of
success at Athens, goes on to Corinth alone ; in that
great commercial and specially wicked city he is " in

weakness and in fear and in much trembling " (1 Cor. ii. 3) ; and the narrative of the Acts indirectly confirms this (xviii. 1–11). He is working at his tent-making in order to pay his way, and only uses the Sabbaths in the Jewish synagogue for quiet " reasoning and persuading " ; " but when Silas and Timothy come down from Macedonia," Paul is " pressed in the spirit " (A.V.), or " constrained by the Word " (R.V.), and *then* begins that mighty work which shows that the Lord had " much people in that city " (verse 10). In this work we might anyway be sure that Timothy had his share ; but we are expressly told so in 2 Cor. i. 19 : " The Son of God, Jesus Christ, was preached among you by us, even by me and Silvanus and Timothy."

We next meet with Timothy at Ephesus, in that long period of " three years " during which St. Paul worked in that great city (Acts xix. 22 ; xx. 31). From here he is sent, with a companion, Erastus, into Macedonia (xix. 22), where he would no doubt visit the Churches of Philippi, Thessalonica, and Berea. He is also to go on to Corinth, as St. Paul announces in a letter to the Corinthians (1 Cor. iv. 17), and further (xvi. 10, 11) specially commends him to them. " If Timothy come, see that he be with you without fear ; for he worketh the work of the Lord, as I also do ; let no man therefore despise him." Clearly the Apostle is a little afraid of the reception Timothy may meet with there, knowing his gentle and naturally timid character. I have already suggested, in the preceding talk, that Timothy failed to correct the evils rife at Corinth (if he ever reached there), and that then St. Paul sent Titus instead.

Afterwards, when St. Paul himself is at Corinth

(Acts xx. 2), Timothy is with him, as appears from the Epistle to the Romans, which was written from that city at that time, and which contains a message to the Roman Christians from the young evangelist (xvi. 21).[1]   Then when St. Paul starts on his journey to Jerusalem with the " collection," Timothy and others go on before him and wait for him at Troas (Acts xx. 4, 5).   But there is no indication that he went all the way to Judæa, as certainly Luke and Trophimus did (xxi. 15, 29) ; nor that he was with the Apostle during the latter's two years' detention at Cæsarea (xxiv. 27) ; nor that he was in the ship wrecked at Melita, as Luke was (xxviii. 1).   But we find him afterwards at Rome, as his name is joined with the Apostle's in three of the Epistles written during the two years there (Phil. i. 1 ; Col. i. 1 ; Philem. 1.) ; and St. Paul hoped to send him to Philippi, as appears from a passage already quoted : " I hope in the Lord Jesus to send Timothy shortly unto you "—words followed by a beautiful testimony to his character : " I have no man likeminded, who will care truly for your state. . . . But ye know the proof of him," etc. (Phil. ii. 19–22).

The rest of our knowledge of Timothy's career is derived (with one exception) from the two Epistles to him.   During one of the later journeys of St. Paul, after his release at Rome, the Apostle leaves Timothy at Ephesus to superintend the work there (I. i. 3) ; and thither he sends the First Epistle.   The Second Epistle is written from the Roman dungeon during

---

[1] If it should ever turn out, as some think, that the last chapter of Romans does not belong to that Epistle, but to another written to Ephesus, Timothy's message would be all the more natural.

the second more rigorous imprisonment, and it begs Timothy to come to Rome quickly. The one addition to our knowledge is in the Epistle to the Hebrews (xiii. 23), " Know ye that our brother Timothy hath been set at liberty." It may be that Timothy did reach Rome, either before or soon after St. Paul's execution, and was there arrested himself, and that the writer of Hebrews (assuming it was not St. Paul), hearing of his release, proposed going with him to the Jewish Christians (whoever they may have been) to whom this Epistle was written—" with whom, if he come shortly, I will see you."

Tradition makes Timothy " Bishop " of Ephesus after this, and relates his martyrdom, the Ephesian mob attacking him on account of his protest against a festival in honour of Diana, and killing him with clubs.

4

ENVIRONMENT AT EPHESUS AND IN CRETE

IT will greatly help our appreciation of the Pastoral Epistles if we can realise, however imperfectly, the environment of Timothy at Ephesus and of Titus in Crete. It is impossible in brief Talks like these to draw such a picture as would adequately furnish the reader's mind in this respect. The various commentators devote many pages to the subject. But a bare sketch must be attempted.

Ephesus was the greatest of the cities of that large territory which we now call Asia Minor, occupying the position that Smyrna does to-day : being the most easterly point of the whole Asiatic Continent, but with a host of flourishing cities and towns behind it, and a prosperous country presenting a very different aspect from the decay and misery and neglect now to be seen under Turkish rule.   Through Ephesus flowed the bulk of the trade between East and West, greatly enriching its citizens.   Does not the description of the mystical " Babylon " in Rev. xviii. owe something to St. John's experience in Ephesus ?—

" Merchandise of gold, and silver, and precious stone, and pearls, and fine linen, and purple, and silk, and scarlet ; and all thyine wood, and every vessel of ivory, and every vessel made of most precious wood, and of brass, and iron, and marble ; and cinnamon, and spice, and incense, and ointment, and frankincense, and wine, and oil, and fine flour, and wheat, and cattle and sheep ; and merchandise of horses and chariots and slaves ; and souls of men."

Significant indeed, and appalling, are those last words, lifting the veil from the external splendour to reveal the black moral darkness beneath.

And then there was the far-famed temple of Artemis or Diana, one of " the seven wonders of the world," almost as large as St. Paul's Cathedral, with its 127 columns sixty feet high, each the free gift of some princely devotee. This great representative of the finest Ionic architecture would naturally suggest the architectural metaphors in St. Paul's letters written both from and to Ephesus ; see 1 Cor. iii. 9–17, Eph. ii. 19–22, 1 Tim. iii. 15, vi. 19, 2 Tim. ii. 19, 20. Ephesus gloried in the title of "temple-keeper of Artemis," and of the hideous many-breasted image said to have fallen down from Jupiter—as the "town-clerk" reminds the mob in Acts xix.[1] There was an extensive trade in the small "silver shrines" referred to in that chapter, and we get there a graphic illustration of Ephesian money-making.

In that chapter we have also a glimpse of the sorcery and superstition for which Ephesus was famous. We see Jewish exorcists actually outdoing the Greek by using the name of Jesus. Every kind of magical imposture was practised ; and there is nothing surprising in the value of the costly books of charms and incantations burnt by the converts being "fifty thousand pieces of silver," or nearly £1, 800—for they were much sought after and fetched fancy prices.

Sir W. Ramsay[2] gathers from the pages of the Roman satirist Juvenal suggestive references to the Greeks who poured into Rome from the Ephesian coast and neighbourhood. Juvenal, he says, uses such "ugly and repulsive terms" as often to "defy quotation," but corresponding exactly with the language used by St. Paul in these Epistles : "evil men and impostors" (II. iii. 13), "overthrowing whole houses, teaching things which they ought not, for filthy lucre's sake" (Tit. i. 11), "creeping into

---

[1] "Temple-keeper" is "worshipper" in the **A.V.** ; but the Greek νεώκορος is a well-known word answering to our "warden."

[2] *Expositor*, August, 1909, p. 174.

houses and taking captive silly women " (II. iii. 6),
whose " mind and conscience are defiled " (Tit. i. 15) ;
and so on.

No wonder, then, that the moral condition of Ephesus was unspeakably bad. One of its citizens, Heraclitus, was said to have been called, as he was, " the
weeping philosopher," because he constantly wept
over the abominable vice and wickedness of the people.
Farrar in his Life of St. Paul gives a terrible picture
of it. We cannot forget that it was in a letter
addressed to the Churches of which Ephesus was the
chief that St. Paul wrote the words, " It is a shame
even to speak of those things which are done of them
in secret " (Eph. v. 12). The Epistles to the Seven
Churches (largely the same group) also indicate their
moral surroundings.

Now among these wealthy, superstitious, and vicious
communities the Gospel had met with remarkable
success. " Mightily," says St. Luke (Acts xix. 20),
" grew the word of God, and prevailed." " Almost
throughout all Asia " (the Roman province), said
Demetrius to his fellow silversmiths, " this Paul
hath persuaded and turned away much people "
(ver. 26). The " three years " of " night and day "
work (xx. 31) had borne fruit indeed. But in that
very farewell address to the elders in which St. Paul
looks back to that time of blessing, the looking forward is very different. " After my departure, grievous wolves shall enter in among you, not sparing the
flock " ; and not from outside only, not merely from
the immoral heathenism of Ephesus, but " from among
your own selves shall men arise, speaking perverse
things, to draw away the disciples after them." And

it was in those predicted times, " fightings and fears within, without," that the timid and gentle-spirited Timothy was set to preside over the Church thus to be troubled.

To warn Timothy against these " grievous wolves," and to strengthen his hands in dealing with them, was the immediate purpose of the First Epistle ; especially those who were themselves professing Christians. He is to " charge certain men not to teach a different doctrine, neither to give heed to fables and endless genealogies "—referring to Jews in the Church who are " desiring to be teachers of the law, though they understand neither what they say nor whereof they confidently affirm " (I. i. 3, 4, 7). St. Paul speaks of " profane babblings and opposi- tions of the knowledge (*gnosis*, A.V science) which is falsely so called " (vi. 20) ; of " men corrupted in mind and bereft of the truth " (vi. 5) ; of some " giv- ing heed to seducing spirits and doctrines of devils," " branded in their own conscience as with a hot iron " (iv. 2). We shall have to look more closely at these false teachers by and by, for there is a great deal about them in these Epistles. Here let me only quote one phrase from the 2nd Epistle (iii. 5), " hold- ing the form of godliness but denying the power thereof " ; and I borrow from Bishop Moule a sig- nificant incident recorded by him. A friend of his asked " What are the great non-Christian religions ? " and answered his own question thus : " Judaism, Mohammedanism, Brahmanism, Buddhism, and *un- spiritual Christianity.*"[1]   A true epigram indeed !

It is clear that Timothy's efforts to stay the pro-

---

[1] *Second Timothy,* p. 109.

gress of these evils were unsuccessful, at any rate at first ; for in the 2nd Epistle we find the startling statement that " all " who were " in Asia " " turned away from " St. Paul. There has been much discussion as to what this exactly means. To me it seems most likely that the Apostle refers to his arrest, somewhere on the Asiatic coast, after the journeys which followed his first imprisonment. He suffered, I think, just as his Lord and Master had suffered, when all the disciples " forsook Him and fled." It does not mean that the whole Church in Ephesus and the neighbouring country apostatized ; but it does mean that those at least who were present when St. Paul was arrested, or knew of it, made no effort on his behalf, perhaps " turned away " from the appeals of the weeping Timothy, whose " tears " he so constantly " remembered " (II. i. 4) ; and this must have meant a great change of feeling towards him, most likely due to the influence of the false teachers. This 2nd Epistle, accordingly, written from the dungeon at Rome whither he was then conveyed, presses on Timothy more strongly than ever the need of strenuous conflict for the truth of the Gospel.

The position in Crete seems to have been very similar. Its external prosperity, like that of Asia Minor, was quite different from its condition to-day. It had advancing civilisation in very early times. Homer credits it with a hundred cities. But the character of the people is very significantly shown by St. Paul's quotation from Epimenides in chap. i. 12, " Cretans are always liars, evil beasts, idle gluttons." [1] That

---

[1] The line quoted, which was a familiar verse among the Greeks, is a hexameter : Κρῆτες ἀεὶ ψεῦσται, κακὰ θηρία,

poet lived in ancient times, being contemporary with Solon of Athens, Nebuchadnezzar, and the Prophet Jeremiah ; yet after 600 years St. Paul emphatically endorses his indictment, " This witness is true." The reputation of the Cretans as to lying is illustrated by the fact that the Greeks coined a verb, *krētizein*, " to act as a Cretan," " to lie " ; just as the reputation of Corinth is shown by the saying " to play the Corinthian," meaning to lead a licentious life.

It is clear that in Crete, as at Ephesus, the troublers were professing Christians. " They profess that they know God, but by their works they deny Him " (i. 16). They had the Cretan character still conspicuous in them. " Reprove them sharply," says St. Paul, not " that they may be converted from heathenism," but " that they may be sound in the faith." It is a humbling picture indeed. We are apt to think of the early Christians as more perfect than ourselves ; and we are prone to expecting that African and Asiatic Christians to-day shall be examples of faith and love. But the Greeks and the Cretans of old had, and the Negroes and the Chinese to-day have, heathen notions and tendencies ingrained in their very nature. " Heredity," of which there is so much talk in our day, was, and is, all against their Christian consistency. And as for the particular evils dealt with in these Epistles, we shall see by and by that

---

γαστέρες ἀργαί. Conybeare cleverly renders it in an English hexameter : " Always liars and beasts are the Cretans, and inwardly sluggish." Tindale rendered the last two words " slow bellies," which the A.V. adopted ; but "slow" does not convey the meaning of ἀργαί, which the R.V. correctly renders " idle," as we have it in I. v. 13.

they are true foreshadowings of evil tendencies in modern England.

There never has been a " golden age " in the history of Christendom, as Dr. Plummer impressively points out.[1] There always have been errors in doctrine and failures in life.   The difference between Christian men now who are face to face with such evils, and Timothy and Titus in the first century, is, as Bishop Moule reminds us, that while we have " a long Christian history behind us, full of illustrations of the self-recovering power of the Gospel, and of the immortal vitality of the living heart of the Church "—*they* could only " fall back . . . on their Lord, known, trusted, taken at His word, felt and followed in the dark."[2]

Note.—With regard to the quotation from the old Cretan poet Epimenides, " Cretans are always liars, evil beasts, idle gluttons," my attention has been called to a remarkable fact which will certainly interest some at least of my readers. In the *Expositor* of October, 1912, Professor Rendel Harris described a recent discovery of his. He had been studying certain old Syriac books, one of them a commentary on the Acts of the Apostles by a Nestorian divine which contains large extracts from Theodore, Bishop of Mopsuestia, a voluminous writer of the 4th century whose works are lost. These extracts in their turn quote passages from the poem called " Minos," by Epimenides, one of them containing the famous line quoted by St. Paul. Now it seems that the reputation of the Cretans as liars was chiefly based on their affirming that the great god Zeus, " the father of gods and men," was dead, and that his tomb was in Crete.   The poet represented Minos, king

---

[1] *The Pastoral Epistles*, p. 264.
[2] *Second Timothy*, p. 132.

of Crete, who was supposed to be the son of Zeus, as resenting this assertion, and using about the Cretans the language of the famous line. All this would not have much interest for us but for what follows. This Syriac commentary reveals the fact that the very passage in the old poem which contains the familiar line contains also another line, equally familiar, which St. Paul also quoted, not in an Epistle, but in his speech at Athens. We read in that speech (Acts xvii.) : " He is not far from each one of us : *for in him we live and move and have our being ;* as certain even of your own poets have said, *For we are also his offspring.*" These last words we know to be from the Greek poet Aratus ; but the other words which I have also put in italics have never been supposed to be a quotation, but to be St. Paul's own. But they now turn out to be another line from the same poem " Minos " of Epimenides, close to the familiar one quoted in Titus ! Professor Harris thus renders the passage :—

They have fashioned a tomb for thee, O Holy and High !
The Cretans are always liars, evil beasts, idle bellies ;
For thou diest not ; for ever thou livest and standest ;
For in thee we live and move and have our being.

5

COUNSELS TO TIMOTHY: FLEE, FOLLOW, FIGHT

IT is evident that of all St. Paul's friends and fellow-workers Timothy was the nearest and dearest. The Apostle's love for him shines out in these two Epistles. He calls him his " true child "

(I. i. 2), " my child Timothy " (verse 18), " my beloved child " (II. i. 2), " my child " (ii. 1). It is
" child," not " son," every time. How dear Timothy
was to him we see from his " longing "[1] to see him
(II. i. 4, iv. 9, 21), and his " unceasing " prayer for
him (i. 3). He again and again, as we have seen,
recalls the incidents of Timothy's past life, so many
of which we only know of from these letters. And
how pathetic are St. Paul's appeals to his young
comrade : " O Timothy, guard that which is committed unto thee " (I. vi. 20) ; " O man of God, flee
these things " (vi. 11) ; " I charge thee in the sight
of God and Christ Jesus and the elect angels " (v. 21) ;
" I charge thee in the sight of God . . . and of Christ
Jesus " (vi. 13) ; " I charge thee in the sight of God
and Christ Jesus " (II. iv. 1). Happy is the young
Christian worker who has such a leader, and happy
is the Christian leader who " hath his quiver full " of
such " true " children !

The two Epistles are full of instructions and counsels to Timothy regarding his teaching, and the
Church he is to superintend, many of which will
come before us by and by. Here let us just glance
at some of these which are concerned with his personal
conduct. And we may conveniently arrange them
under three heads, indicated by three words which
occur in both Epistles—Flee, Follow, Fight. In
I. vi. 11, 12, we read, " But thou, O man of God, *flee*
these things ; and *follow* after righteousness, godliness, faith, love, patience, meekness. *Fight* the good
fight of the faith." In II. ii. 22 we read, " *Flee*

---

[1] Bishop Moule renders it " home-sick yearning," adding
" the Greek verb means no less." (*Second Timothy*, p. 40.)

youthful lusts, and *follow* after righteousness, faith, love, peace "; while in iv. 5–7 St. Paul encourages Timothy by his own example to "*fight* the good fight."

I. FLEE.—What is he to flee? The former of these two passages says "these things," and the latter "youthful lusts." "These things" may include many evil ways previously alluded to, but the immediate reference is to the love of money and discontent with one's lot. Some had gone wrong through seeking "gain" in wrong ways. Might not Timothy now and then meet with a Simon Magus, who, "supposing that godliness is a way of gain," would offer him money for a share in Timothy's spiritual gifts? Might he not meet some who, recognising him as a "prophet,"[1] would offer to pay for having their fortunes told? Even in the present age of enlightenment are there not many such? Love of money, says St. Paul, is "a root of all kinds of evil" (I. vi. 10), specially of "many foolish and hurtful lusts" (ver. 9) : "Flee these things ! "

There are other evils and dangers he is particularly to avoid ; "prejudice" and "partiality" in judgment (I. v. 21) ; undue haste in choosing men for spiritual office (22) ; being drawn into a share in "other men's sins" (22). He is to "shun profane babblings" (II. ii. 16) and "foolish and ignorant questionings" (23), about which we must inquire more closely by and by. In controversy he "must

---

[1] The "gift" that Timothy was to "stir up" may have been in part a gift of prophecy, which may account for St. Paul addressing him as "man of God," the title of a prophet in the O.T.

not strive," " but be gentle towards all."   He is to
beware of a " spirit of fearfulness,"[1] and not to be
" ashamed " of the Gospel, or of " Paul the prisoner "
(II. i. 7, 8).   Also he is to avoid undue asceticism, to
which such a man was likely to be prone.   This is
the meaning of the famous suggestion to " use a little
wine " (I. v. 23) ; not " Drink no longer water " (A.V.),
as if he were never to touch it, but " Be no longer a
drinker of water "—that is, plainly here, a total
abstainer, which, however good and useful in certain
circumstances, was in his case not wise, and in no
case obligatory.

II. FOLLOW.—First note the word " follow "
itself—*diōke*.   St. Paul uses it of his own life in Phil.
iii. 12, " Not as though I had already attained . . .
but I follow after " (*diōkō*) (R.V., " press on ") ;
upon which Dr. Chadwick cites a saying of Luther's,
" He that *is* a Christian is no Christian, but he who is
becoming such." [2]   Never in this life must we rest
satisfied, but ever " press on," " pursue," " stretch
forward."   The virtues and graces which in both the
Epistles Timothy is enjoined to follow will be studied
further on in detail ; but let me here quote Liddon's
analysis of those in I. vi. 11, " righteousness, godliness,
faith, love, patience, meekness."   They provide,
he says, " (1) for the soul's right relation to
God, (*a*) as the perfect Moral Being (righteousness), (*b*) as the supreme object of devotion (godliness) ;
(2) for the deepest moving principles of the Christian

---

[1] Alford renders δειλία " cowardice," and compares the
phrase in II. i. 7, πνεῦμα δειλίας, with the πνεῦμα δουλείας
(spirit of bondage) of Rom. viii. 15.
[2] *Pastoral Teaching of St. Paul*, p. 192.

life (faith and love) ; (3) for the true temper in which to deal with opponents, (*a*) patience under provocation, (*b*) mildness of feeling."[1]

But look at another enumeration in I. iv. 12. Timothy is to be an example, " in word, in manner of life, in love, in faith, in purity " ; outwardly in speech and conduct, inwardly in three beauteous qualities, love (toward man), faith (toward God), purity (in oneself). What a pattern to set, and to imitate ! This is the verse on which is modelled a prayer in the Service for the Consecration of Bishops : " a wholesome example, in word, in conversation, in love, in faith, in chastity, in purity." " In conversation," says this prayer, following the A.V. ; " in manner of life," more correctly says the R.V. The English word " conversation," 300 years ago, meant, not merely intercourse by word of mouth, as now, but conduct generally. The Greek work is *anastrophē*, and the R.V. translates it in various ways, sometimes " manner of life " or " of living," sometimes simply " life " or " living," sometimes " behaviour " ; see 2 Cor. i. 12, Gal. i. 13, Eph. ii. 3, iv. 22, Heb. xiii. 7, Jas. iii. 13, 1 Pet. i. 15, 18, ii. 12, iii. 1, 2, 16, 2 Pet. ii. 7, iii. 11.

Then, again, St. Paul calls on Timothy to " neglect not," but to " stir up " (literally, kindle into flame), the " gift " bestowed upon him (I. iv. 14, II. i. 6).[2] He is to be, as we sometimes say, " on fire." Was this " gift " the office or ministry to which he was ordained ? Surely not ; but, rather, special power from God to fulfil its duties. The Greek word is

---

[1] *Explanatory Analysis of* 1 *Tim.*, p. 82.
[2] See p. 29, note.

charisma, which is almost anglicised among us. It means a gracious gift, a gift from grace (*charis*). It occurs sixteen times in St. Paul's Epistles, and only once elsewhere (1 Pet. iv. 10). It is especially, though not exclusively, used of the Pentecostal gifts bestowed on the Early Church ; but for our own instruction we may rightly take St. Paul's appeal and apply it to any " gifts," however humble, with which it may have pleased God to entrust us.

The " following " is further pressed in I. iv. 15 : " Be diligent in these things ; give thyself wholly to them " (R.V.) ; but literally the words are " Be ever pondering on these things, and *be in them* " ;[1] in fact, *be absorbed* in your solemn and responsible work. Then his " progress " would be " manifest unto all." Not that Timothy was to be thinking of this. On the contrary, the more he was absorbed in his work, the less would he think of men's opinion. But all the more would a really good example be set. A word for us all !

Once more : " Continue in these things ! " (I. iv. 16). As Bishop Moule once said at Keswick, " Daniel *continued* " (Dan. i. 21). There are few more interesting studies than a comparison of the 170 occurrences of the words " continue," " continual," etc., in the English Bible. Of course they stand for different Hebrew and Greek words ; but the meaning is the same, and the lesson most impressive. And see here the result of " continuance " in " following " :

---

[1] " Be diligent " is μελέτα, which the A.V. renders " Meditate on," which is too mild. The word would sound significantly in Timothy's ears after the " Neglect not," μὴ ἀμέλει, of the preceding verse. " Give thyself wholly to them," though not literal, is a good paraphrase of ἐν τούτοις ἴσθι.

"thou shalt save both thyself and them that hear thee."

III. FIGHT.—Timothy is summoned to a soldier's life in both Epistles (I. i. 18, II. ii. 3, 4) ; but that is not the figure here. It is the athlete who contends in the arena, the wrestler or the gladiator, who is set up as the model. We will examine the words by and by ; meanwhile we only note that Timothy is to grapple with the work entrusted to him, to " agonize " in it, as the Greek means, in the resolute spirit of the winner in the most strenuous games.

Now, in Timothy's case, one of the chief obstacles to his success was the tendency to timidity and undue self-suppression of which we have before seen signs. Hence St. Paul's frequent appeals to him to be " strengthened," to " fulfil his ministry." He is to assert his authority when necessary. As the Apostle has " charged " him, he is to " charge " others (I. i. 3, vi. 17), to " command " as well as to exhort and teach (I. iv. 11, v. 7), to reprove and rebuke (II. iv. 2), yes, publicly (I. v. 20). Then, " Let no man despise thy youth." When St. Paul wrote similar words to the Corinthians about Timothy (1 Cor. xvi. 11), he was exhorting *them* not to despise him ; but now he exhorts Timothy himself not to act so as to bring contempt upon himself. " Don't be too boyish ; don't unduly humble yourself ; act worthily of thy high commission." No doubt there is such a thing as undue self-assertion, as what we colloquially call " uppishness " ; but on the other hand, there is such a thing as a timid over-humility and consequent shrinking from responsibility. That would not do in the Greek arena, any more than in captaining a Test Match Eleven ; and it will not do if we are to fulfil the functions God lays upon us.

So we see that Timothy, with all his personal goodness, was not quite the ideal man for his post. And yet St. Paul gave it to him. He did not pass over him, or supersede him. He bore with him ; he encouraged him ; he diligently instructed him ; if we may so express it, he gave him a fair chance. Here is a lesson for the seniors among us, and those in authority.

And what for the juniors ?—indeed, for all of us average folk ? As we read the exhortations to Timothy, do we not all feel how sorely we need them too ? Yet surely it is a real encouragement to find one so relatively weak doing such splendid service. Do we feel utterly unfit for this or that position of trust in the Church of God ? Let us remember that not Timothy only, but St. Paul himself, deeply felt his unfitness. " Not," he wrote (2 Cor. iii. 5), " that we are sufficient of ourselves . . . but our sufficiency is from God." So is ours !

6

PAUL ON HIMSELF:
THE LORD'S SERVANT

WE turn now from the two younger men to whom these Epistles were written, and think of the older man who wrote them. To attempt, indeed, an " appreciation " of St. Paul is quite beyond my intentions. He is confessedly one of the greatest characters in history, and far abler pens than mine might well fail to do him justice. But we must see what the writer of these letters says of himself. He is accustomed to introduce himself to his correspondents under certain titles. Sometimes he calls himself a " servant " of the Lord ; sometimes as His " apostle." In one of our three Epistles, that to Titus, he uses both words, and he does so in only one other case, in writing to the Church at Rome. In the two Epistles to Timothy he only calls himself an apostle. We will examine both these titles, and as " servant " is a humbler one for a Christian worker than " apostle," we will take it first.[1]

In Tit. i. 1 St. Paul calls himself " a *servant* of God." In 1 Tim. i. 12 he thanks God for " appointing him to His *service* " (A.V. ministry). In II. i. 3 he says " I thank God, Whom I *serve* from my forefathers." Now in these three passages the Greek words belong to three different groups, with different meanings. When St. Paul calls himself " a servant of God " he uses the word *doulos*, which means a bond-servant or slave, absolutely at the disposal of his Master. When he thanks God for appointing him to his " service " he uses a word, *diakonia*, which means some definite work of " ministry," whether done by a slave or anyone else. When he declares

---

[1] In a little book entitled *The Servant*, published by the S.P.C.K., I have examined the different words used for " service " and " serving " in the Bible, which together occur 1,800 times.

that he has " served " God from his forefathers he uses a word, *latreuō*, which refers to allegiance, loyalty, worship ; and it is as if he said " This God is my God."   Let us look at these three groups of words.

1. First, the bond-servant, or slave, *doulos*.   St. Paul introduces himself as a *doulos* of God or of Christ at the beginning of his Epistles to the Romans, the Philippians, and Titus ; also in writing to the Galatians (i. 10).   He gives the title also to Timothy (Phil. i. 1) and to Epaphras (Col. iv. 12).   In 2 Cor. iv. 5 he speaks of himself and his colleagues as the *douloi* of the converts : " Ourselves your servants for Jesus' sake."   He speaks of our Lord Himself as " taking the form of a *doulos* " (Phil. ii. 7).   The word is used about forty times in the N.T. of the servants of God or of Christ, and it indicates, not any particular form of service, but the status of the servant.   What is that status ?   Is it bondage ?   There is a word, *douleia*, which means the bondage of the literal *doulos*, but it is never used of the service of God.   Our familiar Collect is right in reminding us that God's " service " is " perfect freedom " ; and emphatically does St. Paul write to the Galatians (v. 1, R.V.), " With freedom did Christ set us free : stand fast, therefore, and be not entangled again in a yoke of bondage."   Nevertheless, the essential point in the status of a slave is that he is his master's property ; and St. Paul never forgot, neither must we forget, that our Divine Master has *purchased* us " with His own blood " (Acts xx. 28, Eph. i. 7, 1 Peter i. 18-19, Rev. v. 9).

The spirit of true service is beautifully indicated

in one passage in our Epistles, II. ii. 24.   Even with
" those that oppose themselves " " the Lord's servant
must not strive, but be gentle towards all, apt to
teach, forbearing, in meekness instructing " them.
The other occurrences of this group of words are in I.
vi. 1-2, and Titus ii. 9, where the literal servants of
earthly masters are referred to ; and in Titus ii. 3,
" Enslaved to much wine," and Titus iii. 3, " Serving
divers lusts and pleasures "—a contrast indeed !

2. Secondly, the servant as minister, *diakonos*.
The word, and its cognate verb, occur in I. iii., where
the office of a deacon is described ; but this office, or
rather order, will come before us by and by, and I
pass it over now.   The words are also used, however,
in the general sense of service.   Both the A.V. and
the R.V. sometimes render them "service," " servant,"
" serve," and sometimes " ministry," " minister,"
" to minister."   But the points to be noted are (1)
that these words stand, not for the status of a servant,
like the *doulos* group, but for definite work, service,
or ministry ; and (2) that this service is not the
direct service of God in the sense of allegiance or of
worship, but either the service of God among men or
the direct service of man.   The *diakonos* is a *doulos* in
status, commissioned by his Divine Master to serve,
diakonein, in a certain service, a *diakonia*.   The
distinction is well illustrated in the little parable of
the Servant returning from the Field, in Luke xvii.
The servant is called a *doulos*, but when he comes in
from the field and the master says " Gird thyself and
serve me," the word " serve " is *diakonai*.

Turning now to our Pastoral Epistles, we find St.
Paul thanking the Lord for " putting him into the

ministry " (A.V.), or " appointing him to His service " (R.V.), the word being *diakonia*.   He tells Timothy what he must do to be a good *diakonos* (I. iv. 6) ; appeals to him to " fulfil " (R.V. ; A.V. " make full proof of ") his *diakonia* (II. iv. 5) ; reminds him of the good example of Onesiphorus, whose " ministering " (*diakonein*) to the Apostle at Ephesus Timothy well knew of (II. i. 18) ; and directs him when coming to Rome to bring Mark also, who would be " useful for ministering " (R.V. ; A.V. " profitable for the ministry," *diakonia*), II. iv. 11.

What, then, was the *diakonia*, the service or ministry, to which St. Paul was called, and for which he thanks his Divine Lord ?   We find the answer in several other utterances of his, but I need only mention one.   In 2 Cor. v. he describes that ministry in wonderful language—" the ministry (*diakonia*) of reconciliation, to wit, that God was in Christ, reconciling the world unto Himself."   " Now then," he adds, " we are ambassadors for Christ, as though God did beseech you by us."   It was, indeed, worth while to be the Lord's *doulos*, in order to be fitted to be also a *diakonos* for such a *diakonia* !

This, then, is the greatest of all ministries, to preach a world-embracing Gospel.   But St. Paul had others too.   He had to care for men's material needs as well as for their spiritual needs.   Twice was he the bearer of a " collection for the poor saints " at Jerusalem (Acts xi. 27-30, xii. 25. xxiv. 17 ; Rom. xv. 25-31 ; 1 Cor. xvi. 1-4 ; 2 Cor. viii., ix.), and in both cases the work is called a *diakonia*.   Indeed, all kinds of spiritual and benevolent service are included in Christian *diakonia* ; and St. Paul himself speaks of " diversities of ministrations " (1 Cor. xii. 5). Even secular rulers are twice called by him *diakonoi* of God (Rom. xiii. 4-6).

One other point of deep interest must not be passed over. We have seen that our Lord Jesus Christ took on Him the form of a *doulos* ; and He also accepted the work of a *diakonos*. " The Son of Man," He said, " came not to be ministered unto, but to minister " (Matt. xx. 27), the word being *diakonein*. On the very occasion when He most touchingly took the part of the *doulos* by washing the disciples' feet (John xiii.) He also used those memorable words, the Archbishop of York's text at the Coronation of King George, " I am among you as he that serveth " (Luke xxii. 27). The verb again is *diakonein*. It is for us to remember another sentence uttered by Him that same night, " I have given you an example, that ye also should do as I have done to you " (John xiii. 15) ; and yet another, spoken only two days earlier (John xii. 26), " If any man serve Me (*diakonē*) let him follow Me, and where I am there shall My servant be (*diakonos*) ; if any man serve Me (*diakonē*), him will My Father honour."

3. Both these groups of words are largely used by St. Paul, the *doulos* group fifty-six times, the *diakonos* group fifty-five times. The third group, to which we now come, we only meet with in his Epistles six times, and twice in his speeches in the Acts. Three times he speaks of " God . . . Whom I *serve* " (Acts xxvii. 23 ; Rom. i. 9 ; 2 Tim. i. 3). In Acts xxiv. 14 he says, " So *serve* I the God of our fathers." In Rom. xii. 1 he speaks of " your reasonable *service*." And there are also Rom. i. 25, ix. 4 ; and Phil. iii. 3. In these cases the word for " serve " is *latreuō*, and for

" service " *latreia.* These words refer neither to bond-service nor to definite ministry. They stand for allegiance, acknowledgement, loyalty, worship. When St. Paul says three times (as above), " Whom I serve," he means " Who is my God, to Whom I render worship and allegiance." We can see at once how impressive this would be in the storm-tossed corn-ship in the Mediterranean, when he told the despairing officers and crew, probably all heathen, how the angel had come to him from God, " the God Whose I am, and Whom I serve, my God, the great Creator Who rules over winds and waves." Neither *douleuō* nor *diakoneō* would have the force that *latreuō* had in those circumstances. So again, when he stood before Felix, and declared that he " served " the God of his fathers, his meaning was, " I am no heretic ; the God of our fathers is my God."

Let us see for ourselves (1) that we acknowledge and worship the one true God our Father, (2) that we are His willing bond-servants, (3) that we are ready for any ministry to which he may call us.

One other point—the conscientiousness of St. Paul's " service." In II. i. 3 we read, " I thank God, Whom I serve . . . . in a pure conscience." The same phrase, " pure conscience " occurs in I. iii. 9 ; and St. Paul speaks of " a good conscience " in I. i. 5, 19. The word " conscience " is, in fact, used by St. Paul more often than in all the rest of the New Testament. He uses it twenty-two times (including two speeches, Acts xxiii. 1 ; xxiv. 16) ; and it only occurs elsewhere nine times. Let us copy him in the habit he spoke of to Felix : " I *exercise myself* to have a conscience void of offence to ward God and men alway."

7

PAUL ON HIMSELF:
THE APOSTLE

HAVING viewed St. Paul as the Lord's " servant," in the three senses of " service," let us next see him as an " apostle," by which title he describes himself in both Epistles to Timothy.

The Greek word *apostolos* simply means one who is sent, the verb " send " being *apostellō*. Our word " missionary," which is Latin in origin, has exactly the same meaning, the Latin verb " send " being *mitto*. St. Paul realised that the central point of his life was his being one who was " sent." " As My Father hath sent Me, even so send I you," said the Risen Lord to His disciples ; and St. Paul himself, in his defence before Agrippa, recounts the Lord's words to him upon his conversion, " Unto whom [the Gentiles] I *send* thee " (*apostellō*).

Let us refer to the original appointment of the first Twelve Apostles, recorded in Mark iii. 13-19. " He appointed twelve, that they might be with Him, and that He might send them forth (*apostellē*) to preach." In the parallel passage, Luke vi. 13, the words are added " whom also He named apostles " ; and some MSS. have these also in Mark, which Hort insists is the true reading, though most editors reject it.[1] The passage shows that there was a needed qualification for the office before the " sending." They had first to be " with Him." For the " apostle " is more than a mere messenger ; he is a delegate or ambassador, as St. Paul calls himself in 2 Cor. v. 20 and Eph. vi. 20 ; he represents him that sends him. To be

---

[1] *Christian Ecclesia*, p. 22.

qualified for this, the Twelve must be " with " their Master, to receive His teaching and imbibe His spirit. They had to be " disciples " before they could be " apostles."[1]   And was it not so with St. Paul ? Was not that period " in Arabia " (Gal. i. 17) a time of being " with " Christ in spirit and of learning from Him ?

It is interesting to note the use of the two terms " disciple " and " apostle " in the New Testament. The former word occurs about 230 times in the Four Gospels, and in about 160 of these cases it refers definitely to the Twelve (all of them or some).   It occurs thirty times in the Acts, but never to indicate the Twelve ; and it does not occur in the Epistles at all.   On the other hand, the word " apostle " only occurs eight times in the Gospels, seven of them indicating the Twelve ; but thirty times in the Acts, twenty-seven of these cases indicating the Twelve ; and forty times in the Epistles.   What does this mean ?   It means that the period of our Lord's ministry was, for the Twelve, the *disciple-period.* After His Ascension, it was for them the *apostle-period.*

What is the lesson for us ?   (1) No one can be an " apostle " till he has first been a " disciple " ; (2) no one should be content to be a " disciple " only, but should ask the Lord to " send " him also as an apostle," in however humble a sphere.

Timothy himself illustrates the distinction.   He is first introduced to us in Acts xvi. 1 as a " disciple." Then he is called to work of an " apostolic " kind.

---

[1] Dr. Chadwick has some impressive remarks on this, *Pastoral Teaching of St. Paul,* p. 115.

In 1 Thess. ii. 6 St. Paul writes concerning the ministry at Thessalonica of himself and Silas and Timothy, whom he calls " we," and uses the phrase " as apostles of Christ." But Timothy did not have quite the status of an apostle. The Epistle to the Philippians begins " Paul and Timothy, servants of Christ Jesus," because both were " servants "; but the Epistle to the Colossians begins " Paul an apostle . . . and Timothy our brother "; just as in Philemon, " Paul a prisoner . . . and Timothy our brother," because Timothy was not a prisoner.

In both the Epistles to Timothy St. Paul, when mentioning his appointment as an Apostle, refers also to two of his apostolic duties. In I. ii. 7 we read, " I was appointed a preacher and an apostle . . . a teacher . . ."; and the same words occur also in II. i. 11. Let us look at these two functions, the Preacher and the Teacher.

1. *A Preacher*. The Greek word so rendered, *kērux*, occurs only in these two passages and in 2 Pet. ii. 5, where Noah is called " a preacher of righteousness." The R.V. margin suggests " herald "; and the cognate verb, *kērussō*, which is common, means to proclaim or publish. Thus, in Matt. x. 27, " proclaim upon the house-tops "; and the cases where sick persons healed by Christ " published " it abroad. St. Paul, when first converted, at once " proclaimed Jesus, that He is the Son of God," in the synagogue at Dasmascus. But the R.V. often follows the A.V. in rendering it " preach," thus :

Matt. iv. 17. From that time began Jesus to preach.
xxiv. 14. This gospel . . . shall be preached in the whole world.

Luke xxiv. 47.   Repentance and remission of sins should be preached in His Name unto all the nations.

Rom. x. 14, 15.   How shall they hear without a preacher ? and how shall they preach except they be sent ?

1 Cor. i. 23.   We preach Christ crucified.

We find this word twice in our Epistles :

I. iii. 16.   Preached among the nations.
II. iv. 2.   Preach the word.

Another connected word, *kērugma*, means " the preaching," that is, either the act of preaching or the thing preached. Thus, in 1 Cor. i. 21 St. Paul speaks of " the foolishness of the preaching," through which " it was God's good pleasure . . . to save them that believe." This word occurs twice in our Epistles, and is both times rendered " message " in the R.V. (A.V. " preaching ").

II. iv. 17.[1]   That through me the message might be fully proclaimed.
Tit. i. 3.   Manifested His word in the message.

There is another group of words used for preaching in the N.T., from which we derive our words " evangel," " evangelize," etc. The verb is often rendered

---

[1] This R.V. rendering is interesting. The Greek is ἵνα δι ἐμοῦ τὸ κήρυγμα πληροφορηθῇ. The A.V. has " that by me the preaching might be fully known." " Fulfilled " would be the natural translation. But the R.V., to get in the idea of proclamation implied in κήρυγμα, renders it as above.

" preach-the-Gospel."[1] These we shall examine by and by.

II. *A Teacher.* The Greek word *didaskalos* only occurs three times in our Epistles, viz., in the two passages above quoted and in II. iv. 3. But an adjective, *didaktikos,* " apt to teach," occurs twice (I. iii. 2, II. ii. 24), and nowhere else in the N.T. ; the verb *didaskō* five times (I. ii. 12, iv. 11, vi. 2 ; II. ii. 2, Titus i. 11) ; and the two nouns *didaskalia* and *didachē* (which we shall examine by and by) fifteen times and twice respectively. There are also three notable compound words : *hetero-didaskaleo,* " teach a differ-/ ent doctrine " (I. i. 3, vi. 3) ; *kalo-didaskalos,* " a teacher of good " (Titus ii. 3) ; and *nomo-didaskalos,* " a teacher of the law " (I. i. 7) ; the two former not elsewhere in the N.T.

This was a title by which our Lord was often addressed. In many places where we find Him called " Master," the Greek is *didaskalos,* and " Master " means, not " Lord," but " Teacher." In one place the English is " doctor," where the boy Jesus is found in the midst of the " doctors." Evidently the Revisers were unwilling to alter a rendering so familiar. Nicodemus said to the humble Galilean whom he only dared to visit by night, " We know that thou art a *teacher* come from God " ; and our Lord presently said, " Art thou *the teacher* of Israel, and knowest not these things ? "

---

[1] The verb is εὐαγγελίζω. But the original of " preach the Gospel " in our English versions is not always this verb. It is sometimes κηρύσσω τὸ εὐαγγέλιον, as in Matt. iv 23, ix. 35, Mark i. 14, xvi. 15. In Luke viii. 1 we have the two verbs together, κηρύσσων καὶ εὐαγγελιζόμενος, " preaching and bringing the glad tidings."

In the early Church the teacher was a man with definite functions. " First apostles," says St. Paul (i Cor. xii. 28), " secondly prophets, thirdly teachers." But St. Paul combined in himself the various offices and functions. He was an apostle, a prophet, a preacher, a teacher. He was regularly engaged in both preaching and teaching. Thus, at Antioch with Barnabas, " teaching and preaching " (Acts xv. 35) ; and during those two years of the detention at Rome, " preaching the Kingdom of God and teaching the things concerning the Lord Jesus Christ " (xxviii. 31). At Corinth, after the first " preaching of Christ crucified," he dwelt " a year and six months, teaching the word of God among them " (xviii. 11 ; see i Cor. i. 23, ii. 1-4). At Ephesus, for three years, he was " preaching the Kingdom " and " teaching publicly from house to house " (xx. 20, 25, 31). In combining the preaching and the teaching, he followed his Divine Exemplar, whose ministry combined " teaching in the synagogues and preaching the Gospel of the King- dom " (Matt. iv. 23) ; and he obeyed the Lord's own instructions, " Go . . . and make disciples of all the nations "—which is mainly by " preaching " in some form—" teaching them to observe all things whatso- ever I commanded you " (Matt. xxviii. 18-20).

Two lessons are plainly taught us :

(a) Distinguish between preaching and teaching. Sunday school teachers are often rightly warned not to " preach." Many a man can preach, after a fashion, say in a Mission Hall, setting forth the claims of Christ and the way of salvation ; but it is quite a different thing to give daily or weekly instruction to learners, inquirers, converts, or to sit or walk with an individual and deal wisely with his questions and difficulties. Justly does St. Paul, in Rom. xii., call on " him that teacheth " to give himself " to his teaching."   So again a preacher may take a text as a motto and then, without referring to it, speak for twenty minutes on some modern or current topic, when the congregation need *teaching* by careful expository sermons.

(*b*) " Preaching," pure and simple, is *proclamation*. Of what ?   Of God's messages to men.   How many sermons do that ?   What we sorely need is the authoritative word of Christ's ambassador, heralding forth His love, and the gross ingratitude of ignoring it. " I have a message from God unto thee "—*that* is the preacher's true attitude.

It would be an interesting study to examine St. Paul's sermons in the Acts and his teaching in the Epistles ; but that would take us far beyond our present limits.

8

PAUL'S RETROSPECT
AND HIS CHARGE TO TIMOTHY

WE have seen St. Paul as Servant and Apostle. Let us now look at his retrospect of his past life, that wonderful passage in the first chapter of the First Epistle.   He has referred (verse 11) to the Gospel " committed to his trust."   If we look on to verse 18 we see that this trust, " this charge," he now " commits " to Timothy. The intervening verses, 12-17, are a parenthesis ; and what a parenthesis !   He cannot think of the charge committed to him without breaking out into thanksgiving and praise. " I thank Him ! " he exclaims.

For he can never forget his past. He had been, he says (ver. 13), " a blasphemer, and a persecutor, and injurious." This last word " injurious " seems to us comparatively mild, but it is really the strongest of the three. It occurs elsewhere only in Rom. i. 30, where the A.V. has " despiteful " and the R.V. " insolent." Dr. Plummer reads it as indicating " pleasure in outraging the feelings of others." St. Paul, he says, confesses that " in his misguided zeal he had punished innocent people " " not with pitying reluctance, but with arrogant delight." [1]

Nay, more, he calls himself the " chief of sinners." And not that he *was* so, but *is* : " of whom I *am* chief." Was this a mere rhetorical expression ? Ah, no ; many of the holiest saints have said the same thing. They, in fact, see the hatefulness of sin as the average man cannot, and see its especial hatefulness in themselves. We may be sure St. Paul meant what he said, and his saying it is the best proof of his holiness. Did he refer particularly to his persecution of the Christians ? I doubt it. For *that* sin he does almost make an excuse : " I did it ignorantly, in unbelief "—*i.e.* " in my unbelieving state." But he knew the proud and bitter feelings of his heart, his self-sufficiency and self-righteousness ; and he knew that Divine grace alone now kept him. " But for the grace of God, there goes John Bradford ! "

---

[1] *Pastoral Epistles*, p. 54.

And when he looked back on that past, he was overwhelmed with the thought of " the grace of the Lord." It " abounded exceedingly," he says ; a rare word, found nowhere else in the N.T. St. Paul was fond of using compound words beginning with *hyper*. Indeed, he was fond of the preposition *hyper* itself, using it 106 times, more than twice as often as all the other N.T. writers together. And no less than twenty-one different compound words of the kind occur in his Epistles, only two of which are used (once each) elsewhere in the N.T. The word rendered here " abounded exceedingly " is one of the twenty.[1] John Bunyan, when he gave the title *Grace Abounding* to his own spiritual story, well knew what the phrase meant.

We shall look more closely at the word " grace " in a future Talk ; also at the " faith and love " which came " with " the grace, which in fact grace produced in St. Paul ; also at the great verse which is the centre of the passage, the centre of the Gospel itself, " Christ Jesus came into the world to save sinners."

But now observe the Apostle's conviction of the reason why the forgiving and converting grace of God fastened on him individually. Verse 16, " For this cause I obtained mercy, that in me *as chief* [same Greek word as " *chief* of sinners "] might Jesus Christ show forth all long-suffering, for an ensample . . ." An exhibition, a display, of that wonderful divine quality, here specially attributed to Christ, " long-suffering," mentioned often in the N.T., and four

---

[1] The word is ὑπερπλεονάζω. The only other two of these in the Pastorals are ὑπεροχή, " high place " (I. ii. 2), and ὑπερήφανος, " haughty " (II. iii. 2).

times in the O.T. (Exod. xxxiv. 6, Num. xiv. 18, Ps. lxxxvi. 15, Jer. xv. 15) ; and frequently set forth as the right attitude for a Christian towards those who try his patience.   And St. Paul says that in him the Lord showed forth " *all* long-suffering," the Greek word here used for " all " being stronger than the usual one, and only once elsewhere used by St. Paul.

Then, " for an ensample " (A.V. pattern).   We speak of " making an example of " some one who has done wrong, by which we mean inflicting special punishment.   Christ " makes an example " by show-ing forth His long-suffering.   And St. Paul glories in it.   Let me, he would say, be an example ; tell it out everywhere what the Lord of glory has done with the chief of sinners !   He is not ashamed, that either his sin or his conversion should be known and talked about.   After all, personal testimony is the most effective mode of preaching and teaching.   Bengel (quoted by Dr. Newport White) happily compares Ps. xxxii. 5, 6 : " Thou forgavest the iniquity of my sin.   *For this* let everyone . . . pray unto Thee . . ." I recall what Moody, the American evangelist, once said in my hearing : " I am not ashamed to say I am a converted man ; *it's no credit to me !* "

But there was something else for which St. Paul renders thanks to his Divine Lord ; and it really comes first in this wonderful retrospect.   For he begins with that call to " service " which we have before looked at : verse 12, " I thank Him that enabled me, even Christ Jesus our Lord, for that He counted me faithful, appointing me to His service." " Counted me faithful " ; he does claim *that* for him-self ; after such an experience he could be trusted.

He knew he could be, and he knew that the Lord knew he could be. But note that in 1 Cor. vii. 25 he attributes this " faithfulness " to God's mercy. " Enabled me," *endunamōsanti*, a word connected with *dunamis*, " power," whence we derive our " dynamic " and " dynamite." St. Paul's thanks were not only that he was saved and forgiven, not only that he was " appointed to service," but also that he was " enabled " to do the service faithfully. Have we not all cause for the same thanksgiving, however feeble and unworthy our service ?

This great digression in the Letter closes with a magnificent doxology in verse 17, ending with an Amen. But at this we shall look hereafter.

St. Paul then returns to the " charge " he is " committing " to Timothy (verse 18), plainly the proclamation of " the gospel of the glory of the blessed God " (verse 11), the " good tidings " for mankind, which had been " committed to his trust." [1] Now see how he expresses this further on. In vi. 20 we read : " O Timothy, guard that which is committed unto thee " ; and these last six words stand for two words in the Greek *tēn parathēkēn*, " the deposit," as in the R.V. margin. " O Timothy, guard the deposit." Again, in II. i. 14 we read " That good thing which was committed unto thee guard "—literally, " The good deposit guard." So the " deposit " is the Gospel, not excluding from the idea the duty and the privilege of preaching it. But now let us look at another verse, a very familiar one, in which that same Greek word occurs.

---

[1] Similar language is used by St. Paul in 1 Cor. ix. 17, Gal. ii. 7, 1 Thess. ii. 4, Tit. i. 3.

It is II. i. 12, " I know Him Whom I have believed, and I am persuaded that He is able to guard that which I have committed unto Him against that day " —literally, " to guard my deposit against that day." What is this " deposit " which St. Paul has " committed " to the Lord's keeping ? Most readers will reply, " his soul," " himself." But the word *parathēkē* occurs in the N.T. only in these three places, and one asks—Must it not be used in the same way in all three ? If so, " my deposit " would not be " that which I have committed unto Him," but " that which He hath committed unto me " ; and this rendering is given in the R.V. margin. The interpretation would then be that St. Paul was " not ashamed," because he knew Him Whom he had trusted ; and although he himself was in prison and could not preach or teach, and although he felt that his career was over (iv. 6), yet the " deposit " which the Lord had committed to him, and which he had now committed to the Lord, was quite safe ; the preaching and teaching of the same Gospel would be carried on by others whom the same Lord would appoint. Then, naturally, in the next verse but one, he appeals to Timothy to guard *his* " deposit," the same " deposit," indeed, the Gospel. " The good thing which was committed unto thee guard."

If this is correct, a most impressive lesson is conveyed. The dying preacher, the sick missionary, the invalided Sunday School teacher or district visitor, who knows that the Lord had entrusted him with the Gospel message to deliver, can be assured that the Lord Himself will take care of it and hand it on to the others. He might even take courage from the

words to believe that the influence of his own teaching
would be guarded by the Divine Guardian, and used
by Him for the profit of those who had received it.
And he could remind his fellow-workers, as St. Paul
reminded Timothy, that they also have " the good
deposit " entrusted to them ; let them guard it too !

A similar thought is expressed in II. ii. 9. St. Paul
reminds Timothy that he, the Apostle, is suffering
even " as a malefactor " ; " but," he adds, " the
word of God is not bound." No chain or prison bars
for the Lord's message ! The Lord would take care
of that ! Indeed, we know what great work has
actually been done in prisons. We remember Luther
in the Wartburg, and Bunyan in Bedford Gaol, and
we rejoice to echo the Apostle's words and say, " Yes,
indeed ! the word of God is not bound ! "

But commentators are not all agreed that this
interpretation is correct. Without entering into the
arguments either way, we may accept the fact that
the Greek allows either explanation ; and, so far as our
own encouragement is concerned, I see no reason why
we should not read the verse both ways. Whichever
St. Paul actually meant, both are true. The Lord
will guard " my deposit," whether that deposit is
myself or the work He has entrusted to me.

9

FIVE FAITHFUL SAYINGS

THERE is a remarkable feature of the Pastoral Epistles which we find nowhere else in the Bible. There are five " faithful sayings." The expression *Pistos ho logos*, literally " faithful [is] the word," is unique. The nearest parallel is in Rev. xxi. 5 and xxii. 6, in both which verses we read " These words are faithful and true." Here are the five passages :—

1. Faithful is the saying, and worthy of all acceptation, that Christ Jesus came into the world to save sinners. I. i. 15.
2. Faithful is the saying, If a man seeketh the office of a bishop, he desireth a good work. I. iii. 1.
3. Godliness is profitable for all things, having promise of the life which now is, and of that which is to come. Faithful is the saying, and worthy of all acceptation. I. iv. 8, 9.
4. Faithful is the saying : For if we died with Him, we shall also live with Him ; if we endure, we shall also reign with Him, etc. II. ii. 11.
5. But when the kindness of God our Saviour, and His love toward man, appeared . . . according to His mercy He saved us . . . that . . . we might be made heirs according to the hope of eternal life. Faithful is the saying. . . Tit. iii. 4-8.

It will be noticed that in Nos. 1, 2, 4 the words " Faithful is the saying " precede the " saying " itself, while in Nos. 3 and 5 they follow it. This is the view of (I think) all the best expositors ; but it is right to add that No. 1 is the only case in which *all* writers agree on this point. In Nos. 2 and 4 the

" saying " has been supposed to be what *precedes* the statement that it is " faithful," while in Nos. 3 and 5 the " saying " has been supposed to be what *follows*. But so far as I have seen no two writers agree in these corrections, so we may confidently adopt the general opinion.

Now what were these " faithful sayings " ? There can be little doubt that they were current sayings among the early Christians, which St. Paul quotes, and endorses with his emphatic " Faithful." One or two may have been from some short creed or catechism, and the others probably include a proverbial maxim, a verse of a hymn, and a mere popular saying. Let us look at them one by one.

No. 1. Nothing is more likely than that some elementary teaching was given to new converts and their children in the form of a short catechism or creed ; and it is possible that there is an allusion to some primitive creed or doctrinal statement in II. i. 13, where St. Paul exhorts Timothy to " hold fast the form of sound words." May we not fairly suppose that the words of No. 1, " Christ Jesus came into the world to save sinners," were a fragment from such " form " ? It is delightful to think of this familiar text, the " comfortable word " of our Communion Service, being thus a kind of motto or watchword in those early days, and learned by the children at their mothers' knees, *before* St. Paul put it into this Letter, stamped with his endorsement, " Faithful is the saying," so that it became a text of Holy Scripture. We must never forget that there was as yet no New Testament. St. Paul's own earlier Epistles were, of course, valued and revered by those who had received them, but they were not yet put on a level with the Scriptures of the Old Testament, the " Bible " of the Early Church ; nor would they yet be widely circulated ; and as for the Gospels, though I personally am inclined to think that one or two at least were already written, they would not be generally known.

No. 2. At first sight it is curious to find such a sentence as this, that seeking a " bishopric " is desiring a good work, elevated to the dignity of one of St. Paul's " faithful sayings." But we shall see by and by that the " bishop " was then the same as the " presbyter " ; and the meaning is that when the infant Churches saw the Apostles ordaining " elders " or " presbyters " or " bishops " to be their pastors and leaders, it became a current saying that for a man to seek this " ordination " was to desire a good or noble (*kalos*) work or calling. We certainly think so now ; how much more then ! St. Paul, in fact, virtually says, " Yes, that popular saying is a true one, for a noble work it indeed is which is thus sought after." Liddon's remark here is worth quoting : " Such a maxim as this belongs to a time when the ministerial office was one of danger and hardship, and when aspirants to it required encouragement from the public opinion of the Church. . . . *Episcopē* here means the oversight of souls, which is described as a *kalon ergon* [good or noble work]. . . . A man may rightly seek after it ; it implies no clutching at honour or dignity ; it is an occupation spiritually honourable."[1]

No. 3. This also would be a current saying, but of a

---

[1] *Expl. Anal. of First Tim.*, p. 23.

different kind, a sort of proverbial maxim. "Godliness," *eusebeia*, was a familiar word among the Greeks, and was applied by them to the service of the gods and to reverent behaviour towards parents or other superiors, like the Latin *pietas*. We can understand how the Greek Christians might take up the word and say, " Ah, we have come to know that true godliness is more profitable than we ever thought. We knew it had the promise of this life ; we now know it has also the promise of the life to come." And St. Paul, calling on Timothy to " exercise " himself, with the energy of a gymnast (as " exercise " means, *gymnaze*), but with a nobler object, " unto godliness," thinks of the saying already current among the Christians as to the real profitableness of godliness, and adds, " Yes, true is that saying, and worthy of all men to be received."

No. 4 seems to be a verse of a hymn, and we will look at it as such in another Talk. Anyway, St. Paul emphatically endorses its bright and encouraging words.

No. 5. This " saying " is a longer utterance, and really embodies a summary of the Gospel. It has been suggested that it also is from a hymn, but there seems to be nothing in the wording to indicate such a source. More probably, like No. 1, it is a fragment of the elementary teaching common in the Early Church in the form of a creed or catechism. If No. 1 was a brief Christian watchword, this may be a fuller yet short paragraph embodying what the converts learned by heart, and rejoiced to know as the truth of God. We shall study the words more closely by and by; but meanwhile let anyone just read aloud, or repeat, verses 4-7, imagining their being learned by those troublesome Cretans as embodying the glorious message they had received and believed, and he will understand how joyfully St. Paul would quote them, and then exclaim, " Faithful is the saying ! " First, there is the source of the salvation of those Cretan Christians—and of us—" the kindness of God our Saviour, and His love toward man (*philanthrōpia*). Then, the disclaiming of human merit : " not by works done in righteousness which we did ourselves " ; no, only " His mercy "—and that " mercy " not merely giving the hope that perhaps we shall be " saved " some day, but assuring us that we *were* " saved." And when ? When we publicly put off the old life and began the new, when we took the decisive step of submitting to Christ's holy ordinance of baptism, and " with the mouth made confession " of Him " unto salvation " ;[1] that " regeneration " being daily followed by " the renewing of the Holy Ghost," " poured out upon us richly "; and all " through Jesus Christ our Saviour "—was it not His Atonement, through which we were " justified by His grace," that rendered all this possible ? And then God's purpose throughout : that we might be made His " heirs," with the sure " hope of eternal life." Grand teaching for those early Christians ! Would that there were more of it now !

But St. Paul adds a caution, needed still as much as ever. " Constantly affirm " these blessed truths, he says to Titus ; but to what end ? To secure orthodoxy, and make those Cretans good " Protestants," or good " Catholics," against error ? No, no ;

---

[1] See Chap. XXIV., on Baptism.

that would not satisfy the Apostle, or the Apostle's Lord. "To the end that they which have believed God may be careful to maintain good works." A sober, righteous, and godly life, not the ground of salvation, but the evidence and fruit of salvation.

Two other points should be noticed in studying these " faithful sayings " :—

1. In all the five cases the word " faithful " stands first in the Greek, and is therefore to be emphasised. " This is a faithful saying," as in the A.V., and " This is a true saying," as in the Communion Service, both fail to express the emphasis. St. Paul's exclamation is, " Faithful is the saying ! "

2. Two of the five " sayings " are followed by the additional remark, " and worthy of all acceptation." The Greek word for " acceptation " does not occur again in the New Testament, but we have " acceptable in the sight of God " twice, both times in our First Epistle, viz., in ii. 3 and v. 4. " All " here has the force of " by all " ; and Cranmer, in our Communion Service, happily paraphrased the sentence thus, " worthy of all men to be received." How St. Paul must have longed that " all men " should hear such " faithful sayings " ! Why have multitudes not heard them yet ?

10

THREE HYMN STANZAS

IN examining the five " Faithful Sayings," we deferred one of them because it appeared to be a verse of a hymn. Let us now look at this " saying," and at two other passages which are also considered to be verses of hymns.

It was quite natural for St. Paul to quote hymns, just as it was natural for him to quote creeds or catechisms or current proverbs. We know that " psalms and hymns and spiritual songs " were already in use in the Church. The Psalms of the O.T. were a pattern for them. In writing to the Churches of Asia Minor, of which the chief was that of Ephesus, where Timothy was in charge, St. Paul had already commended their use (Eph. v. 19, Col. iii. 16) ; St. James does the same (v. 13) ; and we hear of them also at Corinth (1 Cor. xiv. 26). Our Lord Himself and His Apostles sang a hymn after the institution of the Lord's Supper (Matt. xxvi. 30, Mk. xiv. 26). And the Roman Governor of Bithynia half a century later, Pliny the Younger, reported to the Emperor Trajan that the Christians in his province sang hymns " to Christ as God."

1. The " faithful saying " from a hymn is in II. ii. 11-13. St. Paul has been exhorting Timothy to be brave as a soldier, strenuous as an athlete, laborious as a husbandman. He cites the example of Christ, and then his own example : ver. 9, " I suffer hardship unto bonds, as a malefactor. . . . I endure all things for the elect's sake. . . ." And then he encourages

his young colleague by quoting this hymn. If we transliterate the Greek, we shall perceive the poetical form :—

Ei sunapethanomen kai sunzēsomen.	If we died with Him, we shall also live with Him.
Ei hupomenomen kai sun-basileusomen.	If we endure, we shall also reign with Him.
Ei arnēsometha kakeinos arnēsetai hēmas.	If we shall deny Him, He also will deny us.
Ei apistoumen ekeinos pistos menei.	If we are faithless, He abideth faithful.

Now imagine this hymn sung by a band of persecuted Christians. Think of its meaning ! " Are we in danger of death ? Well, we have died to sin already, by our union with Him Who died as our representative ; and in virtue of that same union we shall live with Him. So even if they do slaughter us, the death of our bodies will only bring the fulness of eternal life for our souls. Meanwhile, let us endure all our suffering with patient courage, knowing we are to reign as kings with Him by and by ! " And can we fancy one saying to another, " O brother, deny Him not ! lest He be compelled to deny you ! Dare you risk His saying ' I know you not ' ? " And then the last clause ; it looks comforting : " We may fail Him, but He will not fail us " ; but there is in it also the solemn hint that His very faithfulness may involve His rejection of the faithless ; so St. Paul appends to the stanza his own word of comment, " For He cannot deny Himself " ; His warnings are as certain as His promises. We all know how animating a rousing hymn is : what must a hymn like this have been to Christians liable to be thrown to the lions !

2. The second passage supposed to be a hymn-stanza is in I. vi. 15, 16.   The "appearing of our Lord Jesus Christ " is alluded to—literally His " Epiphany," the *second* one, the Second Advent ; then, " Which in its (or His) own times He shall show," says St. Paul, and then adds, " Who is "—and quotes the hymn :—

Ho makarios	The blessed
Kai monos Dunastēs,	And only Potentate,
Ho Basileus tōn basileuon-tōn,	The King of kings
Kai Kurios tōn kuriĕu-ontōn	And Lord of lords,
Ho monos echōn athana-sian,	Who only hath immor-tality,
Phōs oikōn aprositon,	Dwelling in light un-approachable,
Hon eiden oudeis anthrō-pōn	Whom no man hath seen
Oude idein dunatai.	Nor can see.

And he adds the ascription, " To Whom be honour and power eternal.   Amen."

We shall examine the words of this superb doxology by and by.   Let me only here remind my readers of the wonderful strains of the Hallelujah Chorus, " King of kings and lord of lords " ; does not Handel's incomparable music instantly spring into the memory ? Well, when we next hear that grandest of all choruses sung or played, let us think of the Christians of Ephesus and Philippi and Corinth in the first century chanting in some setting now unknown to us those glorious and animating words.

3. But the third is the most remarkable.   In I. iii. 14-16 St. Paul explains that he writes his letter,

in case his absence should be longer than he hopes, in order that Timothy may know " how men ought to behave themselves in the House of God, which is the Church of the living God, the pillar and ground of the truth." The reference in these words to the Church we shall consider hereafter ; but St. Paul goes on, " And without controversy great is the mystery of godliness." Evidently the answer to the question how men should behave in the Church is " godliness," the *eusebeia* referred to in our preceding Talk. What, then, is that " mystery of godliness " which is so " great " ? He does not mean that the mysteriousness is great. " Mystery " in the N.T. is a *secret*, generally a secret revealed ; and the words are equivalent to " great is the secret of true religion." Not that there is great secrecy, but that the secret thing now revealed is great. Then where is that great revelation of " godliness," that secret or " mystery " of true religion now unveiled, to be found ? It is in reply to this natural question that St. Paul quotes the hymn. His words, as given in the R.V., are " He Who," and then the stanza :—

Ephanerōthē en sarki,	Was manifested in the flesh,
Edikaiōthē en pneumati,	Justified in the spirit,
Ōphthē aggelois,	Seen of angels,
Ekēruchthē en ethnesin,	Preached among the nations,
Episteuthē en kosmō,	Believed on in the world,
Anelēmphthē en doxē.	Received up in glory.

It seems natural to take the first and second lines of the stanza as linked closely together, and also the fourth and fifth lines ; and then the two short lines will be the double climax, " Seen of angels " being the recognition, in the whole heavenly sphere, of the Incarnation of the Son of God, and " Received up in glory,"[1] as the consequence of that recognition and the consummation of His Mission. Thus, as Dr. Horton remarks, the first, second, fourth, and fifth lines refer to earth, and the third and sixth to heaven.

But some of the best expositors arrange the lines differently, associating the third and fourth lines together, " seen of angels," and " preached among the nations " ; and also the two last lines, " Believed on in the world," and " received up in glory." Bishop Bernard entitles the lines one and two " the revelation and its proofs " ; lines three and four " its extent and mode " ; lines five and six, " its consummation on earth and in heaven." Thus (1) Christ was " manifested in the flesh," was incarnate, and became " very man," yet by His " spirit,"[2] His character and life and works, He was " justified," proved to be indeed the Son of God ; (2) the revelation of Him as the God-Man was made to all creation, to the rational creatures that were nearest to God, the angels, and to those that were furthest off, the heathen nations, the two extremes indicating the whole ; (3) the victory of the Lord is shown by the reception of His message

---

[1] The Greek verb here, ἀναλαμβάνω, is the regular word used in connection with the Ascension, Mark xvi. 19, Acts i. 2, 11, 22. The word for " received up " in Luke ix. 51 is connected with it.

[2] " Spirit " cannot here mean the Holy Spirit. It is plainly contrasted with " flesh " in the first line, and obviously means our Lord's human spirit.

by believers on earth, and by the reception of Himself at the Throne of God.

What, then, is the "secret of true religion"? Not a system of ethics, however good in itself, but the Incarnation and mission and glorification of Jesus Christ. So in Col. i. 27 : "God was pleased to make known what is the riches of the glory of this mystery among the Gentiles, which is Christ in you, the hope of glory"; and in Col. ii. 2 : "That they may know the mystery of God, even Christ."

What a glimpse do we thus get into the hymnody of the Early Church !

Here we might stop ; but it may be well to add a few words about the alteration by the R.V. of "God manifest in the flesh," as in the A.V., to "He Who was manifested in the flesh." This is in accordance with all the earliest authorities. The two readings are $\overline{\Theta C}$, the short form in which ΘΕOC (God) was written, and OC (who) ; and the latter is in the best MSS. The Alexandrian, in the British Museum, usually called A, was an apparent exception ; but Bishop Ellicott carefully examined it, and satisfied himself that originally OC had certainly been written, but that a mark on the other side of the paper had made it look like $\overline{\Theta C}$. Barring this, the reading "God" is not found in any Christian writer before the fifth century, nor is it in any of the foreign versions till three or four centuries later. If the passage is a hymn stanza beginning "Was manifested," the preceding stanza may have named our Lord. Suppose some such words came just before as "Let us praise our Lord Christ," then "Who was manifested," etc.,

would come naturally.   Compare our Christian hymn :
if we quoted these lines,

> " Born that man no more may die,
> Born to raise the sons of earth,
> Born to give them second birth "—

we should all understand Who was referred to,
although the actual quotation did not name Him.

This perfectly correct and necessary change in the
R.V. caused at the time an outburst of disapproval,
as if the doctrine of the Deity of Christ had been tam-
pered with ; an outburst as unreasonable as many
other similar ones have been.   The great truth of
the Incarnation of the Son of God is not dependent
upon a disputed reading of the MSS.

11
DOCTRINAL TEACHING:
THE GOSPEL, THE FAITH

I NOW propose to discuss, in several Talks, the
doctrinal teaching of the Pastoral Epistles.   We
have had some glimpses of it already, but we must
now examine it more systematically.

We have seen that the " deposit " which had been
" committed " to St. Paul, and which he " committed "
to Timothy and Titus, and charged them to " commit " to others, is described as " the Gospel of the
glory of the blessed God," the glad tidings of redemp-

tion for mankind. We have now to see, more in detail, what that Gospel was. But there are two things to be done first, by way of introduction. We will examine the Greek word itself which stands for "Gospel," and we will also look at other words which are used by St. Paul in nearly the same or a connected sense—" the Truth," " the Faith," " Sound Doctrine," etc.

The Greek word for " Gospel " is *euaggelion*. It is a prominent Pauline word, occurring sixty times in the Apostle's writings, and only sixteen times elsewhere in the New Testament. The cognate verb, *euaggelizo*, is more especially a Lukan word, occurring twenty-five times in the third Gospel and the Acts ; but St. Paul uses it twenty-three times, and all the other writers only nine times together. Neither word occurs in St. John's Gospel or Epistles.

The word *euaggelion* means literally " good message," or " news," or " tidings." Transliterated into Latin it becomes *evangelium*, from which we derive our " evangel," " evangelize," " evangelist," " evangelical." But instead of " evangel " we commonly use the Anglo-Saxon " gospel " (good-spell or story), and this translation of the Greek word is adopted almost everywhere in both the A.V. and the R.V.[1]

The English verb " evangelize " is not used in our Versions, and in fact would not quite give the sense of *euaggelizō*. The rendering is usually " preach (or bring) good tidings," or " preach the Gospel," or simply " preach." But " preach " is inadequate,

---

[1] The R.V. once has " glad tidings," in Rom. x. 16, the reason of which is obvious.

and it would be better to retain it for the other verb *kērusso*,[1] noticed in a previous Talk. In Eph. ii. 17 we read that Christ " came and preached peace." The R.V. margin suggests " preached good tidings of peace," which gives the full meaning of the Greek *eueggelisato* ; and the R.V. does adopt this in Acts x. 36, altering the " preaching peace " of the A.V. to " preaching good tidings of peace." Three times in the Acts we have the phrase " preach Jesus ' (viii. 35, xi. 20, xvii. 18), and it would be more correct to say " preach good tidings of Jesus." How much more significant is xvii. 18 if we read that St. Paul preached to the Athenians, who were always on the look-out for " some new thing," " good news about Jesus and the resurrection "! But there are a few places where this mode of rendering would not do. For instance, in Gal. i. 11, " the Gospel which was preached " is *to euaggelion to euaggelisthen*, literally " the good tidings which was preached as good tidings."[2] It is a good thing for us to get glimpses of the difficulties of our translators and revisers.

There is another cognate noun, *euaggelistēs*, which occurs three times in the N.T. We read of " Philip the Evangelist " (Acts xxi. 8) and of " evangelists in the Church " (Eph. iv. 11) ; and, coming to the Pastoral Epistles, we find St. Paul exhorting Timothy to " do the work of an evangelist " (II. iv. 5).

This group of Greek words is found also in the LXX.,

---

[1] See Chap. VII.

[2] In Gal. i. 8, 9, the verb is used of preaching false gospels. The Greek there literally means " Though we, or an angel from heaven, should preach good tidings to you other than what we preached to you as good tidings," etc. And so in the next verse.

the Greek Septuagint Version of the O.T., and it is particularly interesting to find them in Isaiah, the " evangelical prophet." In chap. xl. we have the phrase " tellest good tidings " twice, the word being *euaggelizomenos*. Dean Plumptre, in his Commentary on Isaiah, touchingly remarks : " It is not without emotion that we note the first occurrence of the word which, passing through the Greek of the LXX. and the N.T., has had so fruitful a history, as embodying the message of the Gospel—good-spell, glad tidings— to mankind." No doubt Isa. xl. 9 is the place of that exact word's first occurrence, and with a " gospel " meaning ; but we find words of the same group in the " good tidings " expected by David to be brought by Ahimaaz, but which Joab knew would *not* be " good tidings " to the king (2 Sam. xviii.) ; also in what the " four leprous men " in 2 Kings vii. call the " day of good tidings." The instances in Isaiah are as follows :

Chap. xl. 9.   O thou that tellest good tidings to Zion.
,,   ,,   O thou that tellest good tidings to Jeru-
             salem.
,,   lii. 7.   How beautiful . . . are the feet of him
             that bringeth good tidings.
,,   ,,   That bringeth good tidings of good.
,,   lxi. 1.   The Lord hath anointed me to preach
             good tidings.

And in Nahum (i. 15) we find again the words " The feet of him that bringeth good tidings." When we next hear Handel's *Messiah*, let that beautiful chorus, " O thou that tellest good tidings to Zion," remind us that from it come our great words " evangel," " evangelist," " evangelical " ; and let Mendelssohn's equally beautiful and still more familiar chorus in his *Elijah*, " How beautiful upon the mountains," always stir our hearts with the thought of " the Gospel of the glory of the blessed God."

So much for these interesting words.   Let us never for a moment forget that God's Message is a " Gospel," because it is good news.   How often is it said by men of the world about Missions, " Why do you want to thrust your religion down other people's throats ? " We may truly answer, " I could not do that if I would, and I would not if I could " ; but what a misconception of Christianity does the question involve !   I have received good news, not for myself only, but for all men.   Is it not my plain duty to tell them ?   Perhaps they refuse to hear me ; perhaps they disbelieve me and my " good news " altogether.   For that I am not responsible ; but surely I am responsible to tell them !   That Chinese evangelist was not far wrong who said he preached because he had good news meant for his hearers, and if he did not preach them he would be breaking the Eighth Commandment.

And now what is this good news ?   Let the angel answer whose message to the shepherds of Bethlehem is, as a matter of fact, the origin of our Christmas festivities.   " Behold, I bring you good tidings of great joy, . . . for there is born . . . a Saviour, which is Christ the Lord."   A Saviour !   Do we want one ? Some may say No ; but we Christians, as we look sorrowfully on the evils and miseries in the world around us, perceive that they are all, directly or indirectly, the result of sin.   To save us all from sin, and from sin's consequences, the Son of God took our nature upon Him, lived a perfect life, died an atoning sacrifice ; and now He lives and reigns to complete His work by the agency of the Holy Spirit, and to bring us back to God.   Is not that good news ? What good news can compare with it ?   No wonder St. Paul desired that all Timothy's teaching and preaching should be in accordance with " the gospel of the glory of the blessed God " !

Now the first thing needed for the triumph of the Gospel is that it be believed.   Naturally, therefore, much stress is laid by St. Paul on faith.   But in these Pastoral Epistles he uses this word " faith," *pistis*, not only as expressing the confidence with which we receive the Message and our trust in the Saviour it reveals, but as a synonym for the Message itself. That is to say, he gives it an objective sense as well as a subjective one.   He speaks of " *the* faith "—that is, not the act of believing but the doctrine believed. It is well in these cases to use a capital F, " the Faith." Thus :—

I.	i.	19.	Made shipwreck concerning the Faith.
	iii.	9.	Holding the mystery of the Faith in a pure conscience.
	iv.	1.	Some shall fall away from the Faith.
		6.	Nourished in the words of the Faith.
	v.	8.	He hath denied the Faith.
	vi.	10.	Led astray from the Faith.
		12.	Fight the good fight of the Faith.
		21.	Which some professing have erred concerning the Faith.
II.	iii.	8.	Reprobate concerning the Faith.
	iv.	7.	I have kept the Faith.
Tit.	i.	13.	Sound in the Faith.

We find the same objective sense of the word elsewhere ; for instance, " A great company of the priests were obedient to the Faith " (Acts vi. 7) ; " the Churches were strengthened in the Faith " (Acts xvi. 5) ; and see Acts xiii. 8, Gal. i. 23, Phil. i. 27.

" The Faith " is truly a suitable name for the Gospel of Christ. Our religion is no mere system of ethics. The very beginning of it is " I believe," *Credo* ; and what do I believe ? The facts of the Creeds. For they are indeed *facts*. In the very centre of our simplest Creed we come across the name of a historic personage, the mention of whose name actually gives us a date for the events whose actual occurrence we declare that we believe : " Suffered under Pontius Pilate "—a man known in Roman history. Accordingly, we all, whether really Christians or not, reckon our years from the Advent of Him Who thus " suffered." The most blatant atheist dates his letters " 1914." Why ? Because the civilised world has accepted the fact that Jesus Christ lived 1914 years ago, and that His Life and Death were the greatest events in history. Well may we call our religion " the Faith " !

But the references to " the Faith " in the Pastorals, above quoted, are a significant reminder how easy it is to lose hold of it. Of the eleven passages cited, more than half carry a solemn warning of this danger. We may " deny the Faith " ; we may " err concerning " it ; we may be " led astray from it " ; we may " fall away " from it ; we may be " reprobate " concerning it ; we may even " make shipwreck " concerning it. Well may we pray to be kept " sound " in it, and to " hold it in a pure conscience " ; to be enabled to " fight the good fight " of and for it, and thus to be able at the last to say, " I have kept the Faith."

Of " faith " as an attitude of the soul we shall think another time.

12

DOCTRINAL TEACHING:
THE TRUTH

THERE are two Greek words in the N.T. which signify " doctrine " or " teaching "—that is either the thing taught or the act of teaching. These are *didachē* and *didaskalia*. The former only occurs twice in the Pastoral Epistles, though common elsewhere ; while the latter is specially characteristic of them, occurring fifteen times, and only five times elsewhere. The A.V. translates them both " doctrine " in every case ; the R.V. has " doctrine " ten times and " teaching " five times for *didaskalia*, and " teaching " both times for *didachē*. Bishop Bernard reads " doctrine " fourteen times and " teaching " three times, while Dr. Plummer thinks *didaskalia* generally means " teaching " and *didachē* " doctrine." So doctors differ ! Adopting the R.V. here, we have the following cases of *didaskalia* :—

I.   i. 10. The sound doctrine.
    iv.   1. Doctrines of devils.
          6. Nourished in . . . the good doctrine.
         13. Give heed to . . . teaching.
         16. Take heed . . . to thy teaching.

I.   v. 17. Those who labour . . . in teaching.
     vi. 1. That . . . the doctrine be not blasphemed.
          3. The doctrine which is according to godliness.
II. iii. 10. Thou didst follow my teaching.
         16. Every Scripture . . . is . . . profitable for
             teaching.
     iv. 3. They will not endure the sound doctrine.
Tit. i. 9. Able to exhort in the sound doctrine.
      ii. 1. The things which befit the sound doctrine.
          7. In thy doctrine showing uncorruptness.
         10. Adorn the doctrine of God our Saviour.

And the following of *didachē* :—

II. iv. 2. Exhort, with all longsuffering and teaching.
Tit. i. 9. The faithful word which is according to the
           teaching.

Four times, it will be seen, St. Paul speaks of
" sound doctrine." We find also " sound words "
twice (I. vi. 3, II. i. 13), " sound in the Faith " twice
(Tit. i. 13, ii. 2), and " sound speech " once (Tit. ii.
8).[1] This word is very interesting, and means
" healthy " or " healthful," as in the R.V. margin.
The A.V. has " wholesome " in I. vi. 3. The word
(or a connected one) is " whole " in the Gospels,
where sick men are " made whole." The Greek
adjective is *hugies,* and the verb *hugiaino,* and we can
easily see the origin of our word " hygiene."

We are all familiar with the phrases " sound and
unsound teaching," " sound and unsound doctrine,"
" sound in the Faith " ; and we owe them to these
Epistles. But notice that the expressions really
mean healthful, healthy, wholesome. There is such

---

[1] " Sound mind," in the A.V. of II. i. 7, is another word
altogether ; " discipline " in the R.V.

a thing as spiritual hygiene. Am I spiritually sick ? I need spiritual treatment, that will heal me, make me healthy. Am I spiritually well ? I need spiritual food that will keep me in good health. Now, St. Paul not only lays stress on sound doctrine ; he gives us a test whereby to try it. Look at I. i. 10, 11 : " sound doctrine " is doctrine which is " according to the gospel of the glory of the blessed God," that very Gospel, that Glad Tidings, which is committed to our trust, as it was to St. Paul's. Look also at I. vi. 3, where " sound words " are identified with " the words of our Lord Jesus Christ," and with " the doctrine which is according to godliness." Liddon thus analyses this verse :

(1) In its substance, morally healthy discourse.
(2) In its source, coming from our Lord Jesus Christ.
(3) In its standard, corresponding to the needs of piety.

The phrase " even the words of our Lord Jesus Christ " is very interesting. What words would they be ? The three Gospels, even if written (as I for one think), could not then be widely known. But those " narratives " to which St. Luke alludes (i. 1) may have been scattered about ; and most scholars now think many of His discourses were contained in a lost document, which they call " Q." Isolated sayings of Christ were certainly in men's mouths ; one is quoted in Acts xx. 35, and others (called *logia*) have been found in the sands of Egypt.

We saw in our last Talk that the Gospel was sometimes called " the Faith." There is another word in these Epistles used in the same way, a word which assures us that " the Faith " is no collection of " cunningly-devised fables," or even something which has an element of uncertainty in it, something which may possibly be true, but of which we cannot be quite sure. Twelve times in our Epistles does St. Paul apply to the doctrine of the Gospel the word *alētheia*, " the Truth."[1]

I. ii.   4. [God] willeth that all men should . . . come to the knowledge of the Truth.

iii. 15. The Church of the Living God, the pillar and ground of the Truth.

iv.   3. Them that believe and know the Truth.

vi.   5. Men corrupted in mind and bereft of the Truth.

II. ii. 15. Handling aright the word of Truth.

18. Men who concerning the Truth have erred.

25. Repentance unto the knowledge of the Truth.

iii.   7. Never able to come to the knowledge of the Truth.

8. So do these also withstand the Truth.

iv.   4. Will turn away their ears from the Truth.

Tit. i.   1. An apostle . . . according to . . . the knowledge of the Truth.

14. Men who turn away from the Truth.

Now while we naturally speak of *believing* the Gospel, we speak rather of *knowing* the Truth. The Glad Tidings are received into the heart ; the Truth—that is, the doctrine—is grasped by the mind. And so we find it in these Letters. Of the twelve passages just quoted, five are concerned with " knowing " the Truth. And this brings us to the interesting Greek words *gnōsis* and *epignōsis*. The latter word,

---

[1] Besides I. ii. 7, where the word twice refers to speaking the truth.

which is the stronger, and generally means thorough knowledge, and its cognate verb, are found in the five places where " knowledge of the Truth " is referred to ;[1] while the more ordinary word *gnōsis* occurs only in I. vi. 20, where " knowledge (A.V. science) falsely so-called " is mentioned. Very simple faith, if with but little knowledge, is sufficient for salvation ; as with Cowper's cottager in his *Truth* :—

> Just knows, and knows no more, her Bible true—
> A truth the brilliant Frenchman never knew ;
> And in that charter reads, with sparkling eyes,
> Her title to a treasure in the skies.

But we should not be lazily content with a minimum of knowledge. St. Paul's prayer for the Colossians (i. 9–10) was that they might be " increasing in the knowledge of God " and " filled with the knowledge of His will " ; and for the Philippians (i. 9), that their love might " abound yet more and more in knowledge and all discernment " ; and so also for the Ephesian Churches (iv. 13) ; and in all these cases it is the stronger word *epignōsis* that he uses. This word occurs twenty times in the N.T., fifteen of them being in St. Paul's Epistles. The ordinary word *gnōsis* occurs twenty-nine times, twenty-two of which are in St. Paul. Both, therefore, are distinctly Pauline words.

There is, however, a pursuit of " knowledge " which is unsanctified and dangerous. " Knowledge," wrote St. Paul to the Corinthians (I. viii. 1), " puffeth up, but love buildeth up " (see R.V. margin). The day

---

[1] In two of these places, II. ii. 25 and Tit. i. 1, the A.V. has " acknowledging."

came, not many years after his time, when the " Gnostics " arose, who exemplified in their teaching what " *gnōsis* falsely so-called " is. They claimed to lead their disciples (as Bishop Moule puts it[1]) " past the common herd of mere *believers* to a superior and gifted circle who should *know* the mysteries of being, and who by such *knowing* should live emancipated from the slavery of matter, ranging at liberty in the world of spirit." We shall by and by see a little of the teachers who in Timothy's day anticipated these errors, and we shall perceive that the " advanced thinkers " of the first century did not differ much from the " advanced thinkers " of the twentieth.

Our Lord Himself gives us the key of the position. " If ye abide in My word," He said (John viii. 31-32), then are ye My disciples indeed ; and ye shall know the Truth, and the Truth shall make you free." Justly has Dr. Griffith Thomas reminded us, by the title of his popular handbook, that " Christianity is Christ." The Lord Himself said, " I am the Truth." Which reminds me of a once-familiar anagram on Pilate's question put to the Prisoner standing before him (John xviii. 38), " What is truth ? " In Latin this question would be *Quid est veritas ?* and these letters rearranged make *Vir est qui adest,* " It is the Man Who is here before thee."

----

[1] *Second Timothy,* p. 91.

13

DOCTRINE OF GOD

WE now go on to examine the teaching of the Pastorals on particular doctrines. And, first of all, what do they teach us about God, the Creator, the Supreme Ruler, the Father of men ?

1. We have the grand fundamental truth of the One God emphatically stated : " There is one God " (I. ii. 5) ; " the only God " (I. i. 17). This, after all, was the primary message for that period ; and so it is to-day, alas ! for half the population of the world. What a blessing would England be to the world if her sons in Asia and Africa, for purposes of trade, or sport, or government, would but testify by word and life that, in St. Paul's words to the Corinthians, " We know that no idol is anything in the world, and that there is no god but one ; for though there be that are called gods, whether in heaven or on earth . . . yet to us there is one God, the Father, of Whom are all things, and we unto Him " !

2. Then we have twice [1] the striking expression, " the Living God " :—

I. iii. 15.   The Church of the Living God.
  iv. 10.   We trust in the Living God.

The thought thus embodied is a common one in the O.T. We find the exact phrase twelve times there, as when David in his youthful indignation exclaims, " Who is this uncircumcised Philistine, that he should

---

[1] The words " the living " in I. vi. 17 (A.V.) are dropped by the R.V.

defy the armies of the Living God ? " and when Hezekiah speaks of Rabshakeh being sent "to reproach the Living God " ; and when the Psalmist's soul " thirsts for the Living God " ; and when King Darius cries to Daniel in the den, " O servant of the Living God ! " But the solemn asseveration, " As the Lord liveth," occurs over thirty times, and Jehovah Himself uses the phrase " As I live " seventeen times. It was a great and significant thought. The existence of tribal deities was not denied by the Jews ; Baal and Moloch were very real to them ; they had not arrived at St. Paul's perception that an idol is nothing ; but Jehovah alone was " the Living God." In the N.T. we find the exact phrase fifteen times, and once Christ Himself speaks of " the Living Father " (John vi. 57). Peter's great confession is " Thou art the Christ, the Son of the Living God." Caiaphas adjures Jesus " by the Living God." St. Paul appeals to the barbarians at Lystra to turn to " the Living God," and bases his exhortation to the Corinthians to be " separate " from the heathen on their being " a temple of the Living God."

St. Paul, let us remember, was writing to Timothy at Ephesus. Did he so emphatically speak of " the Living God " in contrast with that imaginary deity " whom all Asia and the world worshipped " (Acts xix. 27), " the great goddess Diana " ? And now for centuries not one soul on earth has believed in the famous Ephesian goddess, while our Living God not only lives for ever as the one Supreme Deity, but lives in a special sense in the hearts of tens of thousands. And yet half the world still knows Him not. Whose fault is that ?

3. Then we have two great passages describing God. The first is in I. i. 17, " The King eternal, incorruptible (A.V. immortal), invisible, the only God." " The King eternal," literally " of the ages," a phrase only occurring once elsewhere in the N.T. (Rev. xv. 3), where the R.V. gives the exact translation, " King of the Ages." [1] The R.V. references, always well chosen, send us to Ps. x. 16, " the Lord is King for ever and ever," which in the LXX. is " of the age and the ages." We naturally think of the ages to come, but our Epistles twice mention the ages past, the " times eternal " :—

> II. i. 9. Who saved us, and called us with a holy calling, not according to our works, but according to His own purpose and grace, which was given in Christ Jesus before times eternal.
>
> Tit i. 2. In hope of eternal life, which God, Who cannot lie, promised before times eternal.

The Greek is *pro chronōn aiōniōn*, and the A.V. renders it " before the world began," but " before times eternal " is the literal translation. Here we have a wonderful glimpse of the foreknowledge and eternal purpose of God. He foreknew the Fall of man ; He purposed to stoop down and save man ; it was all of grace ; and it was no mere rescue from the consequences of the Fall ; there was also a promise of eternal life from " God Who cannot lie " ! [2] A

---

[1] The A.V. has " King of Saints," ἀγίων, but αἰώνων is the true reading.

[2] The three words " Who cannot lie " translate one Greek word, ἀψευδής, which simply puts the negative α before the word for lying or false. This word occurs nowhere else in the N.T.

promise to whom ? To mankind ? But mankind did not then exist. No ; but even then, " before times eternal," the Son of God represented the race whose nature He would one day stoop to take, and received the promise for us ! All this is beyond the comprehension of the most learned, but not beyond the faith of the humblest believer.

Then look at the three adjectives. " Incorruptible," *aphthartos*, the same word as we find in Rom. i. 23 (the incorruptible God), 1 Cor. ix. 25 (an incorruptible crown), 1 Pet. i. 23 (the word of God incorruptible seed), 1 Pet. iii. 4 (incorruptible apparel, a meek and quiet spirit). " Invisible," *aoratos*, the word applied to God also in Col. i. 15 and Heb. xi. 27 ; and the fact is stated in other words in John i. 18 and 1 John iv. 12, " No man hath seen God at any time."   " Only," *monos* ; God *is unique*.

4. The other passage is I. vi. 15, " the blessed and only Potentate, the King of kings and Lord of lords, who only hath immortality, dwelling in light unapproachable, Whom no man hath seen, nor can see." Some of these clauses repeat the former statement in varying language, and need not detain us ; but note that " immortality " is *athanasia*, the negative of *thanatos*, " death," occurring elsewhere only in 1 Cor. xv. The name Athanasius is derived from it. Also that " unapproachable,"[1] *aprositos*, occurs nowhere else in the N.T., but is found in the Jewish writers Josephus and Philo. But we must look at two of the other words.

(*a*) " Potentate." The Greek word *dunastēs* only

---

[1] Represented in the A.V. by six English words, " which no man can approach unto."

occurs in two other places, and in them is applied to men.[1] In the Magnificat, " He hath put down the mighty from their seat," " mighty " is the same word ; and the Ethiopian eunuch is described by the same word, there rendered " of great authority." The word is, of course, connected with *dunamis*, " power." " Potentate " is a good rendering ; and God is " the *only* Potentate."

(*b*) " Blessed." This is not the usual word applied to God, *eulogētos*, the participle of the verb " to bless," as in Mark xiv. 61, Luke i. 68, Rom. i. 25, ix. 5, 2 Cor. i. 3, xi. 31, Eph. i. 3, 1 Pet. i. 3. That word means " worthy to be well spoken of," worthy to be praised, adorable. But the word here, and in I. i. 11, is *makarios*, " happy." In Bishop Bernard's words, " God is not only the Object of His creatures' blessing, but has in Himself the fulness of bliss." We are really to think of our Heavenly Father as " happy." Among the Greeks this word was the regular epithet for their gods, and St. Paul does not shrink from applying it to the One Only God, for He indeed alone has a right to it. Is He not pictured in the Old Testament as " rejoicing " ? Thus :—

Deut. xxviii. 63. The Lord rejoiced over you to do you good.

Ps. civ. 31. The Lord shall rejoice in His works.

Isa. lxii. 5. As the bridegroom rejoiceth over the bride, so shall thy God rejoice over thee.

lxv. 19. I will rejoice in Jerusalem and joy in My people.

---

[1] It is applied to God in Ecclesiasticus and the Books of Maccabees.

> Jer. xxxii. 41.　I will rejoice over them to do them good.
>
> Zeph. iii. 17.　The Lord thy God . . . will rejoice over thee with joy . . . He will joy over thee with singing.

Do we wish for the real happiness that God enjoys ? Christ shows us how. His Beatitudes in Matt. v. all begin with *makarios*, " blessed " or " happy."

5. The Fatherhood of God is not so prominent in the Pastorals as in some other of St. Paul's Letters. But each of the three has the phrase " God the Father " in the opening salutation, as is the case in all the rest. In several of the Epistles, however, it is " God *our* Father," which lays stress on the Divine Fatherhood towards His children both by nature and by grace. " God *the* Father " is primarily the expression of the Fatherhood in relation to the Son, the Fatherhood within the Godhead. But there are works attributed to God in these Epistles which may well be regarded as belonging to His Fatherly relation to us. The food which we are to " receive with thanksgiving " is expressly said to be " created " by Him (I. iv. 3). " All things " that are given us " richly to enjoy " are His gift (I. vi. 17). He gives " not a spirit of fearfulness, but of power and love and discipline " (II. i. 7). He " Who cannot lie " has, as we have already seen, " promised " " eternal life."

6. But these Epistles have one very notable feature in their references to God the Father. He is called, repeatedly, " the Saviour." This, however, must occupy our attention in another chapter.

14
GOD, THE SAVIOR

" OUR Saviour " is one of the commonest of religious phrases. Many people who never speak of " Jesus," or even of " Christ," do not mind uttering it. Little less common is " The Saviour." Both seem to imply a certain respectful distance, and certainly the more earnest Christian people, who think of Christ as their Friend and their Lord, do not often use either. This is perhaps curious, for a title more tender, and at the same time more holy, could scarcely be thought of. The surprising thing, however—at least it was surprising to me—is to find the word " Saviour " so uncommon as it is in the N.T. One would expect it to occur a hundred times or more, and it only occurs twenty-four times ; and of these, ten are in these Pastoral Epistles and five in 2nd Peter, leaving only nine in all the other books. Moreover, in eight of the twenty-four cases it refers definitely not to Christ, but to God the Father, and for this reason I take it now, the present Talk being to that extent a supplement to the preceding one on the Doctrine of God.

Of the eight cases of the title being given to God the Father, six are in the Pastorals. This use of it is therefore one of their special features. Here are the six passages :—

I. i. 1. God our Saviour, and Jesus Christ our Hope.
   ii. 3. Good and acceptable in the sight of God our Saviour.
  iv. 10. The Living God, Who is the Saviour of all men.

Tit. i. 3. The commandment of God our Saviour.
  ii. 10. Adorn the doctrine of God our Saviour.
  iii. 4. The kindness of God our Saviour.

The other two cases are particularly interesting :—

Luke i. 47. My spirit hath rejoiced in God my Saviour.

Jude 25. To the only God our Saviour, through Jesus Christ our Lord.

When Mary begins her Magnificat by expressing joy in God her Saviour, it is plain that she refers, not to the Child presently to be born of her, but to the God of Israel Whom she has always worshipped ; and St. Jude's doxology carefully distinguishes, by that word " through," between " God our Saviour " and " Jesus Christ."

It was nothing new for Jews to call the God of their fathers " Saviour." In the O.T. the idea is repeatedly expressed. " Salvation " is frequently attributed to Him, and the word " Saviour " itself is used in the following passages :—

2 Sam. xxii. 3. My high tower, my refuge, my Saviour.
  Ps. cvi. 21. They forgat God their Saviour.
  Isa. xliii. 3. I am the Lord thy God . . . thy Saviour.
  11. Beside me there is no Saviour.
  xlv. 15. O God of Israel, the Saviour.
  21. A just God and a Saviour.
  xlix. 26. I the Lord am thy Saviour.
  lxiii. 8. So He was their Saviour.
  Jer. xiv. 8. O Thou Hope of Israel, the Saviour thereof.
  Hos. xiii. 4. Beside Me there is no Saviour.

In some of these cases it is temporal deliverance or

preservation that is meant.   But, as regards spiritual salvation, we must always remember that its source is the love of God to man, whether by " God " we mean the Father in particular or the " Three Persons in one God."   This is illustrated by other passages in the Pastorals :—

> I. ii. 4. Who willeth that all men should be saved.
> II. i. 9. Who saved us, and called us with a holy calling.
> ii. 25. Peradventure God may give them repentance.
> Tit. ii. 11. The grace of God hath appeared, bringing salvation.
> iii. 5. According to His mercy He saved us.

It is surely a welcome addition to the Doctrine of God to find that He is not only the One God, the Creator, the Living God, the King of the Ages, the Incorruptible, the Immortal, the Invisible, the Potentate, the Happy God, the Father, *our* Father—all which we saw before,—but also the Saviour; not only so in the Person of the Son, and in virtue of the Son's Incarnation and Atonement, but, definitely, " Saviour " in Himself, as the great Originator, in His love and grace, of the salvation of men.

But we will now go on to see how and where in the N.T. the Son of God receives this glorious title. Only twice is He called " Saviour " in the Gospels, viz., by the angel at His birth and by the Samaritans at Sychar ; twice in speeches in the Acts, once by St. Peter and once by St. Paul ; twice by St. Paul in Epistles other than the Pastorals, but in one of the two cases in a special sense, marked by both A.V. and R.V. not using a capital S ; once by St. John in his First Epistle ; and the five times in 2nd Peter. Here are the passages :—

Luke ii. 11.   There is born to you . . . a Saviour, which is Christ the Lord.

John iv. 42.   We . . . know that this is indeed the Saviour of the world.

Acts v. 31.   Him did God exalt . . . to be a Prince and a Saviour.

xiii. 23.   Hath God . . . brought unto Israel a Saviour, Jesus.

Phil. iii. 20.   We wait for a Saviour, the Lord Jesus Christ.

Eph. v. 23.   Christ is . . . himself the saviour of the body.

1 John iv. 14.   The Father hath sent the Son to be the Saviour of the world.

2 Pet. i. 1.   Our God and Saviour Jesus Christ.

i. 11.   The eternal kingdom of our Lord and Saviour Jesus Christ.

ii. 20.   The knowledge of the Lord and Saviour Jesus Christ.

iii. 2.   The commandment of the Lord and Saviour.

18.   Grow in the grace and knowledge of our Lord and Saviour Jesus Christ.

The four occurrences in the Pastorals are :—

II. i. 10.   The appearing of our Saviour Christ Jesus, Who abolished death.

Tit. i. 4.   Grace and peace from God the Father and Christ Jesus our Saviour.

ii. 13.   Our great God and Saviour Jesus Christ.

iii. 6.   The Holy Ghost, which He poured out . . . through Jesus Christ our Saviour.

The third of these, " Our great God and Saviour Jesus Christ," we owe to the R.V.[1] The A.V. has

---

[1] And also the similar words in 2 Pet. i. 1.

" the great God and our Saviour Jesus Christ." From the early ages of the Church the question which was the true meaning has been keenly debated. The Eastern Fathers generally agreed with our R.V., and the Western with our A.V. Modern commentators also differ. Alford, Lord A. Hervey, and Dr. Newport White support the A.V. ; Bishop Bernard, Dean Spence-Jones, Dr. Plummer and Dr. Horton the R.V. The grammar of the Greek is not decisive. The words may correctly be read either way. But the context favours the R.V. St. Paul is speaking of the Second Advent : " Looking for the blessed hope and appearing of the glory of . . ." Whose name should naturally finish the sentence ? Certainly the expected " appearance " is that of the Divine Son. The R.V. was blamed by some orthodox critics for its change of " God " into " Who " in I. iii. 16, which I explained in a previous Talk ; but they may be grateful to it for the change here.

It is surely very remarkable that these Epistles, not written for a doctrinal purpose, should express great fundamental doctrines so clearly and emphatically as they do, though in so incidental a way. When, as here, we see the Father and Son so carefully distinguished, and yet both called the Saviour, and Christ called " our great God and Saviour," we have what is called Nicene theology foreshadowed and abundantly warranted.

We shall have to examine the doctrine of " salvation " by and by, but we may take this opportunity to notice how prominent in the Pastoral Epistles is the group of words of which it is one. We have seen that " Saviour " is characteristic of them and occurs

ten times. If we add the seven occurrences of " save,"
and the three of " salvation," we have twenty of this
group. I have already quoted fourteen of them.
Here are the others :—

I. i. 15.   Christ Jesus came into the world to save
            sinners.
    ii. 15. She shall be saved, if . . .
    iv. 16. In doing this, thou shalt both save thyself
             and them that hear thee.
II. ii. 10. The salvation which is in Christ Jesus.
    iii. 15. Able to make thee wise unto salvation.
    iv. 18. The Lord . . . will save me unto His
             heavenly kingdom.

No other book or group of books has so many occurrences of the three words in proportion. The Book
of Acts has them twenty-one times, but it is more
than twice as long as the Pastorals, and in it the
word " save " does not always mean spiritual salvation. Our Epistles, therefore, occupy a unique
position with regard to these important words. Is
there any reason for this ?

In Dr. Hort's *Christian Ecclesia* (p. 219) there is an
interesting paragraph attributing the prominence of
this group of words in the Pastorals to an increasing
sense in St. Paul's mind, as he grew old, of the danger
to the Church from the new forms of Rabbinism,
" not from the old mistaken zeal for Law and Circumcision, but from the new casuistry and fabling of the
Jewish doctors."   " One   marked   characteristic,"
Hort says, " of the rabbinical spirit was its bitter
exclusiveness, the exclusiveness of men who, as St.
Paul told the Thessalonians (1 Thess. ii. 15), were
' contrary to all men,' ' forbidding us to speak to the

Gentiles that they may be saved.'   And so St. Paul teaches the new Ecclesiæ of God that He Whom they worship is emphatically the Saviour God, who willeth that all men should be saved . . . and thus leads them to feel that the work of an Ecclesia of His as towards the world is likewise *to save*."

Do we not need the same reminder to-day ?   Men talk of the Fatherhood of God and the Brotherhood of Man.   Yes, both of them great facts.   God's Fatherhood led Him to stoop to be Man's Saviour, because He saw that Man *needed saving*.   Let Man's Brotherhood show itself also in bringing men who need saving to God their Saviour.

It should be added that the recent discoveries of papyri in Egyptian sands have shown that the title " Saviour " was often applied to the gods and to the emperors.   This was, of course, known before ; but the new illustrations of it are striking, as we learn from Deissmann's wonderful book, *Light from the Ancient East*.

15

DOCTRINE OF CHRIST

HAVING examined the teaching of the three Epistles concerning God, we now go on to look at their teaching concerning our Lord Jesus Christ. In one respect we have already done so, having traced the word " Saviour " in both its applications in the preceding Talk; and we need not enlarge further on that title.

But now notice the phrases " our Lord " and " the Lord ": to whom do they refer? " Our Lord " occurs twice : in I. i. 14, " the grace of our Lord," and in II. i. 8, " the testimony of our Lord." (I do not include the full phrase " our Lord Jesus Christ.") In both these cases it is clear that Christ is meant. " The Lord," standing alone, occurs sixteen times, all in the Second Epistle (in the R.V. ; in the A.V. not quite so often). Two of these are quotations from the O.T., and no doubt stand for Jehovah ; these are " The Lord knoweth them that are His," and " Let everyone that nameth the Name of the Lord depart from unrighteousness." But in the majority of the other cases Christ is clearly meant ; and probably so in all, in accordance with general N.T. usage :

i. 16.   The Lord grant mercy.
  18.   The Lord grant him to find mercy of the Lord.
ii. 7.   The Lord shall give thee understanding.
  14.   Charging them in the sight of the Lord.
  22.   Them that call on the Lord.
  24.   The Lord's servant must not strive.
  26.   Taken captive by the Lord's servant.
iii. 11.   Out of them all the Lord delivered me.
iv. 8.   The Lord, the righteous Judge.
  14.   The Lord will render to him according to his works.
  17.   The Lord stood by me and strengthened me.
  18.   The Lord will deliver me from every evil work.
  22.   The Lord be with thy spirit.

If these passages do all belong to our Lord Jesus Christ, what a picture they present of His manifold offices and functions !—as the Judge, the Advocate the Deliverer, the Giver of gifts, the Master, the Object of worship. And the greatness of the title has been lately illustrated (like that of Saviour) by the papyri described in Deissmann's *Light from the Ancient East.*

A conspicuous feature of the Pastorals is the phrase " Christ Jesus," as distinct from " Jesus Christ." This particular form of our Lord's Name, " Christ " coming before " Jesus," is emphatically Pauline. St. Paul uses it eighty times in his Epistles, and it only occurs once elsewhere in the N.T.[1] This form, though not in common use among us, has in our ears a specially tender and moving sound, probably owing to two very familiar texts, " Christ Jesus came into the world to save sinners " and " The Peace of God . . . keep your hearts and minds in Christ Jesus." Perhaps there was something tender about it in St. Paul's mind, seeing that his most frequent use of it is in the letters to his dear young colleague Timothy. Twenty-three times in these two letters he says " Christ Jesus " ; only four times " Jesus Christ " ; " Christ " alone, once ; " Jesus " alone, not at all. It is not necessary to quote all the twenty-three passages ; but let these be noted :

> i. 14.   The grace of our Lord abounded exceed-
> ingly with faith and love which is in
> Christ Jesus.
> 15.   Christ Jesus came into the world to save
> sinners.

---

[1] That is, in the R.V. In the A.V. it occurs four times outside St. Paul's writings, but the R.V. changes it in all these cases. On the other hand, the R.V. introduces it in Acts xxiv. 24, the one case alluded to above.

<table>
<tr><td>ii.</td><td>5.</td><td>One Mediator between God and man, Himself Man, Christ Jesus.</td></tr>
<tr><td>II. i.</td><td>10.</td><td>Our Saviour Christ Jesus, Who abolished death.</td></tr>
<tr><td>ii.</td><td>1.</td><td>Be strengthened in the grace that is in Christ Jesus.</td></tr>
<tr><td></td><td>3.</td><td>A good soldier of Christ Jesus.</td></tr>
<tr><td>iii.</td><td>12.</td><td>All that would live godly in Christ Jesus shall suffer persecution.</td></tr>
<tr><td></td><td>15.</td><td>Able to make thee wise unto salvation through faith which is in Christ Jesus.</td></tr>
</table>

Noticing, in our last Talk, the title " Saviour " as applied to Christ, we observed how the R.V. of Tit. ii. 13 emphasised His Deity. But the doctrine that our Lord Jesus Christ is, as our Nicene Creed expresses it, " God of God, Light of Light, Very God of Very God," is not dependent upon the right interpretation of isolated texts. It is implied throughout the N.T., and not least in these Epistles. The very salutations, for instance, " Grace, mercy, and peace, from God the Father and Christ Jesus our Lord," would be impossible if the Father and the Son were not equally divine.

And not less emphatic, though equally incidental, is St. Paul's acknowledgment of our Lord's true Manhood. Especially in I. ii. 5, where the A.V. " the Man Christ Jesus " is altered in the R.V. into " Himself Man, Christ Jesus " ; for Christ is not " a man," or " the man," but " Man," the representative of the whole race of men and women ; so the Greek implies.[1]

---

[1] The words εἷς καὶ μεσίτης θεοῦ καὶ ἀνθρώπων, ἄνθρωπος Χριστὸς Ἰησοῦς, literally " one mediator also between God and man, man Christ Jesus." The R.V. inserts " himself " for clearness.

And the historic associations of the historic Jesus are referred to : His human descent, " of the seed of David " (II. ii. 8) ; His trial and condemnation, " Who before Pontius Pilate witnessed the good confession " (I. vi. 13) ; His death, " Who gave Himself for us " (Tit. ii. 14) ; His resurrection, " risen from the dead " (II. ii. 8).   As noticed in a former Talk, the reference to Pilate actually puts Christ into a chronological table.

In addition to the plain statements of our Epistles on both the Divine and the Human Nature of our Lord, we have His pre-existence clearly indicated in the very verse which is the centre of all the teaching concerning Him, " Christ Jesus came into the world to save sinners."   " Came "—from whence ?   Jesus once gave the answer in words which even His slow-hearted disciples called " plain speaking " (John xvi. 28, 29), " I came out from the Father, and am come into the world."   That is Incarnation. (Comp. John i. 9, ix. 39, xi. 27, xviii. 37.)   Many " Lives of Christ " and " Lives of Jesus " have been published, which begin with the birth of " the Babe of Bethlehem " ; but how rarely are the readers led to think of that Babe as the Eternal Son of God !   Dr. Hastings, in the *Expository Times*,[1] lately called attention to this.   He said he had eighty-one " Lives of Christ " in his own library, and only two or three of these touched His life before He came into the world.   " They occupy themselves with His life on earth as if there were no other ; yet the heavenly life of Christ is longer far, and far more momentous, than the earthly

---

[1] April, May, June, July, 1913.

life." Dr. Hastings proceeded to give hints how to write a " biography " of the pre-existence of our Lord, citing many more passages of Scripture than most of us could have guessed at ; and then Mr. Harrington Lees, seizing on these hints, produced a delightful study of the passages in articles in the *Sunday at Home*.[1]

So " Christ Jesus came into the world." What for ? " To save sinners." It is the " comfortable word," as our Communion Service calls it, which summarises the whole Gospel. We have seen that God the Father is our Saviour, in that His love is the source of the great redemption ; but it is the Son Who has actually done the work, as the " One Mediator between God and man " (I. ii. 5). That word " mediator," *mesitēs*, one who intervenes between two parties, is only elsewhere used of Christ in the Epistle to the Hebrews (viii. 6, ix. 15, xii. 24), as the Mediator of the New Covenant. (It is applied also to Moses in Gal. iii. 19, 20.) This verse, then, I. ii. 5, " one Mediator between God and man," is important as the one place where St. Paul so calls our Lord. His work was, and still is, emphatically mediation. He " suffered for sins once," " that He might *bring us to God* " ; that is the central purpose of redemption. And our Prayer Book realises how appropriate a title it is for Him. When we pray " for clergy and people," we say, " Grant this, O Lord, for the honour of our Advocate and Mediator, Jesus Christ." The guidance we ask for the High Court of Parliament,

---

[1] *Sunday at Home*, October and November 1913. These and other papers, under the title of *Christ in the Home*, are published separately.

" we humbly beg in the Name and Mediation of Jesus Christ." When we use the wonderfully comprehensive prayer for " Christ's Church militant here in earth," we ask all " for Jesus Christ's sake, our only Mediator and Advocate." And so with some of the Collects. Rightly is " Advocate " joined with " Mediator "; and when we read in Rom. viii. and Heb. vii. of Christ " making intercession for us," we realise that this Mediation is His high-priestly work, and, having Him as our " great High Priest," we " come boldly unto the throne of grace " (Heb. iv. 14).

The work that our Lord did, the method of His mediation, is further revealed in our Epistles by the words " ransom " (I. ii. 6) and " redeem " (Tit. ii. 14); but we leave the consideration of these words till we come to the Doctrine of Salvation. Meanwhile, notice that the coming of the Son of God into the world is in II. i. 10 called His " appearing." God, says St. Paul, " saved us, and called us with a holy calling, not according to our works, but according to His own purpose and grace, which was given us in Christ Jesus before times eternal, but hath now been manifested by the *appearing* of our Saviour Christ Jesus." The Greek word is *epiphaneia*, whence our " Epiphany." In Tit. ii. 11 we read that " the grace of God hath appeared," *epephanē*, and in iii. 4, that God's " kindness and love toward man appeared," *epephanē*. The reference in both places is to the coming of Christ into the world; and it is worth noting that in the only two other occurrences of this verb in the New Testament (Luke i. 79, Acts xxvii. 20) it refers to the shining of the sun, as we see in the R.V. The word " manifested," too, in the text above quoted, is the rendering of a cognate verb, and so it is also in Tit. i. 3, and in the great " faithful saying " before noticed, I. iii. 16 ; also in several other places in the New Testament. Our use of the name " Epiphany " for the Visit of the Magi, " the Manifestation of Christ to the Gentiles," is an undue limiting of the meaning of the word.

But *epiphaneia* is not only used, in this one place, for the First Advent. It is still more significantly used for the Second Advent, as we shall see in our next chapter.

16
CHRIST'S SECOND ADVENT

WE saw in our last Talk that the word rendered " appearing," *epiphaneia*, refers once in the Pastorals to the First Advent of Christ (II. i. 10) ; but everywhere else it stands for the Second Advent. It is, indeed, a word only found in these Epistles, except in one remarkable passage to be noticed presently.

> I . vi. 14. I charge thee . . . keep the commandment . . . until the appearing of our Lord Jesus Christ.
>
> II. iv. 1. I charge thee, in the sight of . . . Christ Jesus . . . and by His appearing and His Kingdom.
>
> 8. Unto all them that love His appearing.
>
> Tit. ii. 13. Looking for the . . . appearing of the glory of our great God and Saviour Jesus Christ.

The cognate verb mentioned last time, usually translated by our verb " to manifest," *phaneroō*, is also used of both Advents. In Col. iii. 4, 1 Pet. v. 4, 1 John ii. 28, iii. 2, which refer to the Second Advent, the R.V. changes the " appear " of the Authorised Version to " be manifested."

So there are two Epiphanies, the Epiphany of Grace and the Epiphany of Glory, " the two great limits of the Christian dispensation," as Dr. Plummer remarks. Bishop French, of Lahore, wrote on November 8, 1884, " This morning I am preaching on the two Epiphanies, from Tit. ii. 11, 12 ; the Epiphany of Grace, which began the work of God in us and in all His people, and the Epiphany of Glory, which completes it."[1]

The one other passage where *epiphaneia* occurs is 2 Thess. ii. 8, where we find it in close connection with another word used for the Second Advent, anglicised and more familiar to some of us, *parousia*. The words are *tē epiphaneia tēs parousias autou*, which the Authorised Version renders " by the brightness of His coming," and the R.V. " by the manifestation of His coming." We might say " by the Epiphany of His Parousia." But *parousia* rather means " presence," and perhaps the best rendering would be " the appearing of His Presence."

For that is how we ought to think of the Second Advent. Our Lord is not millions of miles away on some central star in the Pleiades. He is always near us, but not manifested. Most true are those striking lines :

---

[1] *An Heroic Bishop*, by E. Stock, p. 81.

> Soon the whole
> Like a parchéd scroll,
> Shall before my amazéd sight uproll,
> And without a screen
> At one burst be seen
> The Presence wherein I have ever been.[1]

But the word Parousia does not occur in the Pastorals. Another expression referring to the Second Advent occurs three times—" that day " :

II. i. 12. He is able to keep [my deposit] against that day.
     18. The Lord grant unto him to find mercy of the Lord in that day.
 iv. 8. A crown of righteousness, which the Lord . . . shall give me at that day.

The " day of the Lord," or " that day," or " the day," are great words in the O.T. prophets. " The day of the Lord " occurs five times in Joel, three times in the fifth chapter of Amos, six times in Zephaniah ; also in Isaiah, Jeremiah, Ezekiel, and Obadiah. In Zeph. i. 7–16 we have " the day " thirteen times. " In that day " occurs fifteen times in the last three chapters of Zechariah, as well as in many other places. " The great and terrible day of the Lord," which St. Peter in Acts ii. quotes from Joel, is also in the last verse but one of the O.T., Mal. iv. 5. In many of these cases it is the First Advent that is pointed to ; but the fact is that there are many " days of the

---

[1] From a striking poem on the Second Day of Creation, by the Rev. Thos. Whytehead (1815–1847), Fellow of St. John's, Cambridge, who went out to New Zealand with Bishop Selwyn, and died there. There are varying versions of the stanza. I take it from a volume of his *Poetical Remains*, with a Memoir, published in 1877, and lent to me by my friend the Rev. C. A. Goodhart.

Lord," and some of these great utterances will have more than one fulfilment.

But in the N.T. we have the phrases "that day," "the day," "the last day," "the day of Christ," "of wrath," "of judgment," "of redemption," all looking forward to the Second Advent. "The last day" is used by our Lord Himself in a very striking way four times in John vi. But we must not wander from our Epistles.

The identification of "that day" with the "appearing" of Christ is clearly seen in the one verse which contains both phrases, II. iv. 8. The "crown" to be given to the Apostle "at that day" is to be given also to "all them that love His appearing." What is said of the one, therefore, applies also to the other. So, taking the seven passages above quoted, we may say that (1) on "that day" the glory of "our great God and Saviour Jesus Christ" will be manifested; (2) on "that day" He will be "the Righteous Judge"; (3) on "that day" there will be a manifestation of "mercy"; (4) on "that day" His Kingdom will be set up in triumph; (5) on "that day" will the "crowns of righteousness" be distributed; (6) until "that day" we are to "keep His commandment without spot"; (7) until "that day" we can confidently leave our "deposit" in His hands. Might not seven sermons be preached on these seven thoughts? Yet they only touch the fringe of the subject.

On the second of them I wish to add a word or two, as we are still on "the Doctrine of Christ." The Returning Saviour, the Man Christ Jesus, the Brother and Friend, is looked for by St. Paul as "the Righteous Judge" who "shall judge the quick and the dead " (II. iv. 1).[1] When was it that he wrote those words ? It was when he had just been before the Roman Judge (possibly the Emperor Nero himself), and was going before him again. It was, in modern phrase, the psychological moment for his referring to his Divine Lord as Judge. So he adjures Timothy to fulfil his functions faithfully and diligently, by reminding him of the Divine Judge. " I charge thee in the sight of God, and of Christ Jesus, Who shall judge the quick and the dead." And then, when he comes to the retrospect of his own life, and looks forward to a " crown " being given to him, it is " the Lord, the Righteous Judge," on Whom his eyes are fixed. Thus we see that the judgeship of Christ is not to the Christian a cause of fear and dread, but of joyful hope. He may look on himself as the " chief of sinners," but he is a pardoned sinner ; and though he dares not claim merit for his faithful service, he knows that " by the grace of God " he is what he is (1 Cor. xv. 10), and he knows that the Righteous Judge will give him the reward of what that grace has done in and by him.

Why, then, should we always have slow and solemn music, often in a minor key, when we come in the Te Deum to the words, " We believe that Thou shalt come to be our Judge " ? Even in the O.T. the Divine Judge is not dreaded, but longed for. " Judge me, O God ! " exclaim the Psalmists again and again ; " Let the earth rejoice, for He cometh to judge " is the strain of Psalm after Psalm ; and in Isa. xxxiii.

---

[1] Bishop Bernard says that " to judge the quick and the dead," $\kappa\rho\iota\nu\epsilon\iota\nu$ $\zeta\hat{\omega}\nu\tau\alpha\varsigma$ $\kappa\alpha\iota$ $\nu\epsilon\kappa\rho\upsilon\upsilon\varsigma$, is in all the early Creeds. " Quick " simply means " living."

we find the animating words, " The Lord is our Judge. . . . He will save us ! "

Nevertheless, recognising the Judge's unerring and inflexible justice, we must not shut our eyes against the certain judgment on the finally impenitent. St. Paul saw it in the case of Alexander the coppersmith, referred to in this very chapter : " The Lord will render to him according to his works." The A.V. reads as an imprecation, " The Lord reward him . . ."; but the R.V. rightly alters this to " The Lord *will* render. . . ." It is in fact an application of Ps. lxii. 12 to the case.

Do these various passages give any indication of the time of the Second Advent, whether it would be soon or long deferred ? Much has been written lately about Eschatology, the " science of the last things," and many wild statements have been current regarding even our Lord's " mistaken expectations " and St. Paul's agreement or disagreement with Him. Now whether we are or are not justified in thinking that the First Epistle to the Thessalonians reveals the Apostle's belief, at the time when they were written, that the Lord's return was imminent, the Pastoral Epistles, written several years later, certainly indicate nothing of the kind. In I. iv. 1, St. Paul speaks of " later times," that is, " the future " ; and in II. iii. 1 of " the last days," which would be further off still, though the phrase probably means the whole of the dispensation, the whole period to the Second Advent. But he could not tell that the Advent would *not* be soon. It might come any time.

That St. Paul was conscious that no revelation had been made to him on this point, and that he was quite ignorant about it, is shown by his words in I. vi. 15 : " Which "—*i.e.*, " the appearing "—" in His own times (R.V. marg. and A.V.) He shall show." Whose times ? Who will show them ? I reply, God the Father. This passage is a striking echo of Christ's farewell words in Acts i. (comp. His own expression, " neither the Son," in Mark xiii. 32, and, in the R.V., also in Matt. xxiv. 36). There we read that He said, " It is not for you to know times or seasons, which *the Father* hath set within His own authority." Here we read, " In His own times He shall show, Who is the blessed and only Potentate,"[1] words which we have before seen point definitely to the Father.

" It is no part of the orthodox creed of inspiration," writes Bishop Moule,[2] " if I apprehend it aright, to think that the apostles, as prophets, could at will map out the chronology of the future and say with decision how long the Lord would tarry." If *they* could not, which of us is presumptuous enough to think that *he* can ? Let us leave the " times and seasons "—yes, and the mode and order of events—in our Father's hands. Surely Frances Ridley Havergal was right when she said, " When the Lord does come, no one will be able to say, ' There, I told you so ! ' "

Meanwhile, in Tit. ii. 13, St. Paul exhorts us to be " looking for that blessed hope." The " happy hope," *makarios*,[3] the word we found applied also to God.

---

[1] In the Greek the two sentences have a close resemblance. Besides " the Father," καιρός, " season " or " time," and ἴδιος, " own," appear in both.

[2] *Second Timothy*, p. 106.

[3] Lord A. Hervey, in his Commentary on Titus, says : " This is the only place in the N.T. where μακάριος is applied

" Looking " : let me close this talk by simply suggesting these texts for meditation :

Luke xii. 36. Be ye yourselves like unto men looking for their Lord.

Phil. iii. 20. We look for the Saviour, the Lord Jesus Christ.

Heb. ix. 28. To them that look for Him shall He appear.

2 Pet. iii. 12. Looking for and earnestly desiring the coming of the day of God.

13. We look for new heavens and a new earth.

14. Seeing that ye look for these things, give diligence that ye may be found in peace, without spot, and blameless in His sight.

17
THE HOLY SPIRIT

HAVING examined our three Epistles to ascertain their teaching concerning God the Father and God the Son, we naturally look to see what is said of God the Holy Ghost ; and it is certainly a surprise, when we read so much about Him in other Epistles (Romans and 1 Corinthians particularly), to find only three direct references to Him in the

---

to an object which does not itself enjoy the blessing, but is a source of blessing to others. Of the fifty passages where it occurs, it is applied in forty-three to persons, twice to God, three times to parts of the body (the Virgin's womb and the eyes and ears of those who saw and heard Christ), once impersonally ("It is more blessed to give," Acts xx. 35), and once in this passage, to the hope.

Pastorals, and one indirect.   Here are the passages :—

I. iv. 1. The Spirit speaketh expressly that in later times some shall fall away from the faith.

II. i. 14. That good [deposit] guard, through the Holy Ghost which dwelleth in us.

Tit. iii. 5. According to His mercy [God] saved us, through the washing of regeneration and renewing of the Holy Ghost.

II. iii. 16. All Scripture is given by inspiration of God.   (A.V.)

This last passage (which I purposely give in A.V. words until I come to their consideration) is, of course, the indirect reference.   I must add, to avoid misunderstanding, that the word " spirit " in I. iii. 16 means, not the Holy Ghost, but the human spirit of Jesus, as before explained ; and that in II. i. 7 it means the spirit of the believer under Divine influence.

But the four passages quoted show us the Holy Ghost as the Revealer, the Indweller, the Renewer, the Inspirer.   I take these in a different order.

I. *The Renewer.*—The word for " renewing," *anakainōsis,* only occurs here and in Rom. xii. 2, " the renewing of your mind " ; but a cognate verb occurs in 2 Cor. iv. 16, " our inward man is renewed day by day," and in Col. iii. 10, " the new man which is renewed " ; and these are both connected with *kainos,* one of the two words for " new."[1] So our thoughts naturally go to the many ways in which the " newness " of the Gospel is manifested : the new covenant, the new testament, the new man, the new

---

[1] The other word, *νέος,* is also used in some of these connections.   The ordinary distinction is that *νέος* is new in time and *καινός* in quality. See Trench, *Synonyms.*

spirit, the new creature, the new life, the new name, the new song, the new heavens and earth, yea, " all things new "—all these in the N.T. ; and some of them in the O.T. also, as well as the ' new heart," and the renewing of strength, of youth, and of the right spirit. (I leave my younger readers to find these out.)

Now the agent in all this newness and renewal is the Holy Ghost. It is He Who makes the new man, the new creature, Who gives the new life, the new heart, the new spirit. In the text before us, therefore, the R.V. is better than the A.V. The A.V., by putting a comma after " regeneration," separates it from the work of the Holy Ghost ; while the R.V., by dropping the comma, attributes to Him both " regeneration " and " renewal." So Bishop Bernard points out in a very interesting note.

II. *The Indweller.*—The particular Greek word here for " dwelleth in," the verb *enoikeō*, only occurs four other times in the N.T. We have the Spirit of God " dwelling in " us (Rom. viii. 11) ; God saying " I will dwell in them " (2 Cor. vi. 16) ; the " word of Christ " to " dwell in us richly " (Col. iii. 16) ; faith " dwelling in " Lois and Eunice (II. i. 5). But a cognate word is used for the Spirit's indwelling in Rom. viii. 9, 11, 1 Cor. iii. 16. We think of our Lord's gracious promise to the disciples (John xiv. 17), " The Spirit of truth . . . dwelleth (R.V. abideth) with you, and shall be in you " ; and we remember how frequently is used the image of the " house " or " temple " or " habitation " to picture the " dwelling " of God by the Spirit, both in the Church and in the individual believer. So Timothy is encouraged to guard his " deposit " by the remembrance of this very thing.   Do you feel, virtually says St. Paul, how weak you are to be the guardian and keeper of the " deposit," of the gospel of the glory of the blessed God ?   But you are not left to do it yourself ; you will do it " through the Holy Ghost " the Indweller. For ourselves, we will recall the Apostle's solemn words to the Romans (viii. 9), " Ye are not in the flesh, but in the spirit, if so be that the Spirit of God dwelleth in you.   But if any man hath not the Spirit of Christ, he is none of His."

III. *The Revealer.*—" The Spirit speaketh expressly . . ."   How did He do that ?   That the Holy Spirit speaks to all who have their ears open to hear Him, I do not doubt ; but the reference here, I equally do not doubt, is to the special gift of " prophecy."   We have perhaps not paid sufficient attention to the fact that in the Early Church there were " prophets." When we sing in the *Te Deum* of " the glorious company of the Apostles," " the goodly fellowship of the Prophets," " the noble army of Martyrs," we possibly think of the old prophets like Elijah and Isaiah ; but it is far more likely that the " Prophets " who come in between the " Apostles " and the " Martyrs " belong, like them, to the age of Christianity.   And there are, in fact, many references in the N.T. to these Christian prophets.   Let us recall some.

First, our Lord Himself says, " Behold, I send unto you prophets . . . and some of them ye shall kill and crucify " (Matt. xxiii. 34 ; see Luke xi. 49). Then, at Pentecost, St. Peter announces the fulfilment of Joel's prediction, " I will pour forth My Spirit upon all flesh, and your sons and your daughters shall prophesy."   Then St. Paul tells us that when Christ

" ascended on high " and " gave gifts unto men," He " gave some to be apostles, and some prophets, and some evangelists, and some pastors and teachers " (Eph. iv. 9–11) ; and that " God hath set some in the Church, first apostles, secondly prophets, thirdly teachers " (1 Cor. xii. 28). When he also speaks of the Church being " built upon the foundation of the apostles and prophets " (Eph. ii. 20), it must be to them that he refers ; and in the next chapter (iii. 5) he declares that the great " mystery " or secret, " that the Gentiles should be fellow-heirs," etc., had only " *now* " " been revealed unto His holy apostles and prophets."   Then we find particular " prophets " mentioned, Agabus (Acts xi. 28, xxi. 10) and other leaders at Antioch (xiii. 1) ; Judas Barsabas and Silas (xv. 22, 32) ; the daughters of Philip the evangelist (xxi. 8) ; even half-taught men at Ephesus (xix. 6).

Prophecy, in fact, was one of the special Pentecostal gifts, as 1 Cor. xii. fully explains ; and it was the best of them all, for St. Paul in chap. xiv. says to the Corinthians, " Desire earnestly spiritual gifts, but rather that ye may prophesy."   And why ?   Because, while other gifts might edify him who received them, or might in some cases lead to self-exaltation and to confusion, " he that prophesieth speaketh unto men edification and comfort and consolation " (verse 3). Yet even this specially precious gift needed guidance. Those who received it were to be careful to prophesy " according to the proportion of the faith," *kata tēn analogian tēs pisteōs* (Rom. xii. 6). Even at its best prophecy as a gift would not last as love would (1 Cor. xiii. 8), and St. Paul emphatically declared that with that gift but without love he was " nothing " (verse 2).

The prophets belonged to what is called the *charismatic ministry*, the ministry of special gifts, *charismata*, which was distinct from the regular ministry of presbyters and deacons, and which did not last after the Church had settled down to its permanent course.   This is not the place to enlarge upon it, and something further must be said when we come to the subject of the Church.

Now prophecy is twice mentioned in our Epistles. In I. i. 18 we are told that " prophecies " " went before on " Timothy, that is, that there were prophets who commended him to St. Paul and predicted his usefulness ; and in I. iv. 15 that the " gift " which the Apostle exhorts him not to " neglect " was given him " by prophecy " when " the hands of the presbytery " were laid upon him.   Whatever that occasion was, the " gift " was no doubt one or more of the *charismata*, and very likely it may have been the gift of prophecy. It is possible that St. Paul's addressing him as a " man of God " (I. vi. 11, cf. II. iii. 17), which was an ordinary title of a prophet in O.T. times, may indicate that Timothy was definitely recognised as a prophet. Anyway the gift of prophecy was given by the Holy Spirit, and the whole subject illustrates His Divine influence as Revealer in the Church.

IV. *The Inspirer.*—The prophets through whom the Holy Spirit was the Revealer of God's messages might be truly called " inspired " men ; but as the phrase " inspired of God " is specifically used in II. iii. 16 of the written Scriptures, we may for convenience call the Holy Spirit the Inspirer in this particular respect.

The five words in the A.V., " given by inspiration of God," which the R.V. reduces to three words, " inspired of God," stand for only one word in the Greek, *theopneustos*, literally " God-breathed " or " God-inspired." This occurs nowhere else in the N.T., nor is it used, we are told, by any Christian writer before Clement of Alexandria, about A.D. 200. But if the word was not used, the thing it stood for was recognised. Clement of Rome (perhaps the Clement of Phil. iv. 3), whose epistle to the Church of Corinth was probably written within thirty years after St. Paul's death, exhorts the Corinthian Christians " to look carefully into the Scriptures, which are the true utterance of the Holy Spirit." Justin Martyr, writing in the middle of the second century, speaks of Moses, David, and Isaiah being used by the Holy Spirit as a musician used the *plectrum*, the instrument with which he played on his lyre. Irenæus, Bishop of Lyons, about the same time, says, " The Scriptures are perfect, inasmuch as they are uttered by the Word of God and His Spirit."[1] The Early Church, therefore, regarded the Holy Ghost as the Inspirer of the Scriptures.

And we, remembering how excellent a type *breath* is of Him and His influence, as illustrated in Ezekiel's vision of the dry bones and by our Lord's symbolic breathing on the disciples when He said, " Receive ye the Holy Ghost," cannot but see in that word *theopneustos* a vivid picture of the work of the Holy Spirit in the production of that wonderful and unique library of inspired books which we call the Bible. A library indeed, and yet one Book ; by many human

---

[1] These are only three out of a long catena of similar testimonies given by Westcott in his *Introduction to the Study of the Gospels*, occupying forty pages of close type.

authors, but inspired by one Divine Author.   Theories
of inspiration may vary.   The Bible itself gives no
further definition, nor does the Church.   But the fact
remains.   Much more, however, has still to be said on
this passage.   It will occupy us for two more chapters.

18
THE HOLY SCRIPTURES: MEANING

NO passage in the New Testament is more
familiar than 2 Tim. iii. 15, 16.   It is the
great classical passage on the inspired Holy Scriptures.   Let us read it in both versions :—

A.V.—From a child thou hast known the holy scriptures, which are able to make thee wise unto salvation
through faith which is in Christ Jesus.   All scripture is
given by inspiration of God, and is profitable for doctrine, for reproof, for correction, for instruction in
righteousness ; that the man of God may be perfect,
throughly furnished unto all good works.
R.V.—From a babe thou hast known the sacred
writings, which are able to make thee wise unto salvation through faith which is in Christ Jesus.   Every
scripture inspired of God is also profitable for teaching,
for reproof, for correction, for instruction which is in
righteousness : that the man of God may be complete,
furnished completely unto every good work.

The general teaching is the same, whichever
reading we adopt. St. Paul first reminds Timothy
of his knowledge of the " Scriptures " from infancy ;
literally from infancy, for the Greek word *brephos*
distinctly means a babe ; then he affirms that these

" Scriptures " can make him " wise unto salvation through faith " in Christ ; and then he expounds further the " profitableness " of these " inspired Scriptures." It is a great passage, full of encouragement. Let us bear in mind that St. Paul is referring to the Old Testament only. Some parts of the N.T. were indeed written at this time ; most of his own letters, for instance ; but certainly none were written when Timothy was a " babe "—to say nothing of their recognition as " Scripture." All the more encouraging is the passage to us. We can take up our Old Testament, and, while freely allowing that scholars may discuss questions of date and authorship and sources and the like, we can say to ourselves, " This collection of thirty-nine books is inspired Scripture " ; and whatever particular theory of inspiration we may formulate, we may rest assured that these books contain God's gracious messages and revelations to mankind. We need not doubt that God guided the Jewish scribes and doctors to make a true choice of the sacred writings comprised in the Canon ; and we read every one of them with reverence and thankfulness. We note that the Greek word *graphē*, in ver. 16, occurs fifty times in the N.T., and everywhere means " Scripture " and nothing else. It would be superfluous here to copy out all these fifty passages ; but that we may be the more satisfied, let us at least read those which we find in St. Paul's writings :—

Rom. i. 2.   Which He promised afore by His pro-
           phets in the holy Scriptures.
   iv. 3.   What saith the Scripture ?
   ix. 17.   The Scripture saith unto Pharaoh . . .
   x. 11.   The Scripture saith, Whosoever . . .

xi.	2.	Wot ye not what the Scripture saith of Elijah ?
xv.	4.	Through comfort of the Scriptures we might have hope.
xvi.	26.	The Scriptures of the prophets.
1 Cor. xv.	3.	Christ died for our sins according to the Scriptures.
	4.	Raised on the third day according to the Scriptures.
Gal. iii.	8.	The Scripture . . . preached the Gospel unto Abraham.
	22.	The Scripture hath shut up all things under sin.
iv.	30.	What saith the Scripture ?
1 Tim. v.	18.	The Scripture saith, Thou shalt not muzzle . . .
2 Tim. iii.	16.	All Scripture is given by inspiration of God. (A.V.)

But I shall be asked why I have omitted " From a child thou hast known the holy Scriptures." Because the word there is not *graphē* at all, but *gramma* ; and *gramma*, which occurs fourteen other times in the N.T., nowhere else means " Scripture." Here are the passages, the words that are renderings of *gramma* being in italics :—

Luke xvi.	6.	Take thy *bond* (A.V., bill).
	7.	Take thy *bond* (A.V., bill).
xxiii.	38.	*Letters* of Greek and Latin and Hebrew (A.V. only ; R.V. omits).
John v.	47.	If ye believe not his *writings*.
vii.	15.	How knoweth this man *letters* ?
Acts xxvi.	24.	Thy much *learning* (*lit.* many *letters*).
xxviii.	21.	We neither received *letters* from Judæa.
Rom. ii.	27.	The *letter* and circumcision.
	29.	Not in the *letter*.
vii.	6.	Not in the oldness of the *letter*.

2 Cor. iii. 6. Not of the *letter* . . . for the *letter* killeth.

       7. *Written* and engraven on stones (*marg.* in *letters*).

Gal. vi. 11. How large *letters*.

Clearly the R.V. was compelled in honesty to alter the English rendering " Scriptures " to " writings." Moreover, the Greek word translated " holy " is not the regular word either. The regular word is *hagios*, which is rendered " holy " again and again in the N.T. But the word here is *hieros*, which in no way conveys the idea of holiness of character, and rather means " sacred," in the sense of being connected with sacred or consecrated things. It is closely connected with *hiereus*, " priest," and *hieron*, " temple." It only occurs once elsewhere in the N.T., in 1 Cor. ix. 13, where " sacred things " belonging to the temple services are referred to. The R.V. therefore altered " holy scriptures " into " sacred writings " ; and we have now the exact phrase " holy scriptures " only once in the Bible, viz., in Rom. i. 2, " Which He promised afore by His prophets in the Holy Scriptures," and here we find the right words, *hagios* and *graphē*.

But now the question arises, Why did St. Paul use the phrase " sacred writings," as though he meant something different from the " holy Scriptures " ? I do not think any satisfying answer has yet been given to this question. Some have thought he must mean to include some of the N.T. books, which the Church had not yet recognised to be " Scripture " in the sense in which the O.T. was universally recognised ; but I repeat that when Timothy was a " babe " not one of the books can have been written. But when we read the whole passage the " sacred writings " of verse 15 seem clearly to be identified with the " Scripture " of verse 16. So I am inclined, if I am asked why St. Paul said " sacred writings," to reply with a counter question, " Why should he not ? " Seeing that in his Epistles (those at least which we have) he only uses the phrase " Holy Scriptures " once, why should not both phrases be equally natural to him ? We ourselves speak of " the Bible," " the Scriptures," " the Word of God," " the sacred volume," and we do not mean different things, but the same thing.

Well, then, someone will rejoin, why say so much about it ? Simply that my readers may see the care taken by the Revisers to be absolutely honest in getting the rendering as accurate as possible. It is often said that the R.V. alters the A.V. needlessly, and people complain of losing familiar words. But surely the higher our estimation of inspired books, the more careful we need to be to know exactly what the writers really said. Those who hold to that particular theory of " verbal inspiration " which Dean Wace in the *Record* said was only " a pious opinion," should be the most grateful to the scholars who trace out for them the exact meaning of the words. (Of course, the R.V. may here and there be mistaken. It is not infallible.)

Let us now go on to look at the R.V. changes in verse 16. First, " all Scripture " is altered to " every Scripture." In this correction almost all expositors are agreed, for *graphē* always means a particular " scripture," and when the whole O.T. is meant the plural *graphai*, " Scriptures," is used. And what an impressive alteration it is! Of course, we must understand the word " every " reasonably. It does not mean that recorded utterances of uninspired men, like the speeches of Job's friends, are to be taken as themselves " inspired." But it does mean that God permitted such utterances to be included as being necessary to the general purpose of His revelation.

Then the R.V. alters " is given by inspiration of God, and is profitable " to " [every Scripture] inspired of God is also profitable." The A.V. rendering was originally that of the Geneva Version of 1560, which King James's translators followed. The R.V. has returned to the phraseology—so we are assured—of Origen and Chrysostom, of the Syriac and Latin versions, of Luther, and Wiclif, and Tindale, and Coverdale. It is, therefore, whether right or wrong, in good company. On the word *theopneustos*, " God-inspired " or " in-breathed," I said something in the preceding Talk. But now notice that the little word " is," twice in the A.V. and once in the R.V., is in italics, not being expressed in the Greek ; and the whole question is whether this " is " should be inserted twice or only once. Shall we say " every Scripture is inspired-of-God and is profitable " ? or " every Scripture inspired-of-God is also profit-able " ? The Greek word for " and " in the A.V. is the ordinary one, *kai*, which is in favour of the former ; but those who prefer the latter make the *kai* stand for " also," with what they call an *ascensive* force. Two passages are cited in illustration : Gal. iv. 7, " If a son, *then* an heir," where " then " is *kai* ; and Rom. viii. 29, " Whom He foreknew He *also* fore-ordained," where " also " is *kai*. Bishop Wordsworth's rendering contrives to combine both views : " All (or every) Scripture, *being*-inspired-of-God, is also profitable." Either way, how impressive ! The " breath of God " in each " Scripture " ! Profitable ? How can it fail to be profitable ?

How, then, are we to decide ? Clearly the doctrine of inspiration is not at stake. If we adopt the R.V. the word " also " secures this, bearing in mind that *graphē* never in the N.T. means anything else than the O.T. Scriptures. So we further ask, After all, what is St. Paul driving at ? What is he impressing on Timothy ? Not that all Scripture is inspired of God ; that went without saying ; there was no question or doubt about it. St. Paul is reminding Timothy of his early knowledge of the Scriptures, and calling upon him to use it for himself and for others. " Because they are inspired of God, as you well know, be sure that they are also profitable for all these purposes, teaching, reproof, correction, instruction in righteousness ; and by studying and using them you, O man of God, and everyone else, will be ' complete, equipped completely unto every good work.' " Just as a mother might say to her boy going to school, " Take this Bible ; you know it is God's word ; you will find it profitable at all times and in all circumstances ; don't fail to read it and be guided by it."

But there is more to say of the Scriptures in another chapter.

19
THE HOLY SCRIPTURES: PRACTICAL TEACHINGS

WE have examined the language of the famous passage, II. iii. 15, 16, and inquired as to its exact meaning. We must now come to its practical teachings.

The statement in verse 15, familiar as it is, is really a very striking one. What higher praise could be given to any book or books than to say that it, or they, can " make one wise " ? And what sort of wisdom ? " Unto salvation." We shall see by and by how widespread in St. Paul's day was the desire, at least among thoughtful men, for " salvation." It was the very thing that many were looking for, though few of them had any clear idea what their longings really meant. Then comes St. Paul, and announces that those old Jewish books, of which Greek philosophers thought little—even if they knew them,—could " make wise unto salvation." We must take the words in their true sense. It is not the new Gospel Message that he is referring to. It is the Old Testament alone. And when we Christians in England to-day are asked, as we often are, " What do you really think of the Old Testament ? " ought we not to be ready instantly and confidently to reply, " It is able to make me wise unto salvation " ? Let scholars by all means discuss the sources of Genesis, the date of Deuteronomy, the design of Job and of Jonah, the place in history of Daniel and Esther. I for one am not afraid of their discussions. I am quite sure that, whether or no we may have to correct any old notions of our own not really warranted by the Bible itself, the more those wonderful Scriptures are studied the clearer will be our conviction that they " are able to make us wise unto salvation." Well does Bishop Bernard observe that " the present participle *dunamena* [are able] expresses the continuous and abiding power of Scripture ; it is not only fit *sophizein nepia* [Ps. xix. 7, " to make wise the simple," the babes], but it was as valuable to Timothy the Bishop as to Timothy the child " ; cf. Ps. cxix. 98 (" Thy commandments make me wiser than mine enemies ").

We must not forget the qualifying words " through faith which is in Christ Jesus." There is no mechanical charm about Scripture. It is only believers in Christ who are made by it " wise unto salvation." But the place of faith we shall see by and by. Let us now go on to the four ways in which the Scriptures are " profitable."

These are (*a*) for " teaching " : it will profit us to get our doctrine from them ; (*b*) for " reproof," or refutation of error : it will profit us to use them as our Lord used them against the Tempter ; (*c*) for " correction," that is, of conduct : it will profit us to amend our lives by its precepts ; (*d*) for " instruction," or discipline, " in righteousness." The word here is *paideia*, which is connected with *pais*, a boy or servant, and includes training and chastisement : so it will profit us to be chastised by the rebukes of Scripture in the conscience.

And what is the purpose, the aim, of all this ? " That the man of God may be complete, furnished completely unto every good work." If the phrase " man of God " points specially to " prophets," then

we have here a word for preachers and teachers.
They must derive all their teaching from the Scriptures,
and all their inspiration too—to use the word in its
general modern sense. The Scriptures can " furnish "
them " completely." We know the difference between an unfurnished, and a half-furnished, and a
completely furnished house. The Scriptures can not
only " make wise unto salvation," but equip us
" unto every good work." And remember, this is
said specifically of the Old Testament !

But, then, how much greater are *our* opportunities
of being " profited," who have both the Old and the
New ! And I think we may fairly draw from one
word in these Epistles a lesson touching the New
Testament, although the New Testament, as we understand it, was not yet in existence when St. Paul wrote
to Timothy. That word is " reading," in I. iv. 13 :
" Give heed unto reading, to exhortation, to teaching." This injunction undoubtedly refers to the
public reading of the Scriptures, *i.e.*, the Old Testament, in the Christian assemblies at public worship,
and in this connection we shall notice the words when
we come to consider the Church services. But here
I would remark that we may confidently believe that
at these assemblies would also be read the Letters
which the Apostles had written to the congregations.
The Church at Corinth would have the Epistles to
the Corinthians read to them ; the Church at Philippi
would have the Epistle to the Philippians read to
them ; and so on. There is actually a direction to
this effect in one Epistle, that to the Colossians.
See iv. 16, " When this Epistle hath been read among
you, cause that it be read also in the Church of the

Laodiceans, and that ye also read the Epistle from Laodicea " (*i.e.*, the Epistle which will be handed on to you from Laodicea). That Laodicean Epistle was probably what we know as the Epistle to the Ephesians, being a circular letter to the Churches in Asia.[1] The passage is interesting for the light it throws on the mutual help given by the Churches to one another ; but I only cite it here as evidence of the public reading of the Apostolic Letters.

Did the Christians, then, recognise such Letters as " Scripture," in the sense in which they knew the Old Books to be Scripture ? My answer is, Not at first. We certainly have no right to assume it, and the probabilities are the other way. But undoubtedly they would receive such Letters as authoritative expositions of God's truth and God's will, in virtue of their coming from Apostles. At first, however, each Church would only have its own Letter or Letters, except in the case of a circular letter like that " to the Ephesians " ; and we can imagine the deep interest with which (say) the Christians at Thessalonica would by and by receive a copy of (say) the Epistle to Rome. " How kind of them to send us a copy ! " would be said by one Christian to another.

So also with the Four Gospels. The Hebrew Christians would have copies of St. Matthew, and the Greek Christians copies of St. Luke, long before the former had Luke and the latter Matthew. And imagine the delight of one Church after another

---

[1] The reason for thinking this Epistle to be a circular Letter is that the words in ver. 1, " at Ephesus," are omitted in many MSS. The blank could be filled up with the name of any Church to which a copy was sent. Also there are no personal greetings, as there are in Colossians.

when, perhaps in its second generation, it received
St. John's Gospel, and possibly heard for the first
time of Nicodemus and the Woman of Samaria and
the Man Born Blind and the Raising of Lazarus, and
how the Lord Jesus had spoken of Himself as the
Bread of Life, the Light of the World, the Good
Shepherd, the True Vine. Of course, some of this
may have been part of the regular oral teaching they
had long received, but we may be sure that St. John
revealed to them much that was new. Imagine that
wonderful Gospel, the greatest of all writings ever
produced in the world, read for the first time by Christians in far-off Britain, say at Winchester or at York !
And then think of our high privilege in possessing the
whole blessed Book, and in sending it out to all nations
in all languages ! Well might St. Paul say to us,
" Give heed unto reading " !—not only the reading of
the Lessons in church, but our own personal reading of
both Old and New Testaments as the channels of
God's revelations to our souls.

For we know, and will never forget, what I think
the early Christians only gradually came to know,
that these Apostolic writings are " Scripture "—
are parts of God's inspired revelation to man. And,
as Bishop Moule says, " It is a peculiar and precious
feature of the N.T. revelation . . . that it comes to
us so largely through the sacred channel of the human
heart, the human personality. It does not descend
in oracular thunder from the clouds. It is conveyed
in great measure through a series of Letters signed
with men's names and speaking in the dialect of
man's soul." [1]

[1] *Second Timothy*, p. 24.

A few words must be added concerning another phrase found in the Pastoral Epistles. Thus :—

I.	iv.	5.	It is sanctified by the word of God.
		6.	The words of the faith.
	v.	17.	Labour in the word.
II.	ii.	9.	The word of God is not bound.
		15.	Handling aright the word of truth.
	iv.	2.	Preach the word.
Tit.	i.	3.	Manifested His word.
		9.	Holding to the faithful word.
	ii.	5.	That the word of God be not blasphemed.

Does the expression " the word," or " the word of God," mean the Scriptures ? Remembering that the " Scriptures " then meant the O.T. only, we must reply, No ; at all events not necessarily, or generally. In fact, these two phrases, " the word " and " the word of God," which occur about one hundred times in the N.T., scarcely ever mean the Scriptures as written documents. They almost always mean the Gospel Message. That Message is, indeed, contained or embodied in the Scriptures. In a sense we may say it is conveyed even by the O.T., those " sacred writings " which are " able to make wise unto salvation." But in St. Paul's day " preaching the word " meant preaching the glad tidings of Jesus Christ as we now have them in the N.T.

Are we then justified in speaking of the Bible as " the Word of God " ? I for one hold that we are. The sixty-six books which make up the One Book are the casket which contains the treasure of God's revelations to men ; and those revelations are " the word of God." We are not so foolish and ignorant (as a brilliant friend of mine, George

Warington, said forty years ago) as to picture to ourselves " the Psalmist as a shepherd boy sitting under a tree with an Oxford Bible in his hands." Nevertheless, we may fairly use the beautiful expressions of the 19th and 119th Psalms, composed as they were when only fragments of the Scriptures existed, as truly applicable to the whole Bible, which is to us the supreme Rule of Faith, the lamp to our feet, the lantern to our path.

20
THE GRACE OF GOD

HAVING seen that the Holy Scriptures, or " Sacred Writings," are able to make us " wise unto salvation," it would be natural to take up the subject of salvation itself, and see what our Epistles have to say about it. But I desire first, as a preliminary study, to examine one great word, GRACE. It occurs eleven times in the Pastorals ; but six of these are in the opening and closing salutations, and need not detain us. The other five are as follows :

I. i. 14. The grace of our Lord abounded exceedingly.
II. i. 9. According to His own purpose and grace.
  ii. 1. Strengthened in the grace that is in Christ Jesus.
Tit. ii. 11. The grace of God hath appeared, bringing salvation.
  iii. 7. Being justified by His grace.

The Greek word, *charis*, occurs thirteen times in our Epistles, but in the other two cases it is as part of an

idiom which we translate " I thank God " (I. i. 12 ;
II. i. 3).   For *charis* is a wonderful word ; and, while
our English word " grace " is used in several senses,
charis is used in more.   It occurs in the N.T. 154
times,[1] and in 131 of these places it is rendered
" grace " in the R.V.[2]   In ten places it means
" thank " or " thanks."   Thus, in the familiar words
of 2 Cor. ix. 15, " Thanks be unto God for His un-
speakable gift," and of 1 Cor. xv. 57, " Thanks be
unto God which giveth us the victory," the word for
" thanks " is *charis*.   So our thanks to God before
and after meals is called " saying grace."   In eight
places *charis* is rendered " favour."   Mary " found
favour " with God (Luke i. 30), and the youthful
Jesus grew " in favour with God and man."   St.
Peter, in exhorting household servants to patience
under undeserved ill-treatment (I. ii. 19, 20), twice
calls such conduct " acceptable " (A.V. once " thank-
worthy "), the Greek being simply *charis*.   In 1 Cor.
xvi. 3 it is " bounty " (A.V. liberality), and in 2 Cor.
i. 15 " benefit."   We must not stop over cognate and
compound words ; but I may just mention that
eucharistia (whence our " eucharist ") and its cognates
occur frequently to express " giving of thanks."
In the O.T. the corresponding Hebrew word occurs
in the phrase " find grace [*i.e.* favour] in the sight
of " someone ; but it is used in the N.T. sense twice
in the Psalms, five times in Proverbs, and twice in
Zechariah.   Ps. lxxxiv. 11, " The Lord will give grace

---

[1] This includes Rom. xvi. 24, which verse is omitted in
the R.V.

[2] In 2 Cor. viii. 4 the A.V. has " gift " ; and the two versions differ otherwise in that verse, owing to a various reading.

and glory," and Zech. xii. 10, " the spirit of grace and supplication," are familiar.

It is interesting also to note which of the N.T. writers use the word *charis*, and how often. Of the whole 154 cases of its use, just 100 are in St. Paul's Epistles, and twenty-four in St. Luke (Gospel and Acts). St. Peter has it twelve times, the Epistle to the Hebrews eight, St. John seven, St. James twice, St. Jude once. It does not occur in Matthew or Mark.

Now when we examine all these passages, one notable feature at once emerges from them. This is the contrast between our ordinary use of the word " grace " and its use in the N.T. For example, we use it as a title of honour : a duke or an archbishop is " His Grace." Anything more unlike the force of the word in Scripture it would be hard to imagine. Again, we use it as of a personal quality : it may be a physical quality, as " she walks with such grace." This does correspond with the original meaning of *charis*. Dr. Plummer[1] remarks that the word means " comeliness, winsomeness, from Homer downwards." But this is not its force in the N.T. Then again, we use it of words or deeds, as " He had the grace to apologise," or " to visit so-and-so." This use is not unknown in Scripture ; but only in reference to our Lord Himself : " The Word became flesh, and dwelt among us . . . full of grace and truth " ; " All wondered at the words of grace (R.V.) which proceeded out of His mouth."

Again, we speak of the " graces " of a man's character, as nearly equivalent to " virtues," at least to

---

[1] On St. John's Gospel, in Cambridge Greek Testament, p. 72.

virtues of the gentler kind. The nearest parallels to this in the N.T. are " Grow in grace " and " Let your speech be always with grace " ; besides which we find *charis* as a blessing to be passed on : " Minister grace to the hearers " ; and in 2 Cor. viii. the " collection " is four times called " this grace." But these are exceptions. In almost every other case there is nothing *of man* in the word ; nothing that ascribes grace to the individual man himself. Grace is always a gift, or an announcement or assurance of a gift, or the source of a gift, or the effect of a gift ; and always from God. Dr. Hort says : " The associations connected with the term ' grace ' . . . denoting a spiritual power or influence . . . are only misleading in the interpretation of the Biblical language. . . . The dominant conception of *charis* in the Acts and the Epistles is the free bounty of God. . . ."

Grace has been well defined—I think by Horatius Bonar—as " favour to the unworthy " ; but we must add to this the acts, the effects, the gifts, of that favour. Perhaps the word " favourite " may help us to catch the meaning ; only there is no favouritism with God, not even of the kind involved in the teaching of the old hyper-Calvinists. With Him there is " no respect of persons." For God's " favourites " are all His sinful creatures ; and " grace " is the favour manifested in the Incarnation and Atonement of His Son in behalf of them all.

The divine character of grace is emphatically shown in the five texts from our Epistles above quoted. In II. i. 9 grace is exhibited to us as fore-ordaining the salvation of mankind " before times eternal." Then, in Tit. ii. 11, it " appears," has its epiphany, at the Incarnation. Then, in I. i. 14, St. Paul, in the most fervent language, tells of what John Bunyan called "grace abounding" in his own individual conversion. These three passages we have studied before. Then, in Tit. iii. 7, we see grace at work, "justifying" those who have been described as, a few years before, "foolish, disobedient . . . serving divers lusts . . . living in malice and envy." This "justifying" will demand our attention by and by. In all these four cases grace is seen distinctly as a divine attribute. In the fifth alone, II. ii. 1, do we see the word used in the sense in which we are wont most to use it; yet even here Timothy is exhorted, not to cultivate or to exhibit grace as he might cultivate or exhibit some virtue, such as patience or humility or courage, but to avail himself of an influence external to him. "Be strengthened"; not "Be strong," as in A.V. It is a passive verb. Timothy is just to yield himself to the power of Another, to "the grace that is in Christ Jesus." The word is the same as in I. i. 12, "He that enabled me"; and in II. iv. 17, "the Lord . . . strengthened me"; and in Phil. iv. 13, "I can do all things in Him that strengthened me." The verb is *endunamoō*, connected with *dunamis*, "power," whence our "dynamic" and "dynamite." Perhaps "empower" would be the most literal rendering; but this word with us rather means "authorise," so "enable" or "strengthen" is better.

So grace is a divine thing. And if I had space to refer to passages in other parts of the N.T., I think I could show more in detail that grace is (*a*) the revelation of God's love for His unworthy children;

(*b*) the source of our salvation ; (*c*) the state or position of salvation into which the believing and baptized Christian enters (" this grace wherein we stand " ; " fallen from grace ") ; (*d*) the régime under which the Christian lives (" not under the law, but under grace ") ; (*e*) the privilege, office, service, to which the Christian is called (" unto me was this grace given, that I should preach . . .") ; (*f*) the divine influence on the Christian's heart and life, which is the sense in which we most commonly use the word. Not only is it true that " by grace we are saved " ; God is also " able to make all grace abound toward us," and He says to every believer, " My grace is sufficient for thee." We naturally think, especially of " the grace of our Lord Jesus Christ," the first element in our familiar benedictions ; but we have seen the grace of God the Father too in its wondrousness, and there is one passage where " the Spirit of Grace " is mentioned as being " done despite unto " by those who fell away. It was when the disciples were " all filled with the Holy Ghost " that " great grace was upon them all." Let us therefore " come boldly unto the throne of grace " ; and let us watch and pray, that we " receive not the grace of God in vain."

It is interesting to look through the Prayer Book and to see how often Divine Grace is referred to in our prayers, etc. The word occurs, I think, twenty-three times in the Collects, eight times in the Communion Service, thirty-six times elsewhere, sixty-seven times in all, if I have counted correctly. Perhaps my younger readers would check my calculation. It partly depends on whether one counts the same prayer in different places more than once. I only count " The Grace " once.

There is a hymn of Doddridge's (A.D. 1755) which used to appear in old selections, but has dropped out of most modern hymnals, and which beautifully sums up what in this Talk has been said so inadequately :—

> Grace ! 'tis a charming sound,
>   Harmonious to the ear ;
> Heav'n with the echo shall resound
>   And all the earth shall hear.
>
> Grace first contrived a way
>   To save rebellious man ;
> And all the steps that grace display
>   Which drew the wondrous plan.
>
> Grace taught my wand'ring feet
>   To tread the heav'nly road ;
> And new supplies each hour I meet,
>   While pressing on to God.
>
> Grace all the work shall crown
>   Through everlasting days ;
> It lays in heaven the topmost stone,
>   And well deserves the praise.

21

DOCTRINE OF SALVATION: WHAT AND HOW

WE have seen that the Holy Scriptures are " able to make us wise unto salvation." We have seen also that the word " Saviour " is especially prominent in the Pastoral Epistles, and that it is used both of God the Father and of His Son Jesus

Christ. We must now inquire what these Epistles tell us of the salvation itself, and how it is obtained.

The English word " salvation " occurs 160 times in the Authorised Version, 113 of these being in the Old Testament. Taking also the words " save " and " saviour," we find the three words together occurring 470 times, almost 300 being in the Old Testament. Of course, in a great number of cases in the Old Testament it is some earthly deliverance that is spoken of ; but " salvation " in the Psalms (62 times) and in Isaiah (29 times) often has a spiritual sense. In the New Testament the Greek word for " salvation," *sōtēria*, occurs 44 times, and a cognate word, *sōtērion*,[1] four times ; but the rendering is occasionally " safety," " deliverance," etc. The detailed study of this and cognate words is extremely interesting, but must not now detain us.   I have already quoted all the passages in our Epistles in which these words occur, in Chapter xiv. on " God the Saviour " ; and in other chapters also the great central statement, " Christ Jesus came into the world to save sinners," has come before us.

Let it now be noted that the use of such expressions plainly implies that man has need of salvation, whatever that may mean.   If he needs to be " saved " it is because he is either lost or in danger of being lost. So here, in these Pastoral Letters, not written with any direct doctrinal purpose, but partly personal and partly ecclesiastical in character, we have the fact over and over again stated or implied, that the Race of Man is a Fallen Race.   That is an unpopular

---

[1] This is the neuter of the adjective σωτήριος, " saving " or " healthful," which is also used in Tit. ii. 11, and is there translated " bringing salvation."

doctrine in the present day ; but we may depend upon it, nevertheless, that upon this tremendous fact all true religion is based. It is the first duty of every Christian worker to recognise it and to proclaim it. Not necessarily to explain it. Indeed, we really have not sufficient knowledge to do so. It is quite possible that some of our old notions about it, being only human notions, may be wrong. God may possibly yet reveal to us, in one way or another, that the causes of our sinful condition are not what we have sometimes imagined. Let good and thoughtful men keep their minds open for fresh light on what is confessedly dark and obscure. But let us not for a moment tolerate a doubt upon the *fact*. " All have sinned, and come short of the glory of God."

In a previous Talk (p. 90) I quoted from Hort's *Christian Ecclesia* his view of the reason, or one reason, why St. Paul in his old age laid so much stress on salvation. Let me now refer to Professor Sir W. Ramsay, who gives another reason. In the *Expositor* of April 1911 (p. 359), he showed very graphically how the Greek and Roman world was longing at that time for some kind of " salvation." He himself has found in Asia Minor, " in city after city and village after village," inscriptions expressive of this longing, and praying for *sōtēria*. " Those pagans prayed for they knew not what. They asked for salvation, but they did not know in what salvation lay, or what was its nature. What they ignorantly sought for, Paul declared unto them " . . . " and they found the salvation he declared more satisfying, more perfect, more ideal, than they had been able ever to imagine." He goes on to show that " the evil of the world," for which the pagans had other names, St. Paul called *Sin* ; and that St. Paul found the secret of salvation in the Incarnation and the Cross.

On this " secret of salvation " I desire to say a few words before proceeding to examine the references to it in our Epistles. There has been for many years past a tendency in the theological world to lay stress on the Incarnation rather than on the Cross. With this tendency one naturally connects the really great names of Westcott and Moberly. And seeing that all human thought on this most profound of doctrines is necessarily imperfect, and that all teachers are apt, however unintentionally and unconsciously, to emphasise some one side of truth which specially appeals to them, we may frankly acknowledge that the plain old Evangelical teaching on the Atonement did need supplementing. Unspeakably precious as its view of the Cross was, and is, we did need to be reminded of the virtue and power of the whole mission of the Son of God, His Incarnation, His Life, His Death, His Resurrection, His Session and Intercession. Nevertheless, we have good reason to thank God that if the pendulum was swinging too far in this more modern direction, it is now swinging back in the old Evangelical direction.

I take as an example of this the important lectures delivered at Liverpool in September, 1913, by Canon Simpson, of St. Paul's.[1] No living divine

---

[1] *The Religion of the Atonement.* 1s. I see that Dr. Simpson has issued another work on the same subject, *What is the Gospel ? A Study in the Doctrine of Atonement.* 2s. 6d.

is more definitely " modern " than he. No preacher
has a higher reputation. It is a matter for deep
satisfaction that he is deliberately recalling the mind
of the Church to the propitiatory Atonement of the
Cross. He compares some of his Oxford friends of
the generous younger school with what he calls the
modern Scottish school of Dr. Denney, Principal
Forsyth, and others, and definitely throws in his lot
with the latter. He adopts a happy illustration to
indicate his opinion of the two groups :—

" Some of my Oxford friends remind me of a bowler,
perfect in delivery, in pitch, and everything else, but
invariably off the wicket. When, on the other hand,
I read one of the books of those whom I call the Scots
school, there may be many points on which it is scarcely
possible to agree entirely with them, and yet they seem
to get the middle stump every time."   (p. 30.)

Now how is it that these Scottish divines are thus
successful in bowling down the middle stump ? It
is that " in every one of them the evangelical interest
reigns supreme " (p. 25) ; and Canon Simpson's
conviction is that—

" The reconstruction of Christology in the light of
modern thought, which is to be one of the chief theological tasks of the twentieth century, will not only rescue
the doctrine of the Atonement from the comparative
neglect into which, during the nineteenth century, it
had fallen, but, following the example of all really great
creative periods, will make the work of Christ as Redeemer its guiding and formative principle."   (p. 24.)

Dr. Simpson points out that the divines who have
latterly led theological thought in England " have
avoided the language and ideas proper to an Evange-

lical theology." "Phrases like ' the finished work ' have not dwelt readily upon their lips. Substitution they have either definitely rejected or moralised out of all resemblance to itself. They interpreted sacrifice in terms of self-sacrifice " (p. 28). But, he goes on :—

" They do not help us to understand St. Paul when he declares that ' God commendeth His love toward us in that, while we were yet sinners, Christ died,' or St. John when he finds the warrant and source of love in the fact that God ' sent His Son to be the propitiation for our sins.' . . . Their leading interest is in the Body rather than in the Blood of Christ, in the Consummator of humanity rather than in the Saviour of the world." (p. 29.)

In fact, all depends upon the view we take of Sin. If sin is real, if we are responsible for it, if it involves guilt, pollution, and alienation from God, then we want a Saviour. " He bore our sins in His own body on the tree "—that, says Dr. Simpson, " is the simple gospel of St. Peter." And he describes the Atonement as " God making Himself responsible for that catastrophe in the moral nature of man, which is just as real, whether with the Churches we call it sin or not, and dealing with it at infinite cost to Himself in a way which appeals to what is deepest and most ethical in ourselves."

This is perhaps a digression, but I am sure it will not have been an unwelcome one. I return to the Pastorals.

What do they tell us of the Source of Salvation ? It is the Will of God, " Who willeth that all men should be saved " (I. ii. 4). It is His Promise, given, as we have before seen, to His Blessed Son " before times eternal." It is all of " grace," *i.e.*, of favour to the unworthy (I. i. 14, II. i. 9, Tit. ii. 11). It comes from His " kindness " and " love toward man " (Tit. iii. 4). The five verses in which these words occur are the Second Lesson for Christmas day. A more felicitous selection will not be found in the whole Lectionary; but few people ever hear it because so few go to church that evening. Dr. Plummer justly remarks that it would do well for Trinity Sunday, the Three Persons being all conspicuous in it.

But look at those two words, " kindness " and " love toward man." " Kindness " is *chrēstotēs*, one of the words which we find only in St. Paul's writings, and which is translated both " kindness " and " goodness " (in the sense of benignity). We have God's " goodness " three times in Rom. xi. 22 ; also in Rom. ii. 4 ; and His " kindness " in Eph. ii. 7. And we have man's " goodness " or " kindness " in Rom. iii. 12, 2 Cor. vi. 6, Gal. v. 22, Col. iii. 12. The corresponding adjective, *chrēstos*, is " good " in Lu. v. 39, 1 Cor. xv. 33 ; " kind " in Lu. vi. 35, Eph. iv. 32 ; " gracious " in 1 Pet. ii. 3 ; and " easy " in Matt. xi. 30, where Our Lord says, " My yoke is easy." A cognate word is in 1 Cor. xiii. " Love . . . is kind." The other word, *philanthrōpia*, is, of course, the origin of our " philanthropy." It is only once elsewhere used in the N.T., of the " no little kindness " (R.V. " no common kindness ") shown to St. Paul and his shipwrecked comrades by the " barbarians " of Melita. Now there are people who would commend, and imitate, the " philanthropy " of those Maltese, but who will do nothing for " religious " objects. It would be well for us all to remember that God Himself, according to St. Paul, is the Great Philanthropist, and that He showed His philanthropy by stooping to save men from their sins by the sacrifice of His Son.

22

DOCTRINE OF SALVATION: FIVE METAPHORS

IN dealing, however incidentally, with this great topic, St. Paul uses many metaphors. We also habitually use them, but much more loosely than he does, and often without realising their precise meaning. In grouping them, I am going to follow the order suggested by Professor Deissmann, in his able and interesting book, *St. Paul.*[1] He names five aspects of Salvation, expressed figuratively : Justification, Reconciliation, Forgiveness, Redemption, Adoption. "In all these figurative expressions," he observes, " man stands before God, each time in a different guise before the same God, first as an accused person, secondly as an enemy, thirdly as a debtor, fourthly and fifthly as a slave." The passages quoted by him are all from the earlier Epistles, as he avoids the use of the Pastorals ; but all the five figures are used or implied in the Pastorals, and I shall confine myself to them.

1. *Justification.*—We turn to Tit. iii. 7, and we find the very word, "justified by His grace." What

---

[1] The passages referred to above begin at p. 144 of the English edition.

does " justify " mean ? The verb *dikaiō* is connected with *dikaios*, just, or righteous, and *dikaiosunē*, righteousness. Does " justify," then, mean " make righteous " ? No, it means rather " declare righteous." We can see this at once in these same Epistles.

In I. iii. 16, in that hymn-stanza which we examined before, our Lord is said to have been " manifested in the flesh, justified in the spirit." He was not made righteous, but shown to be righteous ; although " in the flesh," His " spirit " showed that He had no sin. So here, " justified by His grace " does not mean that grace makes us righteous ; that would be " sanctified." It means that God's grace, that is, His free favour to the unworthy, declares that we *are* righteous.   The " accused person " (as Deissmann expresses it) is acquitted, " justified," reckoned (as in Rom. iv.) to be without sin in God's sight ; of course, through the righteousness and the sacrifice of Christ. It is interesting to find two great living expositors, who differ on many things, agreeing on this. Bishop Gore says, " To be justified means to be acquitted, or proved righteous, or reckoned righteous in the trial before God.   This, and not to *make* righteous, is the meaning of the word ' to justify ' ; " [1] and Bishop Moule says, " He pronounces you acceptable, at peace with law . . . for Another's sake." [2]

2. *Reconciliation.*—The great passages on this phase of salvation are, of course, Rom. v. 10, " While we were enemies, we were reconciled to God by the death of His Son," and 2 Cor. v. 18–20, about the " ministry of reconciliation." In our Pastorals the same phase

---

[1] Gore, *Romans*, vol. i., p. 124.
[2] Moule, *Romans*, p. 96.

is expressed by the words, " One Mediator between God and man." These we have considered before, and we need only now remind ourselves that Christ's work both enables God to be at peace with man and brings men to peace with God.

3. *Forgiveness.*—Deissmann regards this as what man receives as a " debtor." No doubt it might also be applied to the " accused person " and the " enemy " ; but in view of the Lord's Prayer (" Forgive us our debts ") and of the parable of the Unmerciful Servant, it is quite reasonable to apply it in this special way. In our Epistles we may connect it with the word " mercy," which occurs in them seven times. We recall St. Paul's beautiful retrospect of his own life, in which he twice says, " Howbeit I obtained mercy " ; and the great passage, Tit. iii. 4–8, which we looked at in the preceding Talk, where we find it said of God that " according to His mercy He saved us." It is in the two Letters to Timothy only that St. Paul links " mercy " with " grace and peace " in his salutation ; and in II. i. 16–18 he twice commends to Divine mercy both Onesiphorus and his household.

4. *Redemption.*—This was a metaphor that would particularly appeal to St. Paul's converts, so many of whom were slaves. They might not be able to hope for redemption from their earthly bondage, but they could rejoice in being redeemed from sin. The word means liberation by purchase, and they would joyfully receive the declaration, " Ye were bought with a price " (1 Cor. vi. 20, vii. 23) ; and what a price ! —" purchased with His own blood " (Acts xx. 28). In his other book, *Light from the Ancient East*, Deissmann draws a delightful picture, suggested by the

lately-discovered inscriptions and papyri, of the
Corinthian slave hearing that letter to the Corinthian
Church read at the Christian meeting. This view of
salvation is clearly taught in our Epistles by the use
of the words " redeem " (Tit. ii. 14) and " ransom "
(I. ii. 6).   These two words we must briefly examine.

We saw before, with surprise, how sparing is the
use in the N.T. of our familiar title, " Saviour " ;
but still more surprising is it to find that our scarcely
less familiar title, " Redeemer," does not occur in
the N.T. at all. Curiously enough, the Greek word
lutrōtēs does occur once, being used in Stephen's
speech of Moses (Acts vii. 35) and translated " deliverer."   But in the O.T. the words " redeem," " redeemer," " redemption," are common. Again and
again is God spoken of as the Redeemer of Israel.
We are familiar with " I know that my Redeemer
liveth " and " O Lord, my strength and my Redeemer." The words " redeem " and " redemption,"
however, we do find in the N.T. seven and twelve
times respectively (but twice it is only " redeeming
the time "). They represent two groups of varying
Greek words.[1]   Now we must carefully note what it is
that, in our one passage in Titus, St. Paul tells us that
we are *redeemed from*.   Is it from guilt, from punishment, from death, from hell ?   He does not say so.

---

[1] " Redemption " is λύτρωσις three times, and ἀπολύτρωσις
nine times ; but the latter occurs a tenth time in Heb. xi. 35,
where it is rendered " deliverance."   " Redeem " is λυτρόω
three times, and ἐξαγοράζω four times. In the A.V. " redeem " also occurs in Revelation three times, where the
Greek is ἀγοράζω, which the R.V. renders " purchase." The
A.V. " redeemed " of Lu. i. 68 is altered by the R.V. to
" wrought redemption."

He says, "from all iniquity"; not merely from the penalty of iniquity, but from iniquity itself. Just as the name of Jesus was given to the Infant Redeemer because He should "save His people from *their sins*." I must in passing refer to another parallel passage, 1 Pet. i. 18, 19, whence we get the familiar words, "redeemed by the precious blood of Christ." A true and most blessed phrase; but, redeemed from what? From guilt and punishment? St. Peter does not say so. He says, "from your vain manner of life handed down from your fathers" (R.V.). The reference is to the "traditions of the elders" in which his Jewish converts had been bound. Have we any old customs and habits of thought and life that hinder our Christian course? From *them* the "precious blood of Christ" is designed to redeem us, by its moral power upon our hearts. And so here. Of course, I do not for a moment mean that we are *not* redeemed from sin's penalty. Thank God, we are, indeed! But it is a grave error to limit the redemption to that. When Christ liberates the slave of sin, sin is to have "no more dominion of him."

Then the word "ransom." The One Mediator, the Man Christ Jesus, "gave Himself a ransom for all." We find the word elsewhere in the New Testament only at Matt. xx. 28 and Mark x. 45, which are two records of the same utterance of our Lord. There the Greek word is *lutron*; here it is *anti-lutron*. Now the usual Greek preposition to express Christ's work "for" us is *huper* (or *hyper*), "in behalf of"; and it is often said by those who object to the doctrine of substitution in the Atonement that the stronger word *anti*, "instead of," is only once used, in that sentence of our Lord's, and that we ought therefore only to use the commoner phrase " in behalf of." But in the passage now before us we have both together : *anti-lutron huper pantōn,* which may fairly be rendered " a ransom instead of and in behalf of all." Bishop Bernard in the Cambridge Greek Testament justly says, " *Both* the elements represented by *anti* and *huper* must enter into any Scriptural theory of the Atonement." Bishop Jackson, in the Speaker's Commentary, quotes Chrysostom as saying " What is this *anti-lutron* ? God was about to punish them ; this He did not do. They were about to perish, but He gave His own Son instead of them. . . . He Himself offered Himself a sacrifice in behalf of His enemies." But we must not push a metaphor too far. The Early Fathers used to ask, " To whom was the ransom paid ? " and they answered their question thus, " To the Devil." This was for many centuries the accepted belief. It was Anselm, Archbishop of Canterbury in the days of William Rufus, who propounded a truer doctrine. But we need not build up a complete theory at all. Let us take Scripture phrases and figures in their simplicity, and not seek to be wise above what is written.

5. *Adoption.*—The custom of adopting children was also a familiar one among the peoples St. Paul preached to, and this likewise is strikingly illustrated from the papyri by Deissmann in his *Light from the Ancient East.* We find it alluded to in our Epistles in Tit. iii. 7, " that . . . we might be made heirs according to the hope of eternal life." It is, of course, more fully stated in Gal. iv. 5–7 and Rom. viii. 15–17.

There is one other view of salvation which is promi-

nent in these Epistles.   It is set forth as *life, eternal
life.* But this must wait for another Talk.

23
DOCTRINE OF SALVATION
LIFE AND FAITH

WE have seen five aspects of salvation, following
Deissmann's arrangement.   But there is
one other view of it which is prominent in the Pastoral
Epistles.   It is set forth as Life, Eternal Life, the
Life Indeed :—

> I. i. 16. Them which should believe on Him unto
> eternal life.
>
> iv. 8. Godliness is profitable . . . having pro-
> mise of the life . . . which is to come.
>
> vi. 12. Lay hold on the life eternal.
>
> 19. That they may lay hold on the life which
> is life indeed.
>
> II. i. 1. According to the promise of the life which
> is in Christ Jesus.
>
> 10. Christ Jesus, Who abolished death, and
> brought life and incorruption to light
> through the Gospel.
>
> ii. 10. The salvation which is in Christ Jesus with
> eternal glory.
>
> 11. If we died with Him, we shall also live
> with Him.
>
> Tit. i. 2. In hope of eternal life, which God, Who
> cannot lie, promised before times eternal.
>
> iii. 7. Heirs according to the hope of eternal life.

Surely this is a grand group of texts to gather out
of these neglected Pastoral Epistles !   It is significant

indeed that in these latest letters of St. Paul, one of them written in prospect of speedy execution, the word " death " only occurs once, and then only as a thing " abolished," or rather " brought to nought."[1] On the other hand, life is a thing " promised," as we see in three of the above passages ; and promised by Him " Who cannot lie." Where, in the religions of the ancient world, or in the non-Christian religions to-day, is Death brought to nought, and Life, Eternal Life, promised ? Even in the partial light of the Old Testament what fear of death do we find ! Look at the Sixth, Thirtieth, and other Psalms, and at Hezekiah's touching prayer in Isa. xxxviii. No wonder even the Jews " through fear of death were all their lifetime subject to bondage." But Christ brought Death to nought, and brought Life to light —" brought it out into light," as Bishop Moule renders what he calls " the radiant Greek."[2] Radiant indeed !—for the three words so close together in II. i. 10, *phaneroō* (manifest), *epiphaneia* (appearing), and *phōtizō* (bring to light), seem, as Dr. Newport White says in the Expositor's Greek Testament, to produce " a blaze of light." He cites Bengel as calling them *illustria verba*, and we must remember that " illustrious " etymologically means lustrous or illuminating. (See the Oxford Dictionary.)

Quite naturally does St. Paul, in view of his imminent condemnation and death, concentrate his thoughts

---

[1] The English verb " abolish " only occurs three times in the A.V., in 2 Cor. iii. 13, Eph. ii. 15, and here. The R.V. has it also in 1 Cor. xv. 24, 26. The Greek verb, καταργέω, is usually rendered " bring to nought " or " do away." It is the " cumber " of Lu. xiii. 7, in the sense of " render useless."

[2] *Second Timothy*, p. 50.

on this aspect of salvation.   Death is the consequence, the penalty, of sin.   God is going to sweep sin out of His universe, and death will be swept away with it. " The last enemy that shall be abolished is death " (1 Cor. xv. 26).   For the believer it is already " abolished," " brought to nought," while something else is " brought to light "—" life and incorruption." What that really means, who can say ?   But of this we may be sure, that it stands for an accession of brightness and glory and expansion of powers that are utterly beyond our imagining, worthy indeed of a Divine " purpose and grace."

We must not leave the subject of Salvation without going on to inquire what is said about Faith, which we are accustomed to think of as the hand stretched out to receive salvation as God's free gift.   We know what stress is laid upon faith in St. Paul's other writings, and we desire to see what he says of it in these Letters.

It is certainly remarkable, and quite an unexpected thing, that the Greek word, *pistis*, occurs more often in the First Epistle to Timothy, in proportion to its length, than in any other book in the New Testament. Romans, in 433 verses, has *pistis* 38 times ; Hebrews, in 303 verses, 32 times (24 in chap. xi.) ; Galatians, in 149 verses, 21 times ; First Timothy, in 113 verses 19 times.   The three Pastorals together, in 242 verses, have it 33 times.   This, however, is due to the fact mentioned in a previous Talk, that the word is several times used in an objective sense as " the Faith," standing for the Christian religion rather than for the attitude of the believer.   But let us now look at the passages in which it bears the more usual sense :—

I. i. 2. My true child in faith.
    4. A dispensation of God which is in faith.
    5. The end of the charge is love . . . and a good conscience and faith unfeigned.
   14. Faith and love which is in Christ Jesus.
   19. Holding faith and a good conscience.
 ii. 7. A teacher of the Gentiles in faith and truth.
   15. If they continue in faith and love.
iii. 13. Great boldness in the faith which is in Christ Jesus.
iv. 12. Be thou an example . . . in love, in faith. . .
vi. 11. Follow after . . . faith, love . . .
II. i. 5. The unfeigned faith that is in thee.
   13. In faith and love which is in Christ Jesus.
 ii. 18. Who . . . overthrow the faith of some.
   22. Follow after . . . faith, love . . .
iii. 10. Thou didst follow my . . . faith, long-suffering, love . . .
   15. Wise unto salvation through faith which is in Christ Jesus.
Tit. i. 1. According to the faith of God's elect.
   4. My true child after a common faith.
 ii. 2. That aged men be . . . sound in faith, in love . . .
iii. 15. Salute them that love us in faith.

These twenty, with the eleven objective cases quoted before,[1] make 31. The two others are I. v. 12, where certain " younger widows " are said to have " rejected their first faith," meaning faithfulness to the Heavenly Bridegroom ; and Tit. ii. 10, where the word is naturally rendered " fidelity."

Further, it is interesting to find that the cognate word *pistos* occurs 17 times in our Epistles : 11 of them in First Timothy, actually more often than in any other book. This word ordinarily means " faith-

---

[1] Some expositors think that in a few of the above cases, I. i. 2, ii. 7, iii. 13, Tit. i. 1, 4, the objective sense is intended.

ful " or " trustworthy," but sometimes it is rendered " believer," or " believing," or " that believe."   Here are the passages :—

        I.   i. 12.   He counted me faithful.
            iii. 11.   Women . . . must be . . . faithful in all
                        things.
             iv.   3.   Them that believe.
                  10.   Them that believe.
                  12.   Them that believe.
              v. 16.   Any woman that believeth.
             vi.   2.   Believing masters.
                   2.   They that partake of the benefit are be-
                        lieving.
       II. ii.   2.   The same commit thou to faithful men.
                  13.   He abideth faithful.
     Tit. i.   6.   Children that believe.
                   9.   The faithful word.
And, five times, " Faithful is the saying."

But the case is quite different with the verb " believe," *pisteuō*.   It only occurs four times in the Pastorals, at least in the ordinary sense, viz. :—

        I.   i. 16.   For an ensample of. them which should
                        hereafter believe on Him.
            iii. 16.   Believed on in the world.
       II.   i. 12.   I know Him Whom I have believed.
     Tit. iii. 8.   That they which have believed God . . .
                        maintain good works.

And twice more in the sense of " commit " (I. i. 11, Tit. i. 3).

We should also notice that the negative words *apistia* (unbelief) and its cognates occur four times in the Pastorals :—

        I.   i. 13.   I did it ignorantly in unbelief.
              v.   8.   Worse than an unbeliever.
       II. ii. 13.   If we are faithless.
     Tit. i. 15.   Them that are defiled and unbelieving.

In passing, it is worth noting that while St. John never once uses *pistis*, " faith," in his Gospel, only once in his Epistles, and four times in Revelation, he uses the verb *pisteuō*, " believe," 104 times; his Gospel having it 94 times, more than twice as often as any other book.

Returning to the Pastorals, we note, on a careful examination of the above-quoted texts, that faith as an instrument of salvation is only once clearly mentioned, in II. iii. 15, " wise unto salvation through faith which is in Christ Jesus." In other cases faith is rather the continuous trust in Christ of His believing people. But we find the verb " believe " three times as indicating the way of salvation, I. i. 16, I. iii. 16, Tit. iii. 8 ; and the adjective *pistos* in a few cases may be taken as used to describe one who has " believed " with a view to being saved.

This, however, is a significant indication of the many-sidedness of faith. It is far from being merely the hand that takes God's great gift. It is the guiding principle of the whole Christian life. The Eleventh of Hebrews would show us that ; but we need not go beyond our Epistles. Look at the texts above, and see how they cover the circumstances and needs of our lives. For instance, in ten out of the twenty, faith is linked with love, which is " the fulfilling of the law," and twice it is linked with a good conscience. There is no real conflict between faith and works, as some who misinterpret St. James think. Let our faith be unfeigned (as two of the above texts suggest), a genuine trust in God, in His promises, in His power, in His love, in His care, and it will bring forth good works as its natural fruit.

24

DOCTRINE OF BAPTISM

FAITH, we have seen, is the instrument of salvation. But faith is not to stand alone. Something else is closely linked with it which is often forgotten. In Rom. x. 9–10, St. Paul in clearest words answers the question, What must I do to be saved? " If thou shalt confess with thy mouth Jesus as Lord, and shalt believe in thy heart that God raised Him from the dead, thou shalt be saved : for with the heart man believeth unto righteousness, and with the mouth confession is made unto salvation."

Faith and confession. What is meant by confession ? Surely it means the public, fearless, deliberate, acknowledgment of Christ as a personal Saviour. When was this done by St. Paul's converts ? It was done at their baptism. And when his words to the Philippian jailer are cited as the one way of salvation : " Believe on the Lord Jesus Christ, and thou shalt be saved," we ought at once to add, " and to confess Him openly," for that is exactly what the jailer did. He was baptized " immediately." Thus we see the point of our Lord's own words, " He that believeth and is baptized shall be saved."

Now this is the reason why, in the fullest statement of the doctrine of salvation which we find in the Pastoral Epistles, Tit. iii. 4–7, Baptism has a conspicuous place. Let us again read the whole passage :—

" But when the kindness of God our Saviour, and His love toward man, appeared, not by works done in righteousness, which we did ourselves, but according to His mercy He saved us, through the washing of regeneration and renewing of the Holy Ghost, which He poured out upon us richly through Christ Jesus our Saviour ; that being justified by His grace, we might be made heirs according to the hope of eternal life. Faithful is the saying. . . ."

We have already looked at several points in this great passage. Let us now see what is meant by " the washing of regeneration." The word for " washing " is *loutron*, which the Revised Version margin, and most commentators, render " laver." The reference to Baptism is indisputable. The only other place where *loutron* occurs is Eph. v. 26, " the washing of water with the word " ; and here, too, it is Baptism that is referred to. Some readers imagine that a spiritual cleansing by " the Word of God," the Scriptures, is there meant ; but in the phrase " the Word of God," " word " is *logos*, while in this verse " word " is *rhēma*, which means an individual utterance ; and " with the word " refers, perhaps to the baptismal formula, " In the Name of . . ." but also, surely, to the candidate's open confession of Christ by word of mouth, as in Rom. x. So also in I Pet. iii., where St. Peter says : " Water, which also after a true likeness doth now save you, even baptism, not the putting away of the filth of the flesh, but the interrogation (Authorised Version, answer) of a good conscience toward God." That " interrogation," or " answer," is the public confession of Christ. " Do you confess Jesus as the Son of God ? " " Yes, I do." Thus, " with the mouth confession is made, unto salvation."

Let us try and imagine what St. Paul was thinking of when he wrote those words to Titus. " According

to His mercy He saved us," himself, and Titus, and
the converts in Crete.   When and how ?   His memory
goes back to that house in " the street called Straight,"
in the ancient city of Damascus.   He recalls his own
blinded eyes, and his prayer in the dark (" Behold, he
prayeth "), and his thoughts in the dark about that
Nazarene carpenter whose execution he had supposed
to be well deserved, whose followers, " men and
women," he himself had " persecuted unto the death,"
but Whom he had seen alive in heavenly glory.   He
recalls how in that room, so dark to him, he heard what
he could not see, a brother Jew coming in, the " devout man," Ananias ; and how that visitor addressed
him as " Brother Saul," restored his sight, told him
of the wonderful work to which that same Jesus was
appointing him, saying, " Arise and be baptized,
and wash away thy sins, calling on the name of the
Lord."[1]   And he feels that in that very hour he was
" regenerated," " born again," came out of the old
life and began the new.   He knows that Titus passed
through the same experience, and many of the Cretans.   Can we wonder that he thinks of the hour of
their baptism as the hour when " according to God's
mercy," " through the washing of regeneration," they
were " saved " ?[2]

---

[1] It is important to combine the three narratives, Acts ix.
xxii., xxvi.

[2] Regeneration is παλινγενεσία, from πάλιν, again, and
γένεσις, birth or beginning. This word occurs elsewhere
only in Matt. xix. 28. There, remarks Alford, it means the
new birth of heaven and earth ; here, the new birth of the
individual man.   The word is not unknown in ancient writers.
Lord A. Hervey, in the *Pulpit Commentary*, says : " It is
used by Cicero of his restoration to political power, by Josephus of the restoration of the Jews under Zerubbabel, and by
several Greek authors."

Are we tempted to think of this as something exceptional ? But exactly the same process is being experienced day by day in Asia and Africa. Sometimes a little band of new converts comes, followed by heathen relatives perplexed and maybe hostile, to the bank of a small stream. On the other side are standing the already baptized members of the Church, ready to welcome them. The new converts make their public confession of their belief in Christ, St. Peter's " answer of a good conscience towards God " ; they step down into the stream ; the minister, very likely one of their own race and colour, standing in the water, solemnly baptizes them " in the Name of the Father, and of the Son, and of the Holy Ghost," and declares them to be " regenerate and grafted into the body of Christ's Church " ; and they come up out of the stream *on the other side* : " old things are passed away ; behold ! they are become new."

Do those converts imagine that some magical power resides in that water, or in the act of dipping in it ? Not if they have been well taught. But they do look upon it as the " outward and visible sign " of an " inward and spiritual grace," " a death unto sin and a new birth unto righteousness " ; and though, perhaps months before, they had believed in Christ as their Saviour and given themselves to Him, this was their enrolment, openly and solemnly, in His Church. " With the heart man believeth unto righteousness, and with the mouth confession is made *unto salvation*."

But St. Paul does not stop at " regeneration." The single act is not enough. " And renewing of the Holy Ghost." Just as our Lord said to Nicodemus, " born of water and of the Spirit." St. Paul recalls how on that memorable day at Damascus, Ananias had also said to him, " that thou mayest . . . be filled with the Holy Ghost." He knows that the Holy Ghost had been pricking his conscience even during his persecuting career, perhaps ever since the martyrdom of Stephen. He is sure that when he " arose and was baptized " the Holy Ghost was upon him and in him. And he realised that he owed all his power and perseverance through the years that have followed to the daily " renewing " of the Holy Ghost. So with Titus ; so with the Cretan converts ; so with us all. As our Christmas Collect expresses it : " Grant that we being regenerate, and made Thy children by adoption and grace, may daily be renewed by Thy Holy Spirit."

Here I might stop ; but it may be well to add a few words in reply to the question, What has all this to do with the baptism of infants ?

Now baptism in the N.T. naturally—we may say inevitably—means the baptism of adults. The Christian Church was a new thing, and those who joined it were, as a matter of course, baptized on their own confession of faith. It is the same in the Mission field to-day. If we ask a missionary how many baptisms he has had, we mean, naturally and inevitably, baptisms of adult converts.

Hence some Christians take our Lord's words before quoted as implying that there can be no real baptism without faith on the part of the person baptized, and on this build the doctrine of " Believers' Baptism." Now it is remarkable that under the Jewish dispensation the same language could have been used about circumcision. In Rom. iv. 9–11 we read, "We say, To Abraham his faith was reckoned for righteousness. How then was it reckoned? When he was in circumcision, or in uncircumcision? Not in circumcision, but in uncircumcision: and he received the sign of circumcision, a seal of the righteousness of the faith which he had while he was in uncircumcision." That is a distinct statement of what might have been called "Believers' Circumcision." It was "a seal of the righteousness of the faith which he had while he was in uncircumcision." He believed, and then, as a believer, he received the sign and seal of circumcision. The analogy is perfect between this and "Believers' Baptism." And yet Jewish boys were by God's command circumcised when eight days old.

It is important to remember how exactly the O.T. dispensation corresponds with the New. We may fairly say that there were two "sacraments" in the former, Circumcision and the Passover. Both were instituted before the Sinaitic Law, and both were essential for every man in Israel. And now, corresponding with these, we have Baptism and the Lord's Supper. There is one difference: in the Christian dispensation there is no distinction of sex. Baptism is for both sexes.

With this striking analogy in mind, let us put ourselves in the position of the early Christians. Let us imagine ourselves at Jerusalem on the Day of Pentecost. Crowds are pressing forward in response to St. Peter's appeal, "Repent, and be baptized, every one of you, in the name of Jesus Christ." A man would quite naturally inquire about his children: "Am I to bring them too?" What would Peter's answer be ?   Can we conceive it possible that he would say, " No, they must wait till they are older, and can make their own confession of faith " ?   " What ! " might well be the man's rejoinder, " will they be worse off in the new dispensation than in the old ?   My children have been in God's covenant hitherto : will they not be in the new covenant ? "   I could indeed imagine Peter hesitating, because he had not yet learned that circumcision was not to be required of other nations, and he might possibly think it sufficient for children without baptism.   But by and by, when the Gentiles came into the Church, and the Council at Jerusalem decided against their being circumcised, what could he say then ?

Then suppose the Apostles discussed the question, " What did the Master say ? "   If we can imagine one of them urging that He gave no express command to baptize children, the answer would at once be, " But if we were *not* to do so, surely He would have told us.   He rebuked us for checking their resorting to Him ; He said ' Of such is the Kingdom of God.' If they can be in the Kingdom of God, why exclude them from the Church which is the representative of the Kingdom ? "

This last consideration would of itself be decisive. What do we think of young children now ?   If they can go to heaven at a tender age—and who doubts that they can ?—how can they be disqualified for admission to the Visible Church on earth ?

We see, therefore, that the question whether the households of Lydia, the jailer, and other early converts, did or did not comprise children, is of no importance at all.   If there were any, they would be baptized ; but there was no reason for expressly mentioning them.

I will only add that the Church of England does provide for the personal faith and public personal confession upon which objectors to Infant Baptism lay stress, in the rite of Confirmation, which is in fact the completion of Baptism.

25

THE CHURCH: MEANING

ALTHOUGH the word " Church " occurs only three times in the Pastoral Epistles, they are largely occupied with what we may call Church matters. The doctrinal statements which we have found to be so numerous are really incidental, and a good deal of the ethical teaching which we have yet to study is scarcely less so ; but the organisation, ministry, worship, discipline of the Church are a leading topic of I Timothy, and, though not prominent on the face of the other two letters, underlie many passages in them.

Let us first examine the word " Church " itself ; and here I take as my guide Hort's interesting Cambridge Lectures, published after his death with the title, *The Christian Ecclesia*. The Greek word *ekklēsia*, whence come our " ecclesiastic " and similar words, was in common use among the Greeks as signifying an assembly. In the Hebrew Old Testament one of the words for " assembly " or " congregation " is *qāhāl*, meaning what is called or summoned. When the Septuagint translators wanted a Greek word to represent it, they thought of the verb *kaleo*, " call," because of its similarity of sound, and this word re-minded them of its compound, *ekkaleo*, which again suggested their own regular word for " assembly," *ekklēsia*, derived from it ; and this they naturally adopted. When the early Greek Christians met, for worship or for conference, they too naturally called their meeting by their own familiar term ; and so we find it in the N.T. Dr. Sanday, indeed, thinks that our Lord Himself indirectly gave the Christian Society this name, by using the old Hebrew *qāhāl* in the words reported in Matt. xvi. 18 and xviii. 17, which the Greek writer would naturally translate, as in the LXX., *ekklēsia*.[1] In our earlier English versions *ekklēsia* in the N.T. is translated " congregation " or " assembly," just as *qāhāl* is in the O.T.   The Geneva Version, in Queen Elizabeth's time, altered this to " Church," which is believed to be derived indirectly from the Greek *kuriakos*, meaning " the Lord's "—a word found in 1 Cor. xi. 20 and Rev. i. 10, " Lord's Supper " and " Lord's day." The Scottish form, " kirk," shows the connection better. The word *kuriakos*, by the way, frequently appears in the papyri and inscriptions described in Deiss-mann's *Light from the Ancient East*, in the sense of " imperial," as " the imperial treasury," etc.

There is one very interesting link between " congre-gation " in the O.T. and " Church " in the N.T., which Hort points out.   We are all familiar with St. Paul's striking phrase in his address to the Ephesian elders in Acts xx., " The Church of God, which He hath purchased with His own blood." This, Hort sug-gests, is an expression adopted by the Apostle from a

[1] *The Primitive Church and Reunion*, p. 70.

passage in the Psalms. Certainly it would puzzle many readers to find such a passage, but it is beautifully significant when found. It is Ps. lxxiv. 2, " Remember Thy congregation, which Thou hast purchased of old, which Thou hast redeemed to be the tribe of Thine inheritance." Here we have an *ekklēsia* " purchased " and " redeemed." The idea of Israel as a redeemed and purchased people is first expressed in the Song of Miriam, Exod. xv. 13, 16, where both words occur, and the verse in Ps. lxxiv. seems an echo of them. " There," says Hort, " fresh significance is given to the Psalmist's language by the way in which St. Paul appropriates it to describe how God had purchased to Himself a new congregation (now called *ekklēsia*) by the ransom of His Son's life-blood."

The word " Church," standing for *ekklēsia*, occurs 109 times in our English N.T., 62 times being in St. Paul's Epistles. It is worth noting that our familiar " Church of Christ " is not used, though we find " Churches of Christ " once, in Rom. xvi. 16. We find " Church of God " nine times in St. Paul's Epistles, besides its occurrence in his address in Acts xx., above referred to. As regards this last, however, the R.V. margin tells us that " many ancient authorities " read " Church of the Lord," which would mean Christ ; and certainly the expression " with His own blood " comes more naturally so.

Turning to our Epistles, the three occurrences of the word " Church " are as follows :—

I. iii.   5.   If a man knoweth not how to rule his own house, how shall he take care of the Church of God ?

> I. iii. 15.   The house of God, which is the Church of the living God, the pillar and ground of the truth.
>
> v. 16.   Let not the Church be burdened.

In the N.T., " Church " sometimes means the congregation of believers in a city, or even in a house ; sometimes the congregations of a province ; and sometimes the whole body of them in the world. In each case it is obviously the Visible Organised Church of baptized persons that is meant. But there are a few passages, especially in the Ephesian and Colossian Epistles, where the word seems to mean rather the whole body of true and living members of Christ, the " Invisible Church " of which Hooker writes so impressively. There are naturally differences of opinion as to some passages, whether they refer to the Visible or the Invisible Church. But in the three passages in 1 Timothy there can be no doubt that the Visible Organised Church is meant. In I. iii. 5, it is the local body or community of which the " bishop " is to " take care." In I. v. 16, it is the local body, the congregation, or congregations, which is to support certain widows and not others. The third passage, I. iii. 15, is more important, and must be examined.

As with doctrinal statements, so here, the Church comes in quite incidentally. St. Paul is explaining that he is giving instructions in case he is unable to go to Ephesus soon : " If I tarry long." Instructions about what ? " That thou mayest know how men ought to behave themselves [1] in the house of God, which is the Church. . . ."

What is meant by " the house of God " ? Not a

---

[1] Not as in A.V., " How thou oughtest to behave thyself."

material building, but rather " household," *oikos*. [1] The idea is the same as in Gal. vi. 10, " the household of faith " ; Eph. ii. 19, " the household of God " ; Heb. x. 21, " the house of God " ; 1 Pet. ii. 5, " a spiritual house " ; and other similar passages. Connected with this is St. Paul's mention of himself as a house-steward, *oikonomos*, in 1 Cor. iv. 1, 2 ; and the same figure occurs once in these Epistles, Tit. i. 7, " the bishop must be blameless, as God's steward."

As, then, in the earlier part of our chapter, a man is said to be unworthy of the episcopal office unless he can " rule his own house "—for if he " knoweth not how to rule his own house, how shall he take care of the Church of God ? "—so here St. Paul explains that all his counsels and injunctions are designed to teach Christians generally " how they ought to behave themselves in the house of God," *i.e.* the household of God, the Church of the living God, consisting of living men.

And every " Church," every congregation, however small, is to be " a pillar " and " a stay " (R.V. marg.) " of the truth." Not " *the* pillar," as if one pillar were supporting a whole building ; nor " the ground " or foundation, but a " stay " or bulwark. [2] So Dr. Hort explains the passage ; but commentators vary

---

[1] The two words οἶκος and οἰκία both mean " house," and are both used in the N.T. for the material building ; but when " house " means " household " or " family " the word is almost always οἶκος and not οἰκία. In the Pastorals the distinction is clear ; see I. iii. 4, 5, 12, 15, v. 4 ; II. i. 16, iv. 19 ; Tit. i. 11, for οἶκος ; and I. v. 13 ; II. ii. 20, iii. 6. for οἰκία.

[2] Bishop Bernard says " ἑδραίωμα is not found elsewhere in the Greek Bible. . . . It seems to mean *bulwark* or *stay*, rather than *ground* or *foundation*.

in their interpretations of it. Dean Spence-Jones, in Ellicott's Commentary, points out that we have here two images or pictures of the Church :

" In the first picture, the Church is painted by St. Paul as a vast congregation, with the living God dwelling in its midst ; in the second, the same Church is painted as a massive pillar, holding up and displaying before men and angels *the truth*—the saving truth of the Gospel. In the first picture, the thought of a great company gathered together for God to dwell among is prominent ; in the second—the thought of the great redemption— truth alone comes to the front, and the Church of God is no longer viewed as a company of separate indivi- duals, but as one massive foundation-pillar, supporting and displaying the glories of redemption."

So, whatever is the " behaviour " in the Church of God to be enjoined—and this we shall see in subsequent Talks—one thing is here made quite clear, that the Church's great function, or at least one of them, is to support and display the Truth.

The figure of *building* is often used by St. Paul, and applied to the building up of the Church of living souls ; and the words " edify " and " edification " mean the same thing, the Greek words being the same or similar. But interesting as this imagery is, it is not used in the Pastoral Epistles, so I pass it over.[1] The figure of a " house," and of its " foundation," occurs again in II. ii., and at this we shall look in our next Talk.

Meanwhile, let us not be troubled because the Visible Church is not perfect. It never has been. Dr.

---

[1] We have " edifying " in the A.V. of I. i. 4, standing for οἰκοδομία, but the best MSS. have a different word there, οἰκονομία, which the R.V. renders " dispensation."

Plummer wisely lays stress on the fact that the
" golden age," which some imaginative souls picture
to themselves at some past date in Church history,
never appeared.   As regards the early Church, " witness the monstrous disorders in the Church at Corinth,
the fickleness of the Galatian converts, the un-Chris-
tian asceticism of the Colossian heretics, the studied
immorality of those at Ephesus. . . . And there is
much more of the same sort, as the Pastoral Epistles
show us."   He calls on us to be encouraged by such a
retrospect : " It may reasonably be contended that at
no era since Christianity was first founded have its
prospects been so bright as at the present time." [1]

26

THE CHURCH: VISIBLE

WE have seen that the Church is called by St.
Paul, in I. iii. 15, " the House of God."   The
same figure is used by him again, but rather differently, in II. ii. 20 : " Now in a great house. . . ."
But this is led up to by another figure, which we must
examine first.   The Apostle has been referring to
certain heretical teachers, who had " erred concerning
the truth," and who " overthrew the faith of some."
They and their teachings will come before us by and by,
when we turn our attention to the heresies and evil
influences revealed in these Epistles.   But St. Paul
then comforts himself, and Timothy, and the Church,
with these striking words :

---

[1] *Pastoral Epistles*, pp. 264–266.

Howbeit, the firm foundation of God standeth, having this seal, The Lord knoweth them that are His, and, Let everyone that nameth the name of the Lord depart from unrighteousness.

First of all, what is this " firm foundation of God " ?[1] One naturally thinks of Christ as the only " foundation " (1 Cor. iii. 11), or of " the foundation of the apostles and prophets " (Eph. ii. 20). But the image is not quite the same here, and expositors are generally agreed that it is the Church that is meant, not the Visible Church with its inevitably mixed membership, but the Ideal or Invisible Church. Bishop Moule calls it " that solid foundation of God, the true Church of the First-born." Dean Spence-Jones suggests that the Church of this dispensation is called a " foundation " because on it will be built " the glorious Temple of the future," " a far grander building, which in the fulness of time will rest upon its massive work." The word " firm," *stereos*, is the " solid " of Heb. v. 12, 14 (A.V. strong), and the " steadfast " of 1 Pet. v. 9. Our " stereotype " is derived from it.

But what makes this foundation firm ? What is it that gives solid strength and steadfastness to the spiritual and living Church ? The answer is in the words with which it is " sealed." The reference here is to the custom of putting an inscription on a foundation-stone, a very ancient custom, as the Egyptian and other monuments show, and one still observed among ourselves. In Rev. xxi. 14, the " new Jerusalem " is pictured as having a wall with twelve

---

[1] This R.V. rendering of στερεὸς θεμέλιός is more accurate than " the foundation of God standeth sure " of the A.V.; but the sense is much the same.

foundations, " and on them the names of the twelve Apostles of the Lamb." Now the spiritual Church is doubly sealed with two supremely great sentences, " The Lord knoweth them that are His," and " Let everyone that nameth the name of the Lord depart from unrighteousness." In these lies the secret of solidity and steadfastness.

It is very interesting to see where St. Paul found the two texts which he cites as the seal of the Church. They are both, I do not doubt—though some expositors miss the second,—from the narrative of the rebellion of Korah in Num. xvi. Korah, Dathan, and Abiram were heterodox and schismatical teachers, like the opposers at Ephesus. " The Lord," said Moses to them, " will show who are His " (verse 5), and the Greek translation of these words in the LXX. O.T. is adopted by St. Paul to assure Timothy, and the whole Church, that the " firmness " of the " foundation " rests on the Lord's unerring knowledge of who among its professing members are really " His." I ask my readers to look at the Greek words. In the LXX. of Num. xvi. 5 it is *egnō ho Theos tous ontas autou*; and here it is *egnō Kurios tous ontas autou. Ho Theos* is God and *Kurios* is Lord[1]; and except for this variation the words are identical. The Septuagint, it will be noticed, has " knoweth " where the Hebrew has " will show "; and, remembering that the Septuagint was the actual " Bible " of St. Paul and the early Greek-speaking Church, we understand how the Apostle would quote the words from the version with which they were familiar.

---

[1] Our A.V. has " nameth the name of *Christ*," which is quite wrong.

But what of the other text on the seal? It is deeply interesting. We look down the narrative of Korah's rebellion, and we find Moses appealing to the people to " depart from those wicked men " (verse 26), and so escape the judgment coming upon them. St. Paul remembers that the Israelites who clave to Moses and Aaron as God's appointed leaders for them had to prove their loyalty by coming away from the rebel tents; and he knows that while " the Lord knows them that are His " in the Christian Church, they must, to prove themselves " His," in like manner " depart from iniquity." So he again adopts, and this time (as often elsewhere) *adapts*, the appeal of Moses, taking the sense rather than the language, for the inscription on the spiritual seal. This is surely one of the most striking and beautiful illustrations of the profitable use of O.T. narratives. The stability of Israel lay in Jehovah's knowledge of the hearts of His true and loyal people; but how could that stability be proved and manifested except by their departing from the rebel section of the camp? And so in the Church. The Lord knows all hearts, and the spiritual Church of believing souls is absolutely firm and solid, comprising the " sheep " that " shall never perish "; but the proof and manifestation of this can only be effected by their departing from all iniquity. The result of St. Paul's citations is a most impressive setting forth of the combination of God's sovereignty and man's responsibility which we find it so difficult to grasp, but which is so important an element in the Divine scheme of redemption.

Some of the expressions in the two texts would be worth further study. " The Lord knoweth ": we remember how God said of Abraham, " I have known him " (Gen. xviii. 19) ; how He twice said to Moses, " I know thee by name " (Exod. xxxiii. 12, 17) ; how the prophet Nahum tells us that " the Lord knoweth them that trust in Him " (i. 7) ; how Christ Himself said, " I know My sheep " (John x. 14, 27). We note that the phrase " nameth the name of the Lord " may be a reminiscence of Isa. xxvi. 13 ("make mention of Thy name "), showing how St. Paul would instinctively use O.T. language even when not actually quoting. And we find a parallel to " depart from unrighteousness " in the prophet's appeal to the exiled people in Isa. lii. 11, " Depart ye, depart ye, go out from thence, touch no unclean thing," which St. Paul quotes in 2 Cor. vi. 17. Most commentators, indeed, think this is the passage adapted by him for the second seal ; but to my mind the double reference to Num. xvi. is far more likely.

But now let us go on to what St. Paul says of the " great house " in the verses that follow. " Now in a great house there are not only vessels of gold and of silver, but also of wood and of earth ; and some unto honour, and some unto dishonour. If a man therefore purge himself from these, he shall be a vessel unto honour, sanctified, meet for the master's use, prepared unto every good work."

What is the " great house " ? Plainly the Visible Church. St. Paul has spoken of the Ideal or Invisible Church of truly believing souls, the " firm foundation" with the double seal. Then he thinks of the actual Church which men can see. Ah ! that is a different thing ! It is a " great house," a mixed body. But in this there is nothing to be surprised at. In a " great house " there are " vessels " of all kinds, " some unto honour and some unto dishonour," golden and silvern, wooden and earthen.   So in the Visible Church.   The " vessels " are the members of the Church ; and if a member would be a " vessel unto honour," he must " purge himself from these," which is a difficult phrase. It does not seem to be the Church that is to be purged from unworthy " vessels," as some commentators interpret the passage ; but the individual member or " vessel " is to be " purged."   Purged from what ? " These," I think, must mean the errors of the false teachers referred to in verses 16–18, and perhaps also the " unrighteousness " from which true members of Christ must " depart."   It is encouraging also to note that even an " earthen vessel " may be " unto honour."   St. Paul humbly calls himself one in 2 Cor. iv. 7 : " We have this treasure [the Gospel] in earthen vessels."   The Greek word there and here is the same, *ostrakinos*, and is only found in these two places.

We must not miss what is implied in being " a vessel unto honour."   Note the words that follow :

(1) " Sanctified," *i.e.*, consecrated, set apart for God's service.

(2) " Meet for the master's use," not only destined for that honour, but fit for it.   " Meet " is *euchrēstos*, the same word which is applied to Mark as being " useful " (II. iv. 11 ; A.V. profitable), and to Onesimus also as " profitable " (Phile. 11).   Dr. Newport White suggests " owner " instead of " master," which seems a happy thought.

(3) " Prepared unto every good work " ; so in Tit. iii. 1, " ready unto every good work " ; and we remem-

ber that it is the inspired Scriptures by which we can be " furnished completely unto every good work."

Well may we take up the prayer with which Bishop Moule concludes his meditation on this passage : " Lord and Master, make us thus fit ourselves . . . that we, when Thou requirest us for Thy purposes, may be found by Thee *handy* to Thy touch, in the place and in the condition in which Thou canst take us up and employ us, in whatever way, on the moment, for Thyself."

27

THE CHURCH: WORSHIP

WE have seen that the allusions to the Church in the Pastoral Epistles are only incidental. But St. Paul's counsels to Timothy and Titus on Church matters are not incidental. In 1 Timothy they are the gist of the letter ; and in Titus they have a prominent place. 2 Timothy is different. Even in 1 Timothy, however, we must not expect to find a complete scheme of the organisation or the ministry or the worship of the Church. On the contrary, both fundamental principles and elementary rules are taken for granted. St. Paul assumes much that is not expressed. He deals with particular matters upon which counsel was needed ; and it does not at all follow that these matters were more important than others which find no mention. For example, there are the two Sacraments ordained by our Lord Himself.   One was the authorised entrance into the Visible Church, and of this we have many examples in the Acts ; while the other was regularly observed from the first (Acts ii. 42, xx. 7) as, in one aspect at least, the condition of continued membership.   Yet Baptism is only alluded to in our Epistles in one doctrinal passage (Tit. iii. 5), and the Lord's Supper is not mentioned at all.   To disparage them on that account would be, to say the least, unscientific.   And we shall have to bear the same consideration in mind as we examine St. Paul's directions touching the worship, the ministry, and the discipline of the Church.

Public worship comes first, at the beginning of I. ii. " I exhort, therefore, first of all," writes the Apostle.   Nowhere else in the N.T. does the exact expression " first of all " occur ; so it must indicate the importance of what is going to be said.   But when we read on we are surprised.   We are not told anything of how public worship is to be conducted, or by whom.   Was it liturgical or extempore ?   What part in it had the reading of the Scriptures, exposition and exhortation, confession, petition, thanksgiving, songs of praise, " breaking of bread " ? By whom was it conducted ? and what part did the congregation take, if any ? No directions on these important points are given. But the reason is that indicated above.   There was already some recognised form or method of service, and there was no need to describe it.   And all that St. Paul does is to lay special stress upon one desirable feature of public worship, and, presently, to lay down certain rules for men and women in the congregation respectively.

1. The special feature which he desires to see in

the Church's worship we may call catholicity. The
Christians are not to be wholly concerned with their
own local and personal needs. They are to take large
views and be guided by large sympathies. Prayer
is to be " for all men." This is in accordance with
our Lord's own teaching. The pattern prayer He
gave us begins significantly, not " my Father," but
" our Father." Sir W. M. Ramsay points out[1] that
St. Paul, in his earlier letter to the Ephesian group of
Churches, had appealed for prayer only " for all the
saints " (vi. 18), but that since then the great Neronian
persecution had begun, so now he virtually adds
" Pray for them that despitefully use you." So our
Litany rises to its climax in the suffrage " That it
may please Thee to have mercy upon all men,"
followed immediately by a prayer specifying " our
enemies, persecutors, and slanderers." And the
Prayer for the Church Militant is actually based on
this passage.

2. But one class to be prayed for is expressly
specified. " For kings and all that are in high place "
(A.V. in authority).[2] It was important that the
Christians should be loyal, and show their loyalty ;
and the need for reminding them of this is illustrated
by the allusions in 2 Pet. ii. 10 and Jude 8 to some
who " despised dominion " and " railed at dignities."
All the commentators remind us that the Emperor
of that day was Nero ; but St. Paul's injunction is a
general one. And he gives a particular reason why

---

[1] *Expositor*, September 1909, p. 272.

[2] This phrase is $\dot{\epsilon}\nu\ \dot{\upsilon}\pi\epsilon\rho o\chi\hat{\eta}$. The word only occurs else-
where in 1 Cor. ii. 1, where $\kappa\alpha\theta$' $\dot{\upsilon}\pi\epsilon\rho o\chi\dot{\eta}\nu\ \lambda\acute{o}\gamma o\upsilon$ is rendered
" with excellency of speech."

rulers should be prayed for: "that we may lead a tranquil and quiet life in all godliness and gravity." So our Collect for the Fifth Sunday after Trinity: "That the course of this world may be so peaceably ordered by Thy governance, that Thy Church may joyfully serve Thee in all godly quietness." Polycarp and Tertullian are cited by the commentators as testifying to the ancient custom of the Church praying for rulers. Chrysostom, commenting on this passage, says, "Every day, both in the evening and morning, we offer prayers for the whole world, for kings, and all in authority"; and the early Liturgies contain such prayers. A Japanese editor who visited England a few years ago told me that he was greatly struck by our Prayer Book containing prayers for the Sovereign, as he had previously supposed Christianity to be a disloyal religion, because the Americans, whom he had mostly met, had no king.

3. St. Paul mentions what at first sight look like four different kinds of prayer to be offered: "supplications, prayers, intercessions, thanksgivings." The distinction, however, is rather that of the suppliant's attitude. The first word, *deēsis*, is connected with *dei*, "must," and implies a sense of need; and it is often used of requests made by one man to another. The second, *proseuchē*, is the usual word for prayer to God. The third, *enteuxis*, does not mean intercession only, as it is the regular word for a "petition" to a superior; but the cognate verb is the one used in Rom. viii. 27, 34, and Heb. vii. 25, of "making intercession." The fourth, *eucharistia* (whence our "eucharist"), is always thanksgiving or thankfulness. Bishop Bernard quotes Origen on these four

words, who arranges them in an ascending scale.
" The needy suppliant (*deēsis*), as he goes on, is led
to ask for larger blessings (*proseuchē*), and then,
becoming bold, he presents his *enteuxis*, which being
granted, his devotion issues in *eucharistia*."

4. St. Paul goes on to set forth in verses 3–7 reasons
why public prayer should thus be made for all men.
Liddon [1] reckons these reasons as seven in number, and
I condense his suggestive notes as follows : (*a*) It is
a noble and beautiful practice (implied in the word for
" good," *kalos*). (*b*) It is acceptable to God. (*c*) It
is in accordance with His will, for He " willeth that all
men should be saved." (*d*) As there is " One God,"
we must believe that He cares for all His creatures.
If He were only one of many gods, He might only care
for His own worshippers. (*e*) Also there is one
Mediator, Who, being " Himself Man," represents
the whole race. (*f*) If the " ransom " is " for all,"
all should be prayed for. (*g*) And one personal
reason, verse 7 : St. Paul's message was a world-
embracing Gospel. We have before noted the great
doctrinal statements of these verses. Here we see
their application to Christian worship.

So we may well be encouraged to lay before the
Lord any public or secular affairs in which we are
interested. The prayer for the High Court of Parliament gives us a good pattern in the case of national
needs or emergencies ; but we need not be limited to
such great matters. " In everything . . . let your
requests be made known unto God " (Phil. iv. 6) ;
and the very next verse tells us that *then* " the peace
of God " will " guard " us.

____

[1] *Expl. Anal.* I *Tim.*, p. 12.

Then St. Paul goes on to give certain directions touching the conduct of public worship, verses 8–12 :

1. The worship is to be conducted by men only ; so, at least, most expositors read the passage. The A.V. " I will that men pray everywhere " is certainly misleading. There is no reference here to personal and private prayer everywhere. It is " *the* men " (R.V.) " in every place "—*i.e.*, the men who are present at any place of worship—not, of course, only a sacred building ; it might be a Roman catacomb, or a Cilician hillside, or a tossing ship. And " men " is not *anthropous* but *andras*. It is not the generic word comprising both sexes, whence our words " philanthropy " and " anthropo-logy," but the plural of *anēr*, which is definitely the male sex, and is sometimes used for " husband."

2. St. Paul indicates the posture of the worshippers, " lifting up holy hands." Clement of Rome, in his Epistle to the Corinthian Church (chap. 29), uses similar language : " Let us approach Him in holiness of soul, lifting up pure and undefiled hands unto Him." This, of course, is not to be taken as a ritual rubric. Lifting up the hands was a symbolic act, not for prayer only, but also for benediction, see Lev. ix. 22 ; 1 Kings viii. 22 ; Ps. xxviii. 2, lxiii. 4, cxix. 48, cxxxiv. 2, cxliii. 6 ; Lam. iii. 41 ; Luke xxiv. 50.

3. St. Paul is not content with enjoining a symbolic act. It must be done by spiritual men. " Lifting up *holy* hands." So says St. James (iv. 8). " Cleanse your hands . . . and purify your hearts " ; and Ps. xxiv. 4 answers the question, " Who shall ascend into the hill of the Lord ? " with the words " He that hath clean hands and a pure heart." And St.

Paul adds, " without wrath and disputing." **If we** are at enmity with men, or engaged in bitter controversy, how can we pray for them ? Or, if we adopt the A.V. " doubting " instead of the R.V. " disputing," how can a doubting man pray acceptably ?

4. Then St. Paul turns to the women of the congregation ; but his words to them must be deferred for another Talk.

Meanwhile, there is another verse in this Epistle referring to public worship which must be just noticed. It is iv. 13, " Give heed to reading, to exhortation, to teaching." The reading in the Jewish synagogues of what we call the Lessons is illustrated by our Lord's reading Isaiah at Nazareth, and the practice at Pisidian Antioch (Luke iv. 16 ; Acts xiii. 15 ; cf. Acts xiii. 27, xv. 21 ; 2 Cor. iii. 14, 15). The early Christians continued this custom, reading the O.T. regularly ; and by and by the Epistles of St. Paul and the other Apostles were read also, and the Gospels, and gradually became recognised as " Scripture." Justin Martyr, in the second century, mentions the reading of the Gospels in public worship. " Exhortation " and " teaching " are the two branches of public preaching ; so here we get what we call the sermon. " Exhortation " is *paraklēsis*, sometimes translated " consolation " or " comfort " (see especially 2 Cor. i. 3-7). The word is connected with *Paraclete*, " comforter " or " advocate."

28
THE CHURCH'S MINISTRY: LEADERSHIP

THE subject of the Ministry and Organisation of the Early Church has come much to the front of late. The great works of Harnack and Duchesne have given an impetus to the study of it. It is, of course, not the part of Plain Talks like these to enter into the discussion, even if the writer were competent to do so. But I desire to mention two recent authorities which might be referred to by any readers who wish to have a general idea of what is going on, but have no opportunity of consulting the larger works. One is the pair of articles by Dr. Headlam in the *Prayer-Book Dictionary*, on " Episcopacy " and " Apostolic Succession," which have caused a reaction from the extreme Tractarian teaching, of which reaction the utterances of the Bishop of Madras on Church Union in India are a conspicuous example. The other is a series of articles by Professor Sanday in the *Contemporary Review*, now published in a thin volume entitled *The Primitive Church and Reunion* (Oxford Press). Dr. Sanday quotes important paragraphs from a contribution by Mr. C. H. Turner to the Cambridge Mediæval History, which draw, in a few words, an admirable picture of the Early Church. What I have said on the subject, however, was written before I had seen this, and is sufficiently in accord with it to obviate any need for correction.

It is evident that the organisation of the Early Church developed very gradually. In the Acts, and in St. Paul's earlier Epistles, we find very little about

it. The hints in the Pastoral Epistles are therefore
all the more welcome, but they themselves show that
there was as yet no cut-and-dried ecclesiastical system.
Still, as Sir W. M. Ramsay justly observes, " the development was natural " ; " the seed grew into the
tree."   " The germ," he adds, " of almost everything
in the second-century Church can be traced in the
earliest stages of that Church's history."[1] It must
be borne in mind that from about A.D. 70 there was
a period of half a century or more concerning
which we know very little. Church history, it is
sometimes said, was " passing through a tunnel."
Dr. Plummer puts it thus : " We are in the light of day
during most of the time covered by the N.T., and we
are again in the light of day when we reach the time
covered by the writings of Irenæus, Clement of
Alexandria, Tertullian, and others. But during the
intervening period we are not indeed in total darkness,
but in a passage the obscurity of which is only slightly
relieved by an occasional lamp or light-hole."
Naturally it follows that writers of varying views fill
up the gap differently. Into the many questions
involved it is not my part to enter. Let us turn to
our Epistles.

We notice at once that St. Paul writes to Timothy
of " bishops " and " deacons," and also mentions
" elders " or " presbyters " (I. iii. 1–7, 8–13, iv. 14, v.
1, 17–22) ; and to Titus, of " bishops " and " elders "
only (Tit. i. 5–9). Leaving the " deacons " aside for
the moment, the first and chief thing to notice is
that the " bishops " and the " elders " or " presbyters "
were not two groups, but one and the same. On

---

[1] *Expositor*, August 1909, p. 168.

this there is no controversy ; it is universally agreed that the ministers we know as " presbyters " were in the first century also called " bishops." The term " elder " or " presbyter " (*presbuteros*) came from the Jewish synagogue ; the term " bishop " or " overseer " (*episcopos*) from the political life of Greece. The former title implied the dignity of age ; the latter indicated the work or function of the office, the oversight of the Church.   The identity of the two could not be better expressed than by Liddon, who says :—

" That these two words were used of the same person is clear from Acts xx. 17 *sqq.*, where St. Paul is said to have sent for the *presbyters* of the Church of Ephesus, and to have addressed them as *bishops* (verse 28) ; from Phil. i. 1, where *with the bishops and deacons* must mean with the *presbyters and deacons*, unless we suppose that there were several *bishops* at Philippi and no *presbyters* ; and, lastly, from Tit. i. 5, where, after saying that Titus had been left in Crete that he might ordain *presbyters* in every city, the Apostle immediately proceeds to enumerate the qualifications to be expected in a ' *bishop*,' meaning a *presbyter*."

I need hardly add that Liddon was the last man to miss any allusion in Scripture to " bishops " in our sense of the word, if there were any.

But, then, what of the three Orders—Bishops, Presbyters, and Deacons—on which the Church of England lays so much stress ?   The Preface to our Ordination Service begins with these words : " It is evident unto all men diligently reading holy Scripture and ancient authors that from the Apostles' time there have been these Orders of Ministers in Christ's Church—Bishops,

---

[1] *Expl. Anal.* 1 *Tim.*, p. 21.

Priests, and Deacons." I need hardly say that " priests " here is merely a short form of " presbyter." There is not a single hint in the N.T. that ministers of the Church are " priests " in the sense of the Greek word *hiereus,* except in so far as all believers form " a holy priesthood." The only one place where St. Paul claims a " priestly " status is Rom. xv. 16, where he describes himself illustratively as " ministering " the Gospel (*hierourgounta*) as a missionary to the Gentiles, the priestly " offering " being the Gentile converts themselves. But were our Reformers mistaken in affirming that the three Orders dated " from the Apostles' time " ?

Suppose for argument's sake that they were mistaken, it would still be true that the Episcopate developed at a very early period into what we may justly call its historic form, which form has lasted from then till now, so that the phrase " Historic Episcopate " would even then be strictly and precisely correct. Moreover, we have the striking fact that the Christian writers of the second century themselves regarded episcopacy as the original and general use. But in point of fact our Reformers were not mistaken, nor were those Christian writers of the second century. For the real point is that *there was an authority above the " bishop-presbyters " and the " deacons."*

Our Epistles themselves bear clear evidence of this. Not only was St. Paul's Apostolic authority obviously supreme over the local ministers, by whatever name they were called, but he actually delegated this authority to Timothy and Titus. To the former he gave definite directions for his oversight of the " bishops " or " elders " (I. iii. 1–7, v. 17–22) and of the deacons

(iii. 8–13) ; the latter he instructed to " appoint elders in every city." Here, then, were three Orders. And when Church history emerges from the " tunnel " above alluded to, we find the word " bishop " applied no longer to the " presbyter," but to the office that was over both the presbyter and the deacon. Certainly it was so in the East. In the West the diocesan Episcopate appears to have come later, though from the first there seem to have been Bishops of Rome. The distinctions are carefully drawn out in Bishop John Wordsworth's *Ministry of Grace.*

It would, however, be a mistake to call Timothy " Bishop of Ephesus " or Titus " Bishop of Crete " (unless they became so afterwards). Their missions referred to in the Epistles were special and temporary. St. Paul's expressions, " if I tarry long " (I. iii. 15) and " till I come " (I. iv. 13), clearly imply this in Timothy's case ; and as for Titus, he was to leave Crete when Artemas or Tychicus arrived, and rejoin the Apostle (Tit. iii. 12), who afterwards sent him to Dalmatia (II. iv. 10).

So far as the N.T. is concerned, the one case in it which looks like a local diocesan bishopric is that of St. James, " the Lord's brother," at Jerusalem. No one doubts that he presided over the Church there. The allusions to him in the Acts are admitted on all hands to point that way. See xii. 17, " Tell these things unto James, and to the brethren " ; xv. 13, 19, " Brethren, hearken unto me," " my judgment is . . ." ; xxi. 18, " Paul went in with us unto James " ; also Gal. i. 19, ii. 9. No one supposes that he bore the title of " bishop " ; but although we have not here the name, we certainly have the thing.

But the important fact is now generally recognised by the best writers that there was in the early days a clear distinction between the local and the itinerant ministry. The local ministers were the elders or presbyters, " appointed in every city," and the deacons. The itinerant ministry was that described in 1 Cor. xii. and Eph. iv. St. Paul writes (1 Cor. xii. 28) : " God hath set some in the Church, first apostles, secondly prophets, thirdly teachers," followed by special gifts, " miracles, gifts of healings, helps," etc. ; and in Eph. iv. 11, " He gave some to be apostles, and some prophets, and some evangelists, and some pastors and teachers." In neither passage are bishops or presbyters or deacons mentioned, unless " helps " in the former and " pastors " in the latter may include them. In the *Didachē*, or " Teaching of the Twelve Apostles," probably one of the earliest of Christian writings outside the N.T., we see the itinerant or missionary ministers, particularly the " prophets," actually at work, going from place to place ; and there are directions about their reception. Naturally these travelling ministers, of whom we may take Timothy and Titus as forerunners, had more influence and authority than the local men ; and as they are mentioned in the N.T. along with the special Pentecostal gifts or *charismata*, their ministry is usually called the " charismatic " ministry. But it did not last. Gradually the leading " bishop-presbyter " in any town became the " bishop " in the later sense, and hence arose the diocesan Episcopate. " It was formed," says Bishop Lightfoot, " not out of the Apostolic order by localisation, but out of the presbyteral by elevation ; and the title which originally was common to all came at length to be appropriated to the chief among them."[1] And then, the Pentecostal and prophetical gifts having ceased, the itinerant ministry came to an end, and the local bishops became the chief authority in the Church.

There is what seems to me a rather unprofitable controversy, as to whether Episcopacy is of the *esse* or of the *bene esse* of the Church ; that is, whether it is " essential " or only " beneficial " to the Church. Some who dispute the *esse* show few signs of believing in the *bene esse*. Their utterances rather suggest that *male esse* would more truly indicate their view, that is, that the Church would be better off without bishops at all. That is quite reasonable on the part of Presbyterians or Congregationalists, but it is not reasonable for professing members of the Church of England. But what of the *esse* or *bene esse* ? On the one hand it is certain that the Episcopate dates from very early times, and that no other system was thought of for many centuries. On the other hand, we have to face the fact that other systems have arisen since the Reformation, and that, indisputably, it has pleased God to own and bless Christian communions that have no bishops. To say, therefore, that there can be no such thing as a non-Episcopal Church is rendered absurd by the logic of facts. But to say that it does not matter at all whether a Church has or has not the Episcopate is to fly in the face of history, and for loyal members of the Church of England, or of Churches in communion with her, ought to be impossible.

Students of Missions, at any rate, should well

---

[1] *On Philippians*, p. 194.

weigh the opinion of the Rev. Norman Maclean, of the Presbyterian Church of Scotland. " Bishop Tucker," he writes concerning Uganda, " has blended Episcopacy and Presbyterianisms [by which latter term he means the C.M.S. church-council system] into a perfect organisation. In so doing, he has laid down the lines on which the Christian Church should be organised in Africa. A Church which has the democratic power which Presbyterianisms can give, and which has also the initiative and unity which the historic Episcopate gives, is the ideal Church for the African."[1] This eloquent Presbyterian has no doubt about the *bene esse* !

29
THE CHURCH'S MINISTRY: BISHOPS

ALL that I said in the last Talk was introductory to the passages in our Epistles which refer to the ministers of the Church. I now invite attention to the passages themselves.

First we take the " bishop," in iii. 1–7, bearing in mind that, as I showed, it is what we should call the ordinary " clergyman " that is really meant. Still, whatever qualifications for the work of a presbyter St. Paul specifies would, *à fortiori*, be required of one chosen from among them to be over them in the later sense, so that the choice of this passage as the " Epistle " in the Anglican service for the consecration of a bishop is quite legitimate.

---

[1] *Africa in Transformation*, p. 228.

The Apostle begins by quoting what we saw in a former Talk was a current saying in the Church,[1] viz., that to " seek the office of a bishop " was to " desire a good work," *kalon ergon*, a noble occupation ; and he confirms this by his exclamation, " Faithful is the saying ! "   We must not read this as if it were praising a man's ambition to attain high office.   It is seeking ordination to the sacred ministry. Farrar renders the words " If any man desires the office of the pastorate."[2]   We ourselves regard this as desiring a noble occupation ; and much more is it so in the mission-field.   It was a great day at Sierra Leone in 1843, when Samuel Crowther returned thither after being " crowned a minister " (as the people called it) in England, the first of that African Christian Church to be chosen for ordination ; and still more when, twenty-one years later, he appeared as a bishop in the fuller sense of the word.   The first native clergymen in India, in China, in New Zealand, in Uganda, were marked men ; and only lately we have seen the deep interest aroused by the consecration of the first Indian Bishop.

So, continues St. Paul, " the *episcopos* must be. . ." The " must," *dei*, stands first in the Greek sentence ; and we might render it " Essential is it, therefore, that the *episcopos*. . . ."   What is essential ?   Is it learning, wealth, influence, the gift of leadership ? Is it physical strength for a post which might involve danger and suffering ?   Of these things St. Paul says nothing. This, however, does not mean that such qualifications were unimportant.   A man might

---

[1] See p. 56.   [2] *St. Pau'*, Vol. ii., p. 520.

well be chosen above his fellows because he had them. But the Apostle is thinking of the elementary qualities essential for every *candidate* " seeking the office " ; those without which a candidate could not even be considered at all. Of these there are seven ; and when we look at them, we see that *personal character* is everything at this preliminary stage. The candidate must be—

1. Irreproachable.   Not only enjoying an unblemished reputation, but deserving it.

2. The husband of one wife. Does this only mean that monogamy, being the rule for all Christians, was especially obligatory on a presbyter who should set a good example ? Or does it mean that while other men might marry again if the wife died, the *episcopos* might not ? On these questions authorities differ. We must remember the terribly low state of morality in the Greek and Roman world, and particularly the frequency of divorce, so that a man might have three or four ex-wives, or a woman three or four ex-husbands, living at the same time. St. Paul's phrase is literally " one woman's man," that is, a man true to his one wife, thus forbidding divorce, but not necessarily forbidding a second marriage if the wife died. A second marriage, however, is thought by Bishop Bernard, Dr. Plummer, and other leading authorities, to be here forbidden, as it certainly was in subsequent ages of the Church. But to my mind, Rom. vii. 3, and 1 Cor. vii. 8, 9, 39, clearly allow it to a woman ; and if so, it is hard to think that it was forbidden to a man. If a second marriage really is forbidden, it is curious that (as Bernard remarks) the Anglican Church has broken the rule by allowing

re-marriage, the Greek Church by forbidding bishops to marry at all, and the Roman Church by forbidding all clergy to marry.

3. With six virtues : " temperate, sober-minded, orderly, hospitable, apt to teach," and " gentle." The first three, and " gentle," we shall examine in a future Talk, when we consider the Christian character in its various aspects.[1] " Given to hospitality " is *philoxenos*, " loving the stranger " ; a virtue enjoined elsewhere on Christians generally (Rom. xii. 13, Heb. xiii. 2, 1 Pet. iv. 9, 3 John 5), but especially important for the leaders. " Apt to teach," *didaktikos*, means, not merely skilled in teaching, but ready and keen to engage in it. Bishop Watts Ditchfield gives good examples in his Cambridge Lectures on *The Church in Action*.

4. Free from four faults : " no brawler, no striker, not contentious, no lover of money." The first two refer to the quarrels of drinking men, and the mention of them is a painful revelation of the social life of the period. Love of money is repeatedly alluded to in our Epistles, and we shall see what is said of it by and by.[2]

5. A good head of a family and household. If he is a married man with children, does he rule them well, " with all gravity," so that they respect and obey him ? In any case, is it so with his servants ? " Gravity " is another important word to be noticed hereafter.[3]

6. " Not a novice " ; not a recent convert, who might be " puffed up " by his promotion, and " fall into condemnation " ; literally " not newly-planted,"

---

[1] See p. 275.   [2] See p. 300.   [3] See p. 275.

neophutos, whence our word " neophyte." The same word, in the LXX, is rendered " young plant " in Ps. cxxviii. 3 and cxliv. 12. A cognate word is used of the " planting " of new converts in 1 Cor. iii. 6–8.

7. Of good reputation even among " them that are without." This is the regular phrase for non-Christians, see 1 Cor. v. 12, Col. iv. 5, 1 Thess. iv. 12. In 1 Cor. v. 12 we have also " them that are within." From the Greek words *exōthen* and *esōthen* we derive our " exoteric " and " esoteric."

Now compare with these the parallel list in Titus i. 6–9, noting in passing that Titus is to " *appoint* elders in every city," not as in A.V. " ordain," which word, in our sense, does not occur in the N.T. In this list some qualifications named to Timothy are omitted, and others added. We find " not self-willed," " not soon angry," " a lover of good " (*phil-agathon,* of good men and good things), " just, holy, temperate." " Temperate " here, *egkratēs,* does not occur elsewhere in the N.T. ; but its cognate noun is the " temperance " on which St. Paul " reasoned " with Felix, and occurs also in Gal. v. 23 and 2 Pet. i. 6 ; and the verb is used in 1 Cor. vii. 9, ix. 25. The words point to general self-control, though with particular reference to sensual passion. Then we have " holding to the faithful word which is according to the teaching " (or doctrine) ; and this with two ends in view, (1) " to exhort in the sound doctrine," (2) " to convict the gainsayers." This is an important addition, referring to the function of teaching and preaching entrusted to the *episcopos.* But why " the faithful word according to the doctrine " ? One rather expects that the doctrine should be according to " the faithful word." But probably this expression means not Scripture, but the elementary creeds or catechisms from which the " faithful sayings " (same Greek) were derived, as I showed in an earlier Talk.[1] *These*, says St. Paul, are to be " held to " *if* according to the general apostolic teaching. One thing more : the children of the *episcopos* must belong to the Christian Church, ver. 6. The A.V. " faithful children " does not give the exact sense. The R.V. " children that believe " is right. Titus is not to appoint any one whose children are still heathen ; nor if " accused of riot " (the " riotous living " of the Prodigal Son) or " unruly " (insubordinate).

Is any reader inclined to think St. Paul's standard a rather low one ? Not low, surely, as regards the elementary and preliminary qualifications for a candidate for the ministry. Moreover, when we come to examine the beautiful Greek words *sōphrōn, kosmios, semnos, epieikēs*, which we inadequately render " sober-minded," " orderly," " grave," " gentle," we shall see what a high standard it really is.[2] But, meanwhile, there are two more points to be noticed.

(1) The *episcopos* is " God's steward " (Tit. i. 7). St. Paul called himself a " steward of the mysteries of God " (1 Cor. iv. 1), who must be " faithful " (ver. 2). Our Lord pronounced a special blessing on " the faithful and wise steward " " set over the household to give them their portion of food in due season " (Luke xii. 42, 43). Thus the " steward is a *dispenser*." " Be thou a faithful dispenser," says the ordaining

---

[1] See p. 55.   [2] See pp. 204, 266, 275.

Bishop in the Church of England to the candidate for priests' (i.e. presbyters') orders, " a faithful dispenser of the word of God and of His Holy Sacraments." Even we laymen may be encouraged by St. Peter's words (1 Pet. iv. 10) implying that we may all be " good stewards of the manifold grace of God," and so likewise earn our Lord's promised blessing.

(2) The *episcopos* is to " take care of the Church of God " (I. iii. 5). It is a striking phrase : the Greek verb rendered " take care of," *epimeleisthai*, only occurs elsewhere in the N.T. in the Parable of the Good Samaritan, who " took care of " the robbed and wounded, and made provision for the host at the inn to " take care of " him. What a picture is here ! The good Samaritan has for nearly nineteen centuries been the accepted pattern of unselfish benevolence and thoughtful kindness, of " neighbourliness " in the highest sense ; while the Priest and Levite are the proverbial types of unfeeling selfishness and neglect of duty. And the *episcopos* is to be the Good Samaritan ; but to whom ? To the poor and the suffering ? Yes, no doubt ; but that is not the point here. " Take care of the Church of God " : how often was the Church of God in those days " fallen among thieves," " stripped," " wounded," and left " half dead " ! and how often since ! Readers will suppose I am thinking of a Church being robbed of material resources. Indeed I am not ! I am thinking of what is far more important, spiritual maintenance and health. Truly the *episcopos* has a *kalon ergon*, a noble work, to do, in " taking care " of the Church of God !

30

THE CHURCH'S MINISTRY: ELDERS

BEFORE we go on to the other order of the Ministry referred to in I. iii., the Diaconate, there are a few verses about " elders " in the latter part of chap. v., which we should look at first. These " elders " or presbyters are of course the same persons as are called " bishops " in chap. iii. ; but as St. Paul here uses the word *presbuteros* and not *episcopos*, we will adopt the same language. Parenthetically I must explain that " elder " (*presbuteros*) in the first verse of chap. v. (" Rebuke not an elder ") does not, as elsewhere, mean the Church officer, but any old man, as the context clearly shows.

The passage now before us, chap. v. 17–25, is perhaps, on the face of it, the least interesting in the three Epistles, and is probably the least familiar (except one verse and half of another). But when examined it proves to be full of practical suggestion that may be useful to us all.

1. First, we have the maintenance of the ministry.

" Let the elders that rule well be counted worthy of double honour, especially those who labour in the word and in teaching. For the Scripture saith, Thou shalt not muzzle the ox when he treadeth out the corn. And, The labourer is worthy of his hire."

" Honour " here means provision for the elder's support, as it does in our Lord's words about children helping their parents (Matt. xv. 6) ; and as we use the word " honorarium." " Double," I suppose,

only means ample.   But there is an " especially."
All the elders " ruled " in the congregation, but
apparently not all gave regular teaching ; and
perhaps all who did teach were not equally zealous
in the work ; so there was to be " especial " care
to provide amply for those who " laboured " in it,
a word implying real toil.   When St. Peter says
" We have toiled all the night," he uses the same
word, *kopiaō*.

St. Paul enforces this counsel by a quotation from
" Scripture," from Deut. xxv. 4, a text he had before
used with the same object, to emphasise the just claim
of the ministry to support by those ministered to
(1 Cor. ix. 6–11).   If the Mosaic law mercifully forbad
the " muzzling " that would prevent an ox in the
threshing-floor from refreshing itself from the corn
under its feet, why should a " labourer in the word
and teaching " be grudged an " honorarium " ?   But
what of the other quotation, " The labourer is worthy
of his hire " ?   The words occur, as spoken by our
Lord, in Luke x. 7 ; and some have thought that
St. Luke's gospel is cited by St. Paul as " Scripture."
But even if that gospel were then written (as I think
likely) it was not yet recognised as " Scripture," nor
could it be widely known ; and the exact phrase, " the
Scripture," as I have before shown, always means
the O.T.[1]   St. Paul is really quoting a familiar popular saying, adding to his citation from Deuteronomy, as
it were, " Besides, we all know the adage . . ."   Our
Lord, as it seems to me, in charging the Seventy,
does the same.   Why not ?   How like His gracious

---

[1] See p. 113.

custom of referring to familiar things ! And he cites
the same saying in slightly varying words in charging the Twelve in Matt. x., " The labourer is worthy
of his food."

In the face of all this, what do we think of modern
English Christians expecting to find churches and
clergy provided for them, and grudging the smallest
contribution towards what is scarcely even a living
wage for those who " labour in the word and teaching,"
to say nothing of " double honour " ?

2. Then we have the duty of impartiality :—

" Against an elder receive not an accusation, except
at the mouth of two or three witnesses. Them that sin
reprove in the sight of all, that the rest also may be in
fear. I charge thee in the sight of God, and Christ
Jesus, and the elect angels, that thou observe these
things without prejudice, doing nothing by partiality."

Not only is an elder not to be condemned upon
mere gossip or individual complaint, as in the Mosaic
law (Deut. xix. 15) ; St. Paul even says, " Do not
receive an accusation, except . . ." How much
friction in parishes, and how much injustice, would
be avoided, if we all acted on this principle ! But
if a charge is found true, the offender, even if a ruling
and teaching elder who has had " double honour,"
is to be publicly reproved ; for the more highly
esteemed he may have been, the greater his responsibility. Of course this does not refer to cases of personal offence ; our Lord Himself said that such
cases were only to be " told unto the Church " if
more private means failed. St. Paul means cases in
which Timothy, as delegated with apostolic authority, has to be judge. But the spirit of it is for us all.

Against two things Timothy is warned with special solemnity. " I charge thee . . ." Three times in writing to him does St. Paul use words of the kind (I. vi. 13, II. iv. 1, and here). What is the duty here enforced with such emphasis ? It is the duty of impartiality. Naturally this is supremely important in a judge of any kind ; and Scripture is full of references to the danger of one-sidedness in men occupying that office. Perhaps it is only in an Eastern country, where bribery of judges prevails, that this can be fully appreciated, or the frequent mention of God Himself as no " respecter of persons." But the principle of this solemn injunction is for us all. No " prejudice " (*prokrima*) *against* either party ; no " partiality " (*prosklisis*) *in favour* of either party. We English folk are justly proud of the inflexible impartiality of our judges ; but in our personal opinions and the expression of them— say political, or religious, or even in private life,— how much of it do we show ? Is St. Paul's " charge " one whit too solemn for us to take home to our- selves ? It is significant that our word " prejudice " (like the Greek *prokrima*) is strictly neutral, meaning judgment beforehand *either way*, and yet we almost always use it in the unfavourable sense.

3. Going forward for a moment to verses 24, 25, we find a caution against judgment which, even if im- partial, may be premature :

" Some men's sins are evident, going before unto judgment ; and some men also they follow after. In like manner also there are good works that are evident ; and such as are otherwise cannot be hid."

The point of this is lost in the A.V., owing to the

word *prodēlos* being translated in two different ways,
" open beforehand " in verse 24, and " manifest beforehand " in verse 25.   The R.V. " evident " makes the
parallelism clear.   On the one hand, some sins are so
" evident " that condemnation of them is obvious,
but others, though unnoticed, may yet pursue the
sinner. On the other hand, some good works
(*kala erga*) are so " evident " that one judges the
character at once, but even if we see none, there may
be good which eventually " cannot be hid."   You may
think a man free from fault, and he may have grave
faults under the surface. You may think another
hopelessly bad, and yet find out good in him which
had not been conspicuous at first sight. Therefore,
avoid hastiness in judgment. There may be sur-
prises in store for us like those of both the righteous
and the wicked in our Lord's picture of the Great
Assize in Matt. xxv.

4. Going back to verse 22, we find that along with
impartiality and caution in judgment, St. Paul enjoins
single-heartedness, purity of motive and purpose :—

" Lay hands hastily on no man, neither be partaker
of other men's sins ; keep thyself pure. Be no longer a
drinker of water. . . ."

The Commentators differ as to what " laying on of
hands " is here referred to. Liddon puts it thus :
" Ordain no man hurriedly ; and do not (by ordaining unworthy persons) become thyself responsible
for other men's sins." So Bishop Bernard, Dr.
Plummer, Bishop Hervey, Dr. Horton, etc.   Hort
and Ellicott explain the words differently, but I think
we may adopt this interpretation, which follows

(according to Bernard) Chrysostom and other Greek Fathers. The whole paragraph is thus explained by Bernard : " Do not lightly entertain accusations against a presbyter (v. 19) ; Do not spare rebuke if he fall into sinful habits (v. 20) ; Be not partial (v. 21) ; Do not admit to the presbyterate without due inquiry (v. 22*a*) ; If you do, you accept responsibility for his sins, which, in a manner, you have made your own (v. 22*b*).   And this last grave thought leads on to the personal warning, *keep thyself pure*." Or, the " partaking of others' sins " may be meant thus : " If you ordain a man too hastily, he may prove unsatisfactory, and then you may feel obliged to trust him too leniently, and so fall into sin yourself." Dr. Plummer prefers this.

We see now the point of our Ember Week Prayer : " At this time so guide and govern the minds of Thy servants the Bishops and Pastors of Thy flock, that they may lay hands suddenly on no man, but faithfully and wisely make choice of fit persons," etc.

Do we not all need a similar caution ? May we not in choosing associates, whether equals in friendship or subordinates in service, be too hasty, or too lenient ? and may not evil result from such haste or leniency, for which we shall be partly responsible ? Then St. Paul gives us the true remedy, " Keep thyself pure." Pure, that is, in principle and motive and purpose ; single-minded and single-hearted ; ruling all our intercourse with others by the one grand principle of doing the right thing, that which is right in the sight of God. That is an important part of true purity. St. James lays down the same principle (iii. 17) : " First pure, then peaceable, gentle, easy to be entreated." ("Pure" here does not mean pure in doctrine, as is oddly supposed by some, but pure in motive and purpose and principle.)

But then, why comes in here St. Paul's caution to Timothy against total abstinence? I explained the meaning of that famous verse before,[1] and need only now show its connection with the context. It is as if the Apostle said, "Don't misunderstand me about keeping yourself pure; you may be *too* ascetic; for instance, don't deny yourself the wine your health requires." How thoughtful! how sympathising! And how delightful to find such relatively small matters not beneath the dignity of Holy Scripture!

31
THE CHURCH'S MINISTRY: DEACONS

WE now come to the other order of the ministry, the Diaconate. Deacons in the early Church were more like the modern deacons in Presbyterian and other non-episcopal Churches than like those of the Church of England, who are commonly regarded as young clergymen waiting for priests' orders and meanwhile ministering in the regular way, except for a few limitations. In the opinion of most scholars there is little doubt that, although the seven men chosen in Acts vi. to superintend the charitable ministrations of the Church are not called deacons,

---

[1] See p. 30.

the office did in fact then begin, and was chiefly concerned with the administration of Church funds. Dr. Gwatkin, however, thinks the Seven of Acts vi. had a higher position than was accorded later to deacons.[1]   We only find deacons definitely mentioned in the chapter now before us, 1 Tim. iii., and in Phil. i. 1, where St. Paul addresses " the saints " at Philippi " with the bishops and deacons." But the Greek word *diakonos*, and its cognates *diakonia* and *diakonein*, are very common in the N.T., and stand generally for " a minister," the " ministry," and " to minister "; or, as often rendered, " servant," " service," " to serve."

In an earlier Talk [2] we saw that St. Paul in our Epistles thanks the Lord for appointing him to His *diakonia* (I. i. 12) ; tells Timothy what he must do to be a good *diakonos* (I. iv. 6) ; appeals to him to fulfil his *diakonia* (II. iv. 5) ; reminds him of the good example of Onesiphorus in ministering, *diakonein* (II. i. 18) ; and directs him to bring with him Mark, who is profitable for *diakonia* (II. iv. 11).   In all these cases, and in many others in the N.T., the words stand for ministry or service without any allusion to the particular order of deacons.   Acts vi., which we regard as recording the initiation of the order, shows this in a striking way.   The " daily *ministration* " to the widows (verse 1) is *diakonia* ; " *serve* tables " (verse 2) is *diakonein* ; and the higher office of prayer and the *ministry* of the word is itself also *diakonia*.   In fact, the original and fundamental idea of a *diakonos* is one who serves, just as the original

---

[1] Art. " Deacon," in Hastings' *Dict. Bibl.*
[2] See p. 38.

and fundamental idea of an *episcopos* is one who over-sees or superintends ; and Dr. Hort suggests that in this third chapter of First Tim. St. Paul is thinking of the two departments of Church ministry, *government* and *service*.[1]

Let us now look at St. Paul's directions as to qualifications for the regular diaconate. He begins with the words " in like manner,"[2] referring to the qualifications just before mentioned which must be required in candidates for the office of *episcopos* or *presbuteros*. Four points of character are first mentioned which are nearly the same as in the former case, but seem to be suggested by the frequent intercourse the deacon would have with all classes of the congregation : " grave," the interesting word *semnos* which we are to look at by and by[3] ; " not double-tongued," saying one thing to one man and another thing to another, a very likely fault in frequent visitation of different families ; " not given to much wine," a possibility of that very kind of life ; " not greedy of filthy lucre," which might well be a temptation to the manager of the funds, as in the case of Judas who " had the bag." How practical it all is !

Then the deacon is to " hold the mystery of the Faith." So was the *episcopos*, but in his case it was that he might teach it and convict opponents (Tit. i. 9). The deacon was not a teacher or preacher, at least not in virtue of his office. Of course he might be so independently of his office, like Stephen and

----

[1] *Christian Ecclesia*, p. 211.
[2] See p. 200.
[3] See p. 275.

Philip.   But he must in any case " hold the mystery of the Faith," the sound doctrine we have examined before ; yet not merely for the sake of orthodoxy ; that would be quite contrary to St. Paul's principles ; there must be " a pure conscience," in which the Faith was to be " held," as a jewel in a casket.   Moreover, candidates for the diaconate are to be " proved," tested, and only admitted if found " blameless " (ver. 10).   And this is to include the blamelessness of their family life : one wife, and children and household well ruled, as in the case of the *episcopos*. Then, if they fulfil the duties of their office well, they will gain a good *bathmos* (ver. 13), " degree " in the A.V., but the R.V. " standing " is probably more correct, meaning a good reputation, which of itself will embolden them to be successful witnesses for their Lord, giving them " great boldness in the faith which is in Christ Jesus "—and no man can have a better reward than that !

Here let me explain that the six words in the A.V. of vers. 10 and 13, " use the office of a deacon," represent only one word in the Greek, the verb *diakonein*.   The R.V. " serve as deacons " is certainly better.

But what of the 11th verse, which we have skipped ? In the very midst of the rules about deacons, we find this : " Women in like manner must be grave, not slanderers, temperate, faithful in all things."   Why this ?   Who are these women, receiving instructions " in like manner " with the *episcopos* and the deacon ? Some think they must be the deacons' wives, and the A.V. so renders the words.   But the phrase " in like manner " does seem to introduce another class of

persons holding some office in the Church.[1] Why
not deaconesses ? The actual word " deaconess "
does not seem to have been then coined, as it was a
little later ; but Phebe of Cenchrea (Rom. xvi. 1)
is called a *diakonos*, and although this word is rendered " servant " in both A.V. and R.V., few doubt
that it stands there, not for " service " in general,
but for a definite office. She was, in fact, a " woman
deacon," and no doubt performed duties similar to
those of the male deacons, visiting and relieving the
poor, etc. It seems that the second century document called the Apostolical Constitutions mentions a
" deacon " with the feminine definite article, *hē
diakonos*, and, later, " the deaconess," *hē diakonissa*.[2]
Pliny, too, mentions " handmaidens who were called
ministræ " (female ministers).

If, then, the " women " of ver. 11 are practically
deaconesses, though not yet called so,—if they were
the female members of the diaconate,—the four
qualifications for them named by St. Paul are very
suitable, and very like the first four for the deacon.
" Grave," the *semnos* which we have not yet examined,
but will by and by ; [3] not to be light in conversation,
not even in thought or feeling, but to realise the intense seriousness of life and of their calling. " Not
slanderers," not " devils " (*diabolous*) ; no commandment is more important for women than the ninth.
" Temperate," that is as in ver. 2 (not the word in

----

[1] This phrase " in like manner ", ὡσαύτως, should be
carefully noted. It occurs in I. ii. 9, iii. 8, 11, Tit. ii. 3, 6,
but the A.V. renders the word in different ways, and even
the R.V. has " likewise " in the two Titus verses. A comparison of the five passages shows that a different class is
intended each time.

[2] Hastings' *Dict. Bible*, art. " Women."   [3] See p. 275.

Tit. i. 8). " Faithful in all things," trustworthy ; probably referring particularly to the distribution of money and account-keeping like their men colleagues ; and also keeping family secrets and personal confidences.

Bishop Lightfoot's comment on Rom. xvi. 1 and 1 Tim. iii. 11 is extremely significant : " If the testimony borne in these two passages to a ministry of women in the Apostolic times had not been blotted out of our English Bibles [i.e., by the word " servant " in one case and " wives " in the other], attention would have been directed to the subject at an earlier date, and our English Church would not have remained so long maimed in one of her hands." This important remark was made by him at a very early period in the discussion on Women's Work, in his Essay urging a Revision of the N.T. published nearly half a century ago. It is quoted by Bishop John Wordsworth in his *Ministry of Grace* (p. 261), whence I borrow it.

In our next Talk we shall look more closely at the teaching of these Epistles regarding the position of women in the Church. Meanwhile, let us remember Priscilla and her instruction of Apollos, and Philip's four prophesying daughters, and God's Pentecostal promise of even His " handmaidens " doing the same.

32

WOMEN IN THE CHURCH

ST. PAUL'S teaching in these Epistles about the position of women in the Church is extremely interesting. It is, like his teaching on other important matters, quite incidental. He does not enter into the whole subject systematically, but just gives his directions and counsels as they are needed. And as he begins with their place in the Christian assemblies for worship, or, as we should say, " in church," we will begin there too.

We saw before that I. ii. 8 contains a definite order that public worship is to be conducted by " the men." Then St. Paul goes on : " In like manner, that women adorn themselves in modest apparel, with shamefastness and sobriety ; not with braided hair, and gold or pearls or costly raiment ; but (which becometh women professing godliness) through good works." As he begins with the expression " in like manner," [1] we naturally expect to have some directions corresponding to the " lifting up holy hands " and the " without wrath and disputing " enjoined on the men ; and it rather startles us to read " adorn themselves." What analogy is there between the spiritual counsel for the men and the injunctions about dress for the women ?

Much, naturally, has been written on this point. To my mind Sir W. M. Ramsay suggests by far the best explanation. [2] He draws a picture of the assembly, men on one side, women on the other, as still custom-

---

[1] See p. 200.   [2] *Expositor*, Sept. 1909, p. 274.

ary in the East. The two groups are to act " in like manner." This, Ramsay thinks, can only mean " pray in like manner," the word " pray " being understood ; but St. Paul, with the grave " woman-problem " before him (as at Corinth), turns aside for a moment to enjoin modest dress. I myself recall the first service I attended at a mission church in Ceylon. The men, all together on one side, were in white garments ; the women, on the other side, were in bright red and yellow. The contrast was striking : one side looked like a college chapel with all the men in sur-plices ; the other side like a gay garden-bed. Of course, there was nothing unsuitable, much less improper. But I can quite understand St. Paul dictating the words " in like manner," and then bethinking himself of the two halves of the congrega-tion. He pictures to himself some of those Ephesian wives and daughters conspicuously dressed like the gay heathen women (though meaning no harm) ; and he suddenly stops in his dictation and goes on, " adorn themselves in modest apparel," etc. Dr. Plummer quotes the comment of Chrysostom on this very passage, addressed to the congregation at Antioch : " What then is modest apparel ? Such as covers them completely and decently, and not with superfluous ornaments. . . . What ? Do you approach God to pray with broidered hair and orna-ments of gold ? Are you come to a ball ? to a marriage feast ? to a carnival ? . . . This is the attire of actors and dancers, who live upon the stage. Nothing of this kind becomes a modest woman." The whole extract is interesting. [1]

---

[1] *Pastoral Epistles*, p. 101.

Let me just analyse the two verses, partly following Liddon.[1]   The dress of Christian women : (1) Its positive characteristics : (*a*) comely apparel ; worn with (*b*) modesty, and (*c*) sobriety. (2) Its negative marks : (*a*) no personal decorations, as braided hair ; (*b*) no gold or pearl ornaments ; (*c*) no costly material. (3) Its ruling principle : suitability for " women professing godliness."   (4) Its best adornment, good works.   So, as Dr. Newport White says, while men conduct the Church's worship, women adorn the Church with good works.   St. Peter's counsels (1 Pet. iii. 2–4) should be compared.

Some of the words in these verses are interesting. " Modest " is *kosmios*, and is connected with *kosmos*, the familiar word for " the world," which has in it the idea of order ; and in I. iii. 2, the only other place in the N.T. where *kosmios* occurs, the R.V. renders it " orderly."   The A.V. there has " of good behaviour," with " modest " in the margin.   The word *kosmos* itself is actually the original of " adorning " in 1 Pet. iii. 3, while the cognate verb *kosmeō* is the original of " adorn " in the verse before us and in Tit. ii. 10.   I borrow " comely " from Liddon.

" Shamefastness "—not " shamefacedness," which is merely a bad blunder in spelling—is Wiclif's translation of *aidōs*, and is justly called by Bishop Bernard a " felicitous rendering."   It is constructed like " stedfastness," and means what is made fast, and " held fast, by an honourable shame."   " Sobriety " is *sōphrosunē*, a word which we shall look at carefully hereafter (as also " godliness " and " good works ").[2]   Of the two renderings together Bernard

---

[1] *Explan. Anal.* p. 17.   [2] See p. 266.

says : they are " as near to the Greek as we can go in English. The Greek words have a long history behind them, and have no exact equivalent in modern speech. Both together well describe the discretion and modesty of Christian womanhood."[1]

Then there is something else besides modesty. Twice over St. Paul adds " quietness." Not " silence ", as A.V. ; and not enjoined only on women. Only a little before (ver. 2) St. Paul has spoken of a " quiet life " for us all ; and the same word, *hēsuchia*, is urged in 2 Thess. iii. 12 as against idleness. St. Peter (I. iii. 4), using the same word, speaks of women having a " quiet spirit." Here it is, " Let a woman learn in quietness with all subjection. But I permit not a woman to teach, nor to have dominion [*lit.* ' lord it '] over a man, but to be in quietness." That St. Paul needed to be stricter in laying down rules of the kind for Ephesus and Corinth in those days (see 1 Cor. xiv. 34, 35) than he would be now in a Christian land, is manifest ; and it is no more reasonable to regard all his rules as necessarily binding on us now, than to recognise domestic slavery as he was obliged to do.

The Church has always obeyed his directions so far as public worship, of which he is speaking here, is concerned ; but the prohibition of women " teaching " must not be applied to such service as these very Epistles elsewhere recognise. In Tit. ii. 3 it is expressly provided that the elder women are to be " teachers " and " trainers " ; in I. v. we find an anticipation of the Order of Widows which was

---

[1] Trench has a full note on these words, *N.T. Synonyms*, § 20.

afterwards instituted ; and in our last Talk we found " deaconesses " included in the Church's Ministry.

It is worth noting that the united meeting of men and women in public worship was of itself a token of the enlarged spirit of Christianity. Bishop Jackson, in the Speaker's Commentary, makes the important remark that " there is no Court of the Women in the Christian Temple," as in the Temple at Jerusalem, an outer court for women to worship in, beyond which they might not enter. In the Christian Church, in regard to the worship of God at least, there is " neither male nor female," but " all one in Christ Jesus."

Nevertheless, however varied may be the right and reasonable customs in various ages and various countries, the principle of " subjection," as laid down here, must always have force in some sense. The phrase " all subjection " is as strong as " all godliness " in ver. 2. And St. Paul bases his teaching about the " subjection " of women on two considerations, in ver. 13, 14. (a) Adam was formed before Eve, and from this is deduced the precedence of the man in power and dignity. (b) It was Eve, not Adam, who was " beguiled " into sin, and so caused the Fall. It must be admitted that the argument is a strange one, and I confess I have no explanation to offer. No doubt its cogency would appeal to readers in those days. The bearing of the allusions on the narratives of Genesis is obvious, but that is a large subject, and this is not the place for its discussion.

And now we come to the important and interesting last verse of the chapter. " But she shall be saved through the child-bearing, if they continue in faith and love and sanctification with sobriety." Evidently St. Paul wishes to close with a word of comfort for the woman. She is not to be down-hearted on account of man's precedence of her, or of her responsibility for the Fall, or of the " subjection " which the Apostle regards as a consequence of these circumstances. She has, normally, *i.e.*, apart from exceptional cases, one great primary function to fulfil, that of Motherhood. But what does this mean ? Many expositors put it very baldly. She is, they say, to provide for the perpetuation of the human race by " child-bearing," and she will find her " salvation," not only the safety and health of her body, but her peace and happiness in life and the favour of her God, if she fulfils her function in the right spirit, in the divine ordinance of marriage ; and just as the man's punishment, bodily toil, becomes a blessing to him if rightly borne, so will it be with the woman's punishment. " In sorrow thou shalt bring forth children " ; it will be to her a blessing and a joy.

Now this exposition of the text, good as it is up to a point, does not satisfy me. There is something defective about it. But Sir W. M. Ramsay, alone among commentators so far as I have seen, enlarges the idea in a beautiful way.[1] He declines to limit the Greek word *teknogonia* to its literal meaning of " child-bearing," and interprets the use of it here as St. Paul's way of speaking of *the maternal instinct* of Motherhood in the largest sense of the term, giving an interesting illustration from Sophocles of this wider sense. " The maternal instinct," he observes,

---

[1] *Expositor*, Oct. 1909, pp. 342–347.

" does not require actual physical motherhood. It may be immensely powerful in a childless woman." That wonderful and powerful instinct, which, I may add, we see in every little girl nursing her doll, and which makes such multitudes of unmarried women ready for " mothering " in some way,—and skilful in it withal,—gives woman her destiny in life, and so proves her " salvation " in the large sense of the word.

An illustration of the " mothering " occurs in this same Epistle, in chap. v. 10.   A widow may be admitted to the order of widows " if she have brought up children."   Not necessarily her own, possibly orphans.   Her " motherhood," whether literal or virtual (*in loco parentis*) will " save " her from the temptations of her state.[1]

This seems to me the plain and beautiful meaning of a verse that has caused much controversy.   But there is another interpretation which cannot be passed over without notice.   Many commentators see in the verse an allusion to the Incarnation.   " She shall be saved through the child-bearing " is interpreted as meaning " saved through the virgin-birth of Christ."   This is apparently helped by the R.V. rendering " through " instead of the A.V. " in." But " through " here does not indicate the cause or instrument of the " salvation," but the sphere in which " salvation " will be found.   It is like " saved through fire " in 1 Cor. iii. 15 ; also " saved through water " in 1 Pet. iii. 20, where water is not spoken of as the instrument that saved Noah and his family, but as the medium or sphere in which they were

____

[1] See p. 214.

saved. Again, it is urged that " saved " must mean spiritually saved ; but we have before seen that the Greek word is as comprehensive as the English one, and must be explained by its context. Then note the " if " : " if they continue in faith and love and sanctification with sobriety." This exactly fits the simpler explanation, especially if " they " may mean the husband and wife in the case of a married woman ; and the last word, " sobriety," the *sophrosunē* of ver. 9, beautifully indicates the modesty, discretion, and self-effacement of the true Christian woman.

But above all, to me it seems impossible that St. Paul would describe the great central fact of Christianity, the Incarnation of the Son of God, by so common and familiar an expression as " the child-bearing," without an additional word. The definite article " the," on which some writers lay stress, and which the R.V. rightly inserts, has the personal note so often found in the N.T. (as readers of Bishop Moule's works will remember), and the meaning is " through *her* child-bearing."

At the same time, I think we may accept Bishop Jackson's quite different way of bringing in the Incarnation. He says, in the Speaker's Commentary, " The woman's sentence of child-bearing involved the appointed means of her own and the world's salvation. *Her seed* was to bruise the serpent's head, and thus in a deeper sense she will be saved through the child-bearing as the instrument of the Incarnation of Him Who . . . was born of a woman."

33

CARE AND SERVICE OF WIDOWS

WE have seen what St. Paul says generally of women. In the 5th chapter of the First Epistle he deals with the case of a particular class, widows. We remember how in the early days at Jerusalem trouble arose about widows (Acts vi.) ; and both from that passage and from this we gather that they were a numerous section of the Christian Church. Perhaps in their sorrow and loneliness they had been specially drawn to a community that believed in the God of the widow and the fatherless, and whose members made such sacrifices for the poor. Also we have to remember the frequency of divorce in those days. We saw that this threw light on the " one wife " question ;[1] and it throws light on the widow question too. A man dying might leave three or four widows.

Let us not think that this chapter contains no lessons for us. We all appreciate the housemaid immortalised by Spurgeon, who after her conversion " swept under the mats." We are not all housemaids or have such duties to perform ; but we see that the story illustrates the great principle of faithfulness in little things, even in unnoticed things. And so St. Paul's rules about widows likewise illustrate great principles for general adoption.

1. Ver. 3. Widows were to be honoured. Honour may be shown in different ways. In Matt. xv. 6 our Lord uses the word to indicate the material

[1] See p. 185.

support of parents ; and it is clear from other verses here that St. Paul had the same kind of " honour " in view.   We have before noticed this use of the word also in ver. 17.[1]

2. But not all widows, ver. 4.   A widow with children or grandchildren was to be supported by them.   Thus they would be " shewing piety " at home and " requiting their parents " ;   and the Church would not be burdened.   (The A.V. has " nephews," which word, three centuries ago when that Version was made, meant grandchildren.   The Greek word, *ekgonos*, means a descendant ;   and the corresponding word *progonos*, which stands here for a parent, means any progenitor, say a grandmother.)

3. In the 8th verse St. Paul adds a striking statement of the general principle in the case of poor relatives not chargeable to the Church.   It is not only that children are to support their widowed mothers.   " If *any* provideth not for his own, and specially his own household, he hath denied the faith, and is worse than an unbeliever."   That is, he falls short even of the moral standard of the heathen, who did recognise the duty.   " Unbeliever," or " infidel " (A.V.), *apistos*, is simply the negative of " believer," *pistos*, the Greek prefixed *a* being a negative.   Here it is equivalent to a non-Christian.

4. It is the " widow indeed," as we should say " the *bonâ fide widow*," the widow bereft, " desolate," lonely, that is to be supported, ver. 5.   But even in her case there are conditions.   St. Paul describes her as one that " hath her hope in God, and continueth in supplications and prayers night and day."   Like

---

[1] See p. 190.

Anna at Jerusalem, who " worshipped with fastings and supplications night and day," and " looked for the redemption." (Luke ii. 37, 38.)

5. There might be some widows at Ephesus who would be excluded by such a condition ; and of them St. Paul utters a solemn judgment in the next verse : " But she that giveth herself to pleasure is dead while she liveth." Such an one would have no claim on the Church's charity. It is a strong expression, " giveth herself to pleasure." The Greek is one word, *spatalōsa*, and it only occurs again in Jas. v. 5, where St. James denounces those who have " taken their pleasure " (A.V. " been wanton "). Liddon renders it " riotous " or " dissipated." It is used by the LXX in Ezek. xvi. 49 of the life of a " daughter of Sodom." But it need not imply literal immorality. It means what is so often expressed in our modern literature by the French phrase *joie de vivre*. " Joy of living," indeed ! And St. Paul says she is " dead " ! Not so said classical Greece by the mouth of Sophocles. Dean Spence-Jones quotes from the *Antigone* this description of a man who gives up his sensual pleasures : " Such a man does not *live* ; he is *a living corpse*." One is reminded of the phrase " seeing life." A young man is to " see life," and in the present day it is not one sex only that desires it. But there are some who " shall not see life," and John iii. 36 tells us who they are. On the other hand, the Psalmist asks (xxxiv. 12), " What man is he that desireth life ? " or, as the older Version of Coverdale (as in our Prayer-book), " What man is he that lusteth to live, and would fain see good days ? " The answer, both in the Psalm and in St. Peter's

First Epistle (where it is quoted), is worth reading !

6. Then St. Paul goes on to refer to certain widows who are " enrolled " (A.V. " taken into the number "). The Greek word might be rendered " catalogued," for our word " catalogue " actually comes from it (*katalegō*). This cannot mean a list of widows whom the Church was to support ; for it would have been a sorry charity that confined itself to those who possessed the strict qualifications that follow. Many would fall short of such a test who would have the strongest claim to assistance. But we know that a little later the Church had a regular " Order of Widows " solemnly set apart for religious and philanthropic work ; and we may almost certainly conclude that some scheme of the kind was already being tried. For the conduct of this " order," therefore, St. Paul gives instructions.

7. Three qualifications for an enrolled widow are laid down.

(1) She must be at least sixty years old.

(2) She must have been the wife of one man. Does this mean that she must only once have been a widow ? Those who recall the esteem in which *univirae*, women who had only married once, were held by the Romans, say yes. But then, St. Paul wishes the younger widows to marry again (ver. 14) [1] ; would such an one, losing her second husband, be debarred from entering the Order at the age of sixty ? More likely the condition only means faithfulness in married life, a condition by no means superfluous in those days of frequent divorce. The literal rendering of the Greek, *henos andros gunē*, would be " one man's

---

[1] See p. 214.

woman "; and Dr. Weymouth well suggests "true to her one husband." [1]

(3) She must be " well reported of for good works," the *kala erga* so often insisted on. Five examples are specified :—

(*a*) " Bringing up children "; if not her own, then having the care of orphans; an example of virtual " motherhood," as we saw in the last Talk. [2]

(*b*) " Showing hospitality to strangers "; " giving them bed and board," as Liddon expresses it.

(*c*) " Washing the saints' feet "; that is, doing even servile work, if need be, after the example of our Lord Himself.

(*d*) " Relieving the afflicted "; as our Lord put it, " I was an hungred, and ye fed Me . . . sick, and ye visited Me," etc.

(*e*) And besides these four particular " good works " towards children, strangers, the saints, and the afflicted, there is " following *every* good work," following " diligently," or perhaps the meaning is continuing work begun by others, not always an easy thing to do. [3]

8. Then follows prohibition. Young widows are not to be admitted to the Order. For two reasons (ver. 11–15) :—

(*a*) A young widow may wish to marry again. In that there is no harm; on the contrary, St. Paul

---

[1] See p. 185.

[2] See p. 208.

[3] Both A.V. and R.V. add the word " diligently " to express the prefix ἐπὶ in the Greek verb ἐπακολουθέω; but Bishop Bernard thinks the prefix means direction rather than intensity. The same verb is rendered " follow after " in the 24th verse.

expressly approves it,[1] so as to " give none occasion to the adversary for reviling "—the " adversary " here being any cavilling and gossiping slanderer. But a widow who is once enrolled is dedicated to Christ for His special service ; and any restiveness under His yoke (which is the literal meaning of " waxed wanton against Christ ") is equivalent to unfaithfulness to Him, and a condemning conscience will be the result (ver. 11). Hence the rule that a candidate must be at least sixty.

(*b*) A young widow, if admitted to the Order, might " learn to be idle," a " tattler," a " busybody," using her function of house-to-house visiting to indulge in this way. " Idle " is *argos :* " work " is *ergon ;* put the negative *a* into the latter word, and you have " no work " ; hence " idle." " Tattler " is *phluaros,* a word not elsewhere in the N.T., but " prating " in 3 John 10 is connected with it. " Busybody " is *periergos,* over-doing, and so intermeddling ; also in 2 Thess. iii. 11. Such conduct St. Paul calls " turning aside unto Satan " (ver. 15).

Then he thinks of one more difficulty, ver. 16. There may be young widows who do not marry, and have no means : what of them ? They are to be cared for by their elder relatives, just as the older widows in similar need by their younger relatives, so that the Church be not burdened.

Four kinds of widows, therefore, are mentioned by

---

[1] It will be noticed that the word " widows " in ver. 14 is in italics, not being expressed in the Greek ; and the A.V. has " women." The original is only " younger " in the feminine form, *νεωτέρας,* so all women may be included ; but the context clearly shows that St. Paul is speaking particularly of widows.

St. Paul : (1) the " widow indeed," to be supported by the Church ; (2) the widow with children or grandchildren to support her ; (3) the widow who is disqualified for support by her frivolous life ; (4) the widow enrolled in the Order.

We must not confuse the " order of widows " with the deaconesses before spoken of. In the later " Apostolical Constitutions " they are quite distinct. The deaconess received the laying on of hands ; the widow did not, and the widows are enjoined to be " obedient to the deaconesses, with piety, reverence, and fear." So Dr. Plummer (p. 157) tells us ; and Bishop John Wordsworth, in *The Ministry of Grace* (chap. v.), gives a full account of both communities.

How practical it all is ! Who could have thought that God's inspired Book for all mankind would have descended to such details about local and temporary arrangements ? But when we look closely at them, we find them full of important teaching ; we find minute directions with seemingly no relation to our modern life based upon principles of universal application, and every line proves worthy of study and pregnant with spiritual profit. Once more we recall God's own words, " My thoughts are not your thoughts, neither are your ways My ways."

34

HETERODOX (FALSE) TEACHERS: INTRODUCTION

HAVING reviewed the teachings of our Epistles touching the Church, its Ministry, etc., we now come to look at certain perils which threatened its purity and its life. These three Letters are full of references and warnings against false or heterodox teachers ; and it is clear that to expose these teachers, and to instruct Timothy and Titus how to deal with them, was one chief object of St. Paul in writing.

It is evident that from the first the Church had to suffer, not only from outward persecution, but from unsound and dangerous teaching from some of its own members. At the very beginning there was the Judaising controversy, of which St. Paul writes so much in his earlier Epistles, especially that to the Galatians. In that struggle he had won a great victory. Even the Church at Jerusalem itself, composed largely of strict Jews, had decided that the Gentiles could become Christians without becoming Jews ; and there was no more difficulty on that score. But other " troublers of Israel " had arisen at the later period with which we are now concerned ; and when we find St. Paul writing to his delegates at two places so different as Ephesus and Crete about almost the same kinds of mischievous teaching, we may be sure that such evil influences were widespread. As regards Ephesus, indeed, St. Paul had declared some years before that " grievous wolves " would " enter in among them, not sparing the flock," and that " even among their own selves should men arise, speaking perverse things, to draw away the disciples after them " (Acts xx. 29, 30). It was expressly to oppose these influences that Timothy was left by the Apostle at Ephesus during one of the later journeys after the first imprisonment (I. i. 3), " that thou mightest charge certain men not to teach a different doctrine."

Thus St. Paul at the very beginning of his letter indicates one purpose of his writing ; and in the last chapter of the same letter he uses the same phrase, " If any man teacheth a different doctrine " (vi. 3). Now the five words " to teach a different doctrine," represent one Greek word, *hetero-didaskalein*, from *heteros*, " other," and *didaskalein*, " to teach." [1] We might, therefore, coin an English word and call these men " hetero-teachers " ; and the word which we actually have in English, and which I put at the head of this talk, is merely a cognate Greek word anglicised, *heterodoxos, doxa* being an opinion ; but this word does not occur in the N.T.

What, then, is the " different doctrine " referred to ?   In I. i. 10 St. Paul uses the phrase " anything contrary to the sound doctrine," and in vi. 3 again contrasts the " different doctrine " with " sound words." What is meant by " sound " or " healthy " teaching we saw in a former Talk. [2]   St. Paul does

---

[1] The word ἑτεροδιδασκαλεῖν does not occur elsewhere in the N.T.   The A.V. has in i. 3, " teach no other doctrine, " and in vi. 3 " teach otherwise " ; but " other " is not a sufficiently strong word to express the Greek, and usually renders the milder word ἄλλος.   So the R.V. uses " different." In Gal. i. 6, 7, ἕτερον εὐαγγέλιον ὃ οὐκ ἔστιν ἄλλο, the A.V. has " another gospel which is not another," but the R.V. rightly alters this to " a different gospel which is not another *gospel.*"   [2] See p. 74.

not specify a particular false doctrine. He rather
calls on Timothy to remember the true and healthful
doctrine he knows so well, and to oppose *anything*
contrary to *that :* an excellent plan !

It is clear that the false and unprofitable teaching
was chiefly Jewish in origin (see I. i. 7, Tit. i. 10, 14).
The Rabbis delighted in minute discussions about the
exact meaning of the Mosaic Law ; but instead of
bringing its solemn warnings to bear upon such actual
sins as St. Paul enumerates in I. i. 9, 10, they argued
interminably over points of little or no importance ;
and further, they built up all kinds of speculations
on wild legends and fables, such as are to be found in
the Talmud. In the next century the Gnostics—
so named from *gnōsis*, " knowledge "—enlarged these
speculations, and proud of their *gnōsis*, of which St.
Paul justly says that it was " falsely so called "
(I. vi. 20), sought to explain such insoluble problems
as the origin of evil. Dr. Plummer [1] quotes the
ecclesiastical historian Eusebius as saying that when
the Apostles had passed away, " the conspiracy of
godless error took its rise through the deceit of false
teachers, who endeavoured with brazen face to
preach their ' knowledge falsely so-called ' in opposi-
tion to the preaching of the truth." It would be
beside our present purpose to inquire further of these
matters, which are of little interest now. But there
is to-day plenty of unprofitable jangling on occult
questions, and we may well apply St. Paul's warnings
to our own times.

One gnostic doctrine, the beginnings of which St.
Paul already saw was, as Dr. Plummer expresses it, [2]

---

[1] *Past. Ep.* p. 37.   [2] Ibid. p. 43.

" that Matter and everything material is inherently evil "; which " involved necessarily a contempt for the human body " as " a vile thing." This involved a denial of both the Incarnation and the Resurrection. " How could the Divine Word consent to be united with so evil a thing as a material frame ? Either the Son of Man was a mere man or the body which the Christ assumed was not real." Again, it was bad enough for the soul to be tied to a vile body in this life; but it was incredible that they should be re-united in the world to come. Hence St. Paul's words in II. ii. 8, " Remember Jesus Christ, risen from the dead, of the seed of David "; and in the same chapter (ver. 17), his denunciation of Hymenæus and Philetus, who declared that " the resurrection was past already," that is, that it was spiritual only, from a death of sin to a life of righteousness.

This doctrine also involved two opposite errors, leading to false asceticism and to sensuality. If the material body was so vile a thing, let its influence be suppressed by strict ascetic rules. On the other hand if it was so vile, why try to purify it ? why not leave it to wallow in excesses ? Some of the false teachers preached the one doctrine and lived the other. While " forbidding to marry and commanding to abstain from meats " (I. iv. 3), they themselves indulged in all manner of licentiousness.

The Roman satirist Juvenal describes adventurers at Rome of this kind. Professor Ramsay[1] cites several passages. They had " quick intellect, unblushing self-confidence, ready oratory," " insinuated them-selves into households," " adapting themselves to

____

[1] *Expositor*, Aug. 1909, p. 174.

every humour of their patrons with cunning hypocrisy," their talk consisting of " empty verbal dialectic " and " pretentious moral theories about the simple life."

The best way of realising what the false teachings were, and what St. Paul thought about them, is simply to put down his references to them word by word :—

I. i. 4. Fables and endless genealogies, the which minister questionings.

6–7. Some having swerved have turned aside unto vain talking ; desiring to be teachers of the Law, though they understand neither what they say nor whereof they confidently affirm.

iv 1–3. Giving heed to seducing spirits and doctrines of devils, through the hypocrisy of men that speak lies, branded in their own conscience with a hot iron ; forbidding to marry, and commanding to abstain from meats . . .

7. Profane and old wives' fables.

vi. 4. Puffed up, knowing nothing, but doting about questionings and disputes of words, whereof cometh envy, strife, railing, evil surmisings, wranglings of men corrupted in mind and bereft of the truth, supposing that godliness is a way of gain.

20. Profane babblings and oppositions of the knowledge which is falsely so called ; which some professing have erred concerning the faith.

II. ii. 14. Strive not about words to no profit, to the subverting of them that hear.

16. Shun profane babblings ; for they will proceed further in ungodliness, and their words will eat as doth a gangrene.

II. ii. 23. Foolish and ignorant questionings refuse, knowing that they gender strifes.

iii. 6. They that creep into houses, and take captive silly women laden with sins, led away by divers lusts.

8. Men corrupted in mind, reprobate concerning the faith.

13. Evil men and impostors shall wax worse and worse, deceiving and being deceived.

iv. 3, 4. Having itching ears, will heap to themselves teachers after their own lusts; and will turn away their ears from the truth, and turn aside unto fables.

Tit. i. 10. Unruly men, vain talkers, and deceivers, specially they of the circumcision.

11. Men who overthrow whole houses, teaching things which they ought not, for filthy lucre's sake.

14. Giving heed to Jewish fables.

15. To them that are defiled and unbelieving nothing is pure; but both their mind and their conscience are defiled.

16. They profess that they know God; but by their works they deny Him, being abominable, and disobedient, and unto every good work reprobate.

iii. 9. Shun foolish questionings, and genealogies, and strifes, and fightings about the law, for they are unprofitable and vain.

This is a tremendous catalogue; and it will be noticed that I have not included two important passages, one (I. i. 9, 10) in which grave sins and crimes are enumerated, and the other (II. iii. 2–5) which gives a long list of personal sins and faults; because in neither case is there any direct reference to the heterodox teachers. But we shall have to look at both passages as indirectly connected with them.

Let us note some of the expressions used in the foregoing passages by St. Paul. He mentions " fables " four times, " genealogies " twice, " questionings " four times, " babblings " twice, " disputes " or " strivings " about words three times, " vain talk " twice. Three times he stigmatises the " fables " or " babblings " as profane ; twice, " to no profit " ; once as " eating like a gangrene."[1] The teachers are described as ambitious, avaricious, ignorant, hypocritical, puffed up, corrupt in mind, bereft of the truth, impostors, deceivers, liars, defiled and unbelieving, disobedient, abominable. They have " swerved " and " turned aside " ; they have " made shipwreck of their faith " ; they " fall away from the faith " ; they " consent not to sound words " ; they " have erred concerning the faith," and " concerning the truth " ; they " turn away from the truth " ; they are " reprobate from the faith." Readers must look at the context of some of the passages quoted above, in order to see the point of these strong words of condemnation. In the aggregate it is a terrible indictment.

Many of the particular words used are very interesting and significant. We shall look at these as we examine the four or five chief passages in which St. Paul deals with the heterodox teachers and their errors.

---

[1] In the A.V. "canker." The Greek is γάγγραινα, of which our "gangrene" is a transliteration. The word is used by Greek medical writers of a sore that eats into the flesh.

35

FALSE TEACHERS:
1 Timothy Chapters 1 & 4

WE now proceed to take up the passages in our Epistles in which St. Paul deals with the heterodox teachers.

1. The first is at the very beginning of the First Letter. He starts at once, after the salutation, by reminding Timothy that he had left him at Ephesus expressly to " charge certain men not to teach a different doctrine, neither to give heed to fables and endless genealogies, the which minister questionings rather than a dispensation of God which is in faith " (I. i. 3, 4). The " fables and genealogies " were Jewish in origin. " Fable " is *muthos*, whence our " myth." The word occurs only in the four verses in these Epistles which I quoted in the preceding Talk (I. i. 4, iv. 7, II. iv. 4, Tit. i. 14), and in 2 Pet. i. 16, " we did not follow cunningly-devised fables." " Old wives' fables " (iv. 7) is literally " old-womanish," *graōdēs*, from *graus*, an old woman. " Genealogy " is of course the Greek word *genealogia* anglicised, a word only found in the N.T. here and in Tit. iii. 9. " Endless " is *aperantos*, interminable, and therefore tiresome. There were Jewish books full of " interminable " legends based on the genealogies of the early patriarchs, and on the supposed genealogies of the angels. These absurdities led to endless " questionings " (I. i. 4, vi. 4, II. ii. 23, Tit. iii. 9). This word, *zētēsis*, only occurs also in John iii. 25 and Acts xxv. 20 ("to inquire "). Connected with the " questionings " we find " disputes of words " (I. vi. 4) and

" strivings " about them (II. ii. 14, 23, Tit. iii. 9). From the word here used, *logomachia*, we derive our " logomachy " to express the same idea. St. Paul brands these " questionings " and " strivings " as " foolish," " ignorant " (or rather, undisciplined, *apaideutos*), and unprofitable.

Then the same men are charged with " vain talking," *mataiologia* (I. i. 6) ; and so are those in Crete (Tit. i. 10). " Babblings " practically mean the same thing, as *kenophōnia* might be rendered " empty voices " (I. vi. 20, II. ii. 16). These " babblings " are both times called " profane," *bebēlos*, and so are the " old-wives' fables " above mentioned. This is the word applied to Esau in Heb. xii. 16. It means literally " what one may step on," and thus " common," " not sacred."

Can we honestly say that these phrases do not apply to some of our modern controversies ? Do not the controversies often hang upon minute verbal distinctions ? and do not some of them border on the profane ? It is true that now and then some great truth may really be involved ; but certainly it often happens that some word on which our forefathers laid much stress has ceased to interest us ; and will it not be so by and by with other words for which we now fight desperately ?

Now the " certain men " of whom St. Paul writes in this passage sought the honourable position of " teachers of the law " (I. i. 7). They " professed " " the knowledge falsely so-called " (vi. 21) ; and Prof. Ramsay considers that this word " profess " (usually rendered " promise " *epaggellesthai*) implies a kind of candidature, a bidding for popular support. But

St. Paul disputes their claim. " They understand neither what they say not whereof they affirm." And he goes on to show that the Law was a more serious and solemn thing than they supposed, i. 8–10.

In doing this he practically cites the Ten Commandments, but using his own language. First, we find general terms, which might be meant to refer to the First Table, " lawless and unruly," " ungodly and sinners," " unholy and profane." These Liddon analyses thus : In relation (1) to law, (a) neglecting it, " lawless," (b) resisting it, " unruly " ; (2) to God, (a) not revering Him, " ungodly," (b) sinning against Him, " sinners " ; (3) to sanctity, (a) being without it, " unholy," (b) being outside its sphere, " profane." Then, referring to the 5th Commandment, " murderers of parents," a phrase to be read as indicating the *dishonouring* of parents, which may bring them " with sorrow to the grave," an interpretation justified, says Bishop Bernard, by the use of the words in Greek literature. Then the 6th, " manslayers." Then, gross breaches of the 7th. Then the worst breach of the 8th, " men-stealers," an explicit condemnation of the slave trade ; then the 9th, " liars " and " false swearers."

What a contrast between the questionings and the splittings of words that chiefly occupied those " certain men " and these grim realities of actual life ! But St. Paul does not stop at the gross sins just referred to. He adds, " If there be any other thing contrary to the sound doctrine " (verse 10), which he goes on to define, as we have before seen,[1] as " the gospel of the glory of the blessed God." And then

----

[1] See p. 75.

comes that wonderful parenthesis, his testimony to the marvel of Divine Grace in his own conversion. That is what is wanted to-day.   Amid all the subtleties of theological controversy, we want the Story of the Cross !

2. We go on to chap. iv.   Here St. Paul refers to "later times," that is, the future, near or far ; but evidently he sees signs of an early development of the errors he proceeds to expose.   His language about the teachers of these errors is stronger than that used in chap. i.   They are " men that speak lies " and are " branded in their own conscience as with a hot iron " ; and " through their hypocrisy " they cause others to fall away from the Faith, to *apostatize*. And as these have become victims through " giving heed to seducing spirits and doctrines of devils or demons," it is plain that he regards the teachers themselves as agents of the devil.   The R.V. should here be carefully looked at, for the A.V. does not at all show the distinction between the teachers and their dupes.   " Hypocrisy " is the Greek word *hupokrisis* anglicised.   " Men that speak lies " is the plural of *pseudologos*.   We in English often use " pseudo " by prefixing it to another word to give the idea of what is false or counterfeit ; and in the Greek N.T. we find *pseud-adelphos*, " false brother " ; *pseudo-didaskalos*, " false teacher " ; *pseud-apostolos*, " false apostle " ; *pseudo-martus*, " false witness " ; *pseudo-prophētēs*, " false prophet " ; *pseudo-christos*, " false Christ " ; and so here, *pseudo-logos*, " false-speaker." The phrase " branded in their own conscience with a hot iron " is well explained by Dr. Horton : " Slaves were marked by a brand on the brow ; so these hereti-

cal teachers would be marked in their own conscience, *i.e.*, they would know that they were guilty." The whole passage is a terrible indictment ; yet it is a true prophecy of some modern deceivers, in Christian lands as well as in heathendom.

One illustration of their evil influence is given, the preaching of a false asceticism in the matter of (*a*) marriage, (*b*) food. " Forbidding to marry, and commanding to abstain from meats."[1] St. Paul does not show the falsity of the former : perhaps that heresy was still in the future. But he does deal with the food question, which we know was an actually burning one (see Rom. xiv., 1 Cor. viii., Col. ii.). There were forbidden foods under the old laws, but now— see Mk. vii. 19 (R.V.), Acts x. 15, Rom. xiv. 14. The governing principle laid down by St. Paul is in both cases the same. And how beautifully he does it ! " To abstain from meats, which God created to be received with thanksgiving by them that believe and know the truth. For every creature of God is good, and nothing to be rejected, if it be received with thanksgiving ; for it is sanctified through the word of God and prayer." " Sanctified through prayer " probably refers to saying " grace " ; and both Jews and early Christians are said to have repeated O.T. texts at their " grace," such as Ps. cxlv. 15,

---

[1] It will be noticed that " and commanding " is in italics, not being expressed in the Greek, which reads " forbidding to marry, to abstain from meats," which is evidently wrong in some way. Now " forbidding " is κωλυόντων, and " commanding " would be κελευόντων, and it is suggested that some copyist may have hastily read the latter as a superfluous repetition of the former, and dropped it out. But we have no evidence of this. The real sense, however, is obvious.

16, which may explain the addition of " the word of God."

I must here present two extracts, both so good, though from such different men. First, Liddon thus analyses St. Paul's argument :—

Arg. 1 from the *purpose of God* in creation. The final cause of all *brōmata* [foods] is, that they should be partaken of (*a*) by the faithful, who, as such, know the real relations of man to God and to nature, and (*b*) with thanksgiving.

Arg. 2 from the *intrinsic nature of all creatures*. Everything made by Him (*pan ktisma Theou*) is good, and conversely none is to be rejected, if it be received with thanksgiving.

Arg. 3 from the *sanctifying power of the word of God* uttered over the   food, and accompanied by prayer.

The other is from Dr. Horton's Commentary :—

The protest is raised under these four heads : (1) God, no other, made these meats (and also instituted marriage) ; (2) He made them with a design (and marriage too) ; (3) viz., to be received by men, not stigmatized as evil in a Manichean sense ; (4) and believing men, who know the truth, should take them with thanksgiving. . . . When the body and its appetites, and the provision made for their satisfaction, are all brought into this creaturely relation, and accepted thankfully as from the Creator . . . then a sanctification falls upon appetite and passion ; they are kept in their proper place, and purged by the Divine Spirit.

It will be seen how clearly the Apostle's reasoning applies to both errors, the prohibition of marriage and the strict rules about food. Those that " believe and know the truth " (ver. 3) will take God's good gifts and use them aright ; but what are we to say of the divines and rulers of the Church of Rome ?

36

FALSE TEACHERS:
1 Timothy 6:3-10, Titus 1:10-16

THE third passage in First Timothy dealing with this subject is chap. vi. 3–10. It introduces men of a different type from those so gravely condemned in chap. iv. They are not charged with being agents of the Evil One, or with having " branded consciences." They are rather stupid than wicked : " puffed up, knowing nothing, but doting about questionings and disputes of words," like the " certain men " of chap. i. " Puffed up," *tetuphōtai, i.e.* " beclouded," from *tuphos*, " smoke " ; we use a different metaphor when we describe conceit as " swelled head." " Doting," *nosōn*, is " sick " or morbid, having an unhealthy appetite for arguing and cavilling ; which reminds us of Bunyan's " Talkative." The influence of such men may not lead others to " fall away from the Faith," like that of the hypocritical liars of chap. iv. ; but St. Paul is justly severe on the " envy, strife, railings, evil surmisings, wranglings," which it causes,—wranglings of men " corrupted in mind," or " depraved," and not only " destitute of the truth " (A.V.), but " bereft " of it, having lost what glimmer of it they had. Severe, too, on the motive that reveals itself in some of them, the hope of " gain " through their profession of " godliness." We cannot help thinking of Dickens's Chadband : " puffed up," " doting," seeking " gain " in that very way ; but are there not some in the Christian Church who, though not so contemptible as he, answer more or less to St. Paul's description ?

Notice particularly what leads to all this : " If any man teacheth a different doctrine,[1] and consenteth not to sound words, even the words of our Lord Jesus Christ, and to the doctrine which is according to godliness, *he* is puffed up," etc. What these " sound words " and this " doctrine " are, we have seen before ; [2] but the point is that they are the secret of an upright, modest, healthy, contented life, and that it is neglect of them that leads to conceit and morbidness and wranglings and covetousness. St. Paul insists, as we have seen, on sound belief issuing in a godly life ; and not less does he insist that the way to a godly life is sound belief. That expression " consenteth " is significant. The verb, *proserchomai,* is a common one in the N.T., but everywhere else it means " approach " in a bodily sense. What is meant by " approach " of the mind ? Bishop Bernard illustrates it by St. Peter's words to Cornelius (Acts x. 28), that it was unlawful for a Jew to " come unto " (same verb) a Gentile house. He had " come unto " Cæsarea in the bodily sense, but his mind also, in consequence of his vision, was " coming unto " those whom he could no longer regard as " common or unclean."

But, as in a former case, how beautifully St. Paul meets the false idea that " godliness " may be " a way of gain " ! (The A.V. " that gain is godliness " is a mistranslation ; the R.V. correctly represents the Greek.) " Yes, indeed," he seems to say, " godliness is great gain " ; and in chap. iv., as we have before seen,[3] he has already quoted as a " faith-

---

[1] See p. 218.   [2] See p. 75.   [3] See p. 57.

ful saying " the maxim that it is " profitable for all things."   But then, if godliness, or a profession of it, is taken up *with a view to gain*, there will be no true gain at all ; for, he carefully adds, the condition of true gain is " contentment."   The Greek word is *autarkeia*, and it only occurs elsewhere in the N.T. in 2 Cor. ix. 8, where it is rendered " sufficiency " ; but the adjective *autarkēs* occurs in Phil. iv. 11, a good parallel text, " I have learned, in whatsoever state I am, therein to be *content*."   Bishop Bernard reminds us that Greek philosophers used these words for the " self-sufficiency " on which they laid stress ; but St. Paul uses it in a humbler spirit, and joins " godliness," *eusebeia*, with it.   Notice the reason he gives for contentment : " for we brought nothing into the world, for neither can we carry anything out." " All very well," an objector may say, " but surely between birth and death we need food and clothing." " Yes," replies St. Paul in effect, " we do ; take care that you are content with them ! "

From First Timothy we will go to Titus, leaving Second Timothy till next Talk.   The passage to be looked at is i. 10–16.   St. Paul's language concerning the false teachers in Crete is very severe.   Some of his words are the same as described those at Ephesus, " unruly men, vain talkers and deceivers " ; those who were Jews being the worst, " specially they of the circumcision."   " Whole houses," or " households," are " subverted " or " overthrown " in their faith, by the influence of these men, just as is said of the teaching of Hymenæus and Philetus (II. ii. 18). They work this destruction by " teaching things which they ought not," an expression left in its vagueness, but suggestive of (at least) indelicacy.[1] Their aim is to make money : it is " for filthy lucre's sake," a graphic phrase of Tindale's, but a little apt to be misleading, because it may be read as if money were " filthy," whereas the meaning is " for shameful gain's sake." No wonder the stern judgment is uttered, " Whose mouths must be stopped." It was not sufficient to refute their immoral and greedy talk ; it must not be allowed at all ; and they must be " sharply rebuked." One almost wonders that the aim of the rebuke is " that they may be sound in the faith," as if that were possible. Did the large-hearted Apostle indulge in the hope of saving even such men as these ?

St. Paul does not forget that " to the pure all things are pure " (verse 15) ; but there is perhaps no familiar maxim more often misapplied. Impure things are to be tolerated because, forsooth, those who enjoy them and even dote upon them pretend that they themselves, being pure (which in most cases they are not), will get no harm from them. It is far more to the point that, as the Apostle justly says, " to them that are defiled and unbelieving nothing is pure." In fact, their " defiled mind and conscience " soil with impurity that which may in itself be quite pure. For instance, the God of infinite purity and holiness made mankind " male and female," and our Prayer-book rightly speaks of " holy matrimony." But what about " sex problems " and " sex novels " and " sex plays " ?

Finally (verse 16), " they profess that they know

---

[1] The Greek here is singularly terse, ἃ μὴ δεῖ, untranslatable in English, literally " which not must."

God ; but by their works they deny Him, being abominable and disobedient and unto every good work reprobate." " Abominable," *bdeluktos*, does not occur again in the N.T., but we have " abomination," *bdelugma*, as meaning something disgusting, particularly in Revelation (xvii. 4, 5, xxi. 27). " Reprobate, *adokimos*, means literally " not approved," that is, tested, but not passing the test, and therefore rejected. It is " reprobate " in Rom. i. 28, 2 Cor. xiii. 5, 6, 7, and " rejected " in Heb. vi. 8 and 1 Cor. ix. 27. This last passage is where the A.V. wrongly makes St. Paul fear lest he be a " castaway."

37
FALSE TEACHERS:
2 Timothy 3:1-13

WE now turn to Second Timothy, in the 3rd chapter of which we find one of the most suggestive of St. Paul's references to the heterodox teachers against whose influence he so solemnly warned the Church. I must in this case print the whole passage :—

Ver. 1. But know this, that in the last days grievous times shall come.

2. For men shall be lovers of self, lovers of money, boastful, haughty, railers, disobedient to parents, unthankful, unholy,

3. Without natural affection, implacable, slanderers, without self-control, fierce, no lovers of good,

Ver. 4. Traitors, headstrong, puffed up, lovers of
         pleasure rather than lovers of God ;
     5. Holding a form of godliness, but having
         denied the power thereof : from these
         turn away.
     6. For of these are they that creep into houses,
         and take captive silly women laden with
         sins, led away by divers lusts,
     7. Ever learning, and never able to come to the
         knowledge of the truth.
     8. And like as Jannes and Jambres withstood
         Moses, so do these also withstand the
         truth ; men corrupted in mind, reprobate
         concerning the Faith.
     9. But they shall proceed no further : for their
         folly shall be evident unto all men, as
         theirs also came to be. . . .
    13. But evil men and impostors shall wax worse
         and worse, deceiving and being deceived.

" In the last days " : this is a prediction. The
words are more definitely future than " in later times "
in I. iv. 1.[1] But when would the " last days "
come ? St. Paul did not know ; but he was taught
by the Spirit that, so far from the whole world gradually improving, the " last days " would be especially
" grievous," *chalepos*, the word applied to the demoniac
of Gergesa, and there rendered " fierce,"—a truly
significant forecast ! But was the peril a certainly
distant one ? Not at all. Look at verse 5, " from
these turn away " ; verse 6, " these are they " ;
verse 8, " these also withstand." We have here
present tenses ! The future " last days " may prove
more " fierce," but their characteristic features, as
here displayed, were to be seen then ; and, I may add,

---

[1] In I. iv. 1, it is ἐν ὑστέροις καιροῖς. In II. iii. 1, it is ἐν
ἐσχάταις ἡμέραις.

had been seen before, and have been seen ever since. Compare Rom. i. 29–31, where several of the same exact words are used. As we look at the details, we shall feel sure that in all subsequent centuries there has never been a single year *not* " grievous " in the sense meant.

First notice the five-fold mention of " lovers " : " lovers of self," " of money," " of pleasure " ; " no lovers of good " ; and, in contrast, " lovers of God." " Lovers of self," *philautoi* ; on which Bishop Bernard writes, " In Greek thought of an earlier age *philautia* had a good sense, expressive of the self-respect which a good man has for himself. But . . . once the sense of sin is truly felt, self-respect becomes an inadequate basis for moral theory." " Lovers of money," *philarguroi* : Trench [1] is very interesting on the distinction between *philarguria*, " avarice," and *pleonexia*, " covetousness." The latter has the wider meaning, and is consistent with squandering, while " avarice " is the miser's sin. " Lovers of pleasure," *philēdonoi*, from *hēdonē*, pleasure of a sensual kind, a word used in Lu. viii. 14, Tit. iii. 3, Jas. iv. 1, 3, 2 Pet. ii. 13, anglicised in our " Hedonism," and illustrated to-day in what actually calls itself " the Smart Set " ! " No lovers of good," *aphilagathoi*, the word for " lovers of good " with the Greek negative *a* prefixed. At this point it may be interesting to note the numerous compound Greek words which are formed from the verb *philein*, to love. There are no less than twenty-six, among the more interesting being *philadelphia*, " love of the brethren," *philanthrōpia*, " love of mankind," and *philosophia*,

---

[1] *Synonyms of the N.T.*, § xxiv.

" love of wisdom " ; from the last two of which we derive our " philanthropy " and " philosophy." Twelve of these occur in the Pastoral Epistles, and in eight cases nowhere else :—

Phil-agathos, lover of good, Tit. i. 8.
Phil-andros, loving the husband, Tit. ii. 4.
Philo-teknos, loving the children, Tit. ii. 4.
Phil-anthrōpia, love of mankind, Tit. iii. 4 ; also Acts xxviii. 2, " kindness."
Phil-arguria, love of money, I. vi. 10.
Phil-arguros, lover of money, II. iii. 2 ; also Lu. xvi. 14.
Phil-autos, lover of self, II. iii. 2.
Phil-ēdonos, lover of pleasure, II. iii. 4.
Philo-Theos, lover of God, II. iii. 4.
Philo-xenos, lover of the stranger, hospitable, I. iii. 2, Tit. i. 8 ; also 1 Pet. iv. 9.

And the two negatives :—

A-phil-agathos, no lover of good, II. iii. 3.
A-phil-arguros, no lover of money, I. iii. 3 ; also Heb. xiii. 5.

" Love," says St. Paul in Rom. xiii., " is the fulfilling of the law " ; and love wrongly directed is the source of law-breaking, and of sin of every kind. And no one can escape from the Apostle's net here ; its meshes are not wide enough. I may be free from love of money or from love of pleasure ; but I am not free from love of self. In our very best actions, words, thoughts, feelings, *that* motive is scarcely ever absent ; mixed, it may be, with what is good, with the love of God and man that may be largely influencing us. When we do meet with a man who at least seems to us to be free from " self," what a goodly sight it is !

I must add some brief notes on the other words.

" Boastful," *alazōn*, and " haughty," *huperēphanos*, are coupled as in Rom. i., the former describing words, the latter thoughts and feelings. " Railer," *blasphēmos* ; but the word stands here, not for blasphemy against God, but for speaking evil of our fellowmen. " Unthankful," *acharistos*, is really that great word *charis*, " grace " or " thanks," on which I enlarged before,[1] with the Greek negative prefixed. The word occurs also in Lu. vi. 35. That same Greek negative makes the words for " unholy," " without natural affection," " implacable," " without self-control," " fierce," by prefixing it to the words for the opposites. " Implacable " in the R.V. replaces the " truce-breakers " of the A.V. ; and it means, not breaking a truce already made, but refusing to make one at all. " Without self-control " is *akratēs*, strength or power being *kratos* ; we should contrast *egkratēs*, " self-controlled " (" temperate " in Tit. i. 8). Neither word occurs again in the N.T., but we have *egkrateia* in Gal. v. 23, " temperance " in both versions, but " self-control " in R.V. margin. All three words have reference to sensual passions generally. " Slanderers " is *diaboloi*. " Headstrong," *propetēs*, is " rash " in Acts xix. 36. " Puffed up " is the " beclouded " noticed before.[2] The *Twentieth Century N.T.* suggests " merciless " instead of implacable, " brutal " for fierce, " reckless " for headstrong.

It is interesting to remember that from this passage Bunyan obtained some of the names of the jurymen at " Vanity Fair." " Heady " and " High-minded " are the A.V. rendering of " headstrong " and " puffed

---

[1] See p. 125.　　　　[2] See p. 230.

up." " Hang him, hang him, said Mr. Heady. A
sorry scrub, said Mr. High-mind." There are also
" Mr. Implacable " and " Mr. No-good." Bunyan
also apparently borrowed " Mr. Malice " and " Mr.
Love-lust " from Tit. iii. 3.

But in one respect Bunyan's jurymen were unlike
the men St. Paul is describing in these verses. The
citizens of Vanity Fair were open enemies of religion ;
but these " hold a form of godliness," though they
have " denied the power thereof." They are not
really godly, but they affect to be so. They are outwardly " religious." But the very word for " form "
indicates unreality. In Phil. ii., Christ is described
as being in the " form of God," *morphē*, and then as
taking on Him the " form of a servant," *morphē*
again, both real ; but the word here (as also in Rom.
ii. 20) is *morphōsis*, which Bishop Bernard explains as
the affectation of the *morphē* of godliness. This,
however, is what gives such men their power. And St.
Paul illustrates that power by mentioning their success
with " silly women." Alford quotes passages from
Irenæus, Jerome, and other early Fathers, in which
the same expression, *gunaikarion*, a contemptuous
diminutive of *gunē*, " woman," is used of some who
came under the mischievous influence of certain
heretics. St. Paul describes such women as " laden
with sins," having an uneasy conscience, and ready
for anything which they think will quiet it, beguiled
by the pretended spirituality and supposed occult
knowledge of these " impostors," or wizards, *goētes*,
as he calls them in verse 13. (The suggestive rendering
of the A.V., " seducers," is hardly too strong.)
These impostors St. Paul compares with the

Egyptian magicians who withstood Moses and Aaron at Pharaoh's court.[1]   Those magicians succeeded in imitating three of the signs worked by Moses, but failed with the rest, and had to acknowledge " the finger of God " (Exod. vii. 22, viii. 7, 18, 19).   So also, says St. Paul, shall the " folly " of these impostors be " evident unto all men " ; and therefore " they shall proceed no further."   Yet a little further on he says they shall " wax worse and worse " : how is that ?   " Proceed " and " wax " are the same verb in the Greek, *prokoptō*, and the latter phrase is literally " proceed towards the worse."   They will grow worse themselves, but for that very reason their influence will diminish.   " Progress " is not always a good thing.   Dr. Horton felicitously reminds us that while Bunyan described the Pilgrim's Progress, Hogarth painted the Rake's Progress.

In the last chapter of this Letter St. Paul alludes to the readiness of some who cannot bear " sound doctrine " to run after more congenial leaders.   They are described (iv. 3) as " having itching ears," a happy rendering of Wiclif's, literally " having the ears scratched " ; and as " heaping up " " teachers after their own lusts," their caprice and vitiated taste.

Now are all these warnings out of date ?   Is it not the case to-day that hundreds of people who feel the want of some sort of religion, but will not have the one true religion of Christ, are an easy prey to the latest craze ?   Are there not plenty of " silly women " in particular, " led away by divers lusts,

---

[1] We have no means of knowing whence St. Paul derived the names " Jannes and Jambres," but they occur in Jewish and early Christian writings.

ever learning, and never able to come to the knowledge of the truth " ?   Is it not true that any superstition is welcomed, if only its votaries can escape from the simplicity and the purity of Christ ?   What of the spiritualists, and theosophists, and " mediums " who pretend to be in communication with the unseen world, and the tricksters repeatedly exposed by Mr. Maskelyne ?   Is it not literally true that " evil men and impostors wax worse and worse, deceiving and being deceived " ?   " Being deceived," yes ; while some are conscious and deliberate impostors, others are indeed themselves deceived ; and is not that the work of the Evil One ? Was St. Paul wrong when he wrote (I. iv. 1) of " seducing spirits and doctrines of devils " ?   Did not our Lord Himself tell us that " false Christs and false prophets " should really show " signs and wonders " that might deceive, " if possible, even the elect " ?

" *But thou*," exclaims St. Paul, again and again (I. vi. 11, II. ii. 16, 23, iii. 10, 14, iv. 5).   Let each one of us take that " But thou " home to him or herself !

38

DEALING WITH HERETICS:
1 Timothy 1:19-20; 4:6-12

I have taken up four Talks with examining the passages in the Pastoral Epistles concerning the "teachers of a different doctrine" at Ephesus and in Crete. But we have yet to see how St. Paul instructs Timothy and Titus as to the methods of dealing with such "troublers of Israel." Let us now look at his counsels in regard to this matter.

First observe that he mentions one case in which he had already acted himself. In I. i. 19, 20, he writes of some who had "made shipwreck concerning the faith," the verb used for "made shipwreck" being the same which he used of his own bodily experience when he told of having "thrice suffered shipwreck" (2 Cor. xi. 25). It is a vivid illustration. We use it too sometimes, of a man's physical health : "What a wreck so-and-so is !" But spiritual shipwreck, how terrible ! how fatal ! Then he goes on to particularise two men, Hymenæus and Alexander, "whom," he says, "I delivered unto Satan, that they might be taught not to blaspheme."

What does this mean ? It is "delivered," not (as in A.V.) "have delivered," implying that St. Paul did this thing at a particular time, no doubt when he was at Ephesus. But what was it that he did ? We must compare I Cor. v., where he instructs the Corinthian Church "to deliver" a certain man who had committed a gross sin "unto Satan, for the destruction of the flesh, that the spirit might be saved in the day of the Lord Jesus." Both passages mean excommunication from Church privileges. Liddon admirably explains it thus : " Exclusion from the Kingdom or Church of God by excommunication implies surrender to ' the prince of this world,' *who reigns outside it and seizes those who pass the frontier.*"   Bishop Bernard points out that in the Book of Job (ii. 6), when God, as it were, hands over Job to Satan under certain conditions, His words in the LXX Greek Version are " Behold, I deliver him to thee," the verb, *paradidōmi*, being the same as here.   In that case bodily suffering ensues, just as the Corinthian was excommunicated " for the destruction of the flesh." That the Apostles had this power is clear from the cases of Ananias and Sapphira and Elymas the sorcerer.

It is not easy in our modern England to appreciate excommunication, although the Thirty-Nine Articles expressly recognise it (see Art. 33) ; but in the young Churches in the mission field it is a very real thing. We should carefully note that the object is not punishment, but correction with a view to repentance and restoration.   The Corinthian was so treated " that the spirit might be saved in the day of the Lord Jesus " ; and St. Paul here tells us the purpose of his sentence on the two men at Ephesus, " that they might be taught not to blaspheme," " taught " being the verb *paideuō*, which we have met before in the sense of discipline or education by chastening.   We do not certainly know the result ; but if Hymenæus is the same person as is mentioned in II. ii. as the denier of the resurrection and as having " overthrown the faith of some," the discipline failed in his case.

Turning now to St. Paul's instructions, we find him using such words as " charge," " command," " reprove," " rebuke," " reprove sharply," " exhort and reprove with all authority " (I. i. 3, iv. 11, v. 20, II. ii. 14, iv. 2, Tit. i. 13, ii. 15). Timothy was to " refuse " unprofitable discussions (I. iv. 7, II. ii. 23), to " turn away " from some (I. vi. 20, II. iii. 5), to " shun " others (II. ii. 16). The word for " sharply," *apotomōs*, is worth noting. It is only once used elsewhere in the N.T., in 2 Cor. xiii. 10 ; but the cognate noun is the " severity " of Rom. xi. 22, referring to the unfruitful olive-branches being *severed*, cut off.

Titus has a special counsel given him about the " man that is heretical " (iii. 10), that is, not so much the unsound teacher as the persistent sectarian. The margin suggests " factious," and the Greek word *hairetikos* indicates a tendency to schism and separation. The cognate noun *hairesis* is the word used in the Acts of the " sect " of the Sadducees, or of thePharisees, or of the " Nazarenes" (v. 17, xv. 5, xxiv. 5, 14, xxvi, 5, xxviii. 22). The word primarily means " choice," and so it came to mean the sect or party which one chooses to join. Titus is to be patient with such an one, " admonishing " him twice. After that, he is to " refuse " him, that is, avoid him (margin), for he is evidently " perverted," and " self-condemned." The word " shun," in the preceding verse, is significant in such a case. It means " stand aloof from," *peri-istanai*, or, as Dr. Plummer suggests, " give him a wide berth." Let us carefully note that it is not " heresy," not unsound doctrine, that is here condemned. It is *the separatist spirit*, which is sometimes seen in the most orthodox. There is a separation which St. Paul does enjoin, separation from a sinful world. " Come out and be separate," he says (2 Cor.

vi. 14–18). But this is a very different thing from separation from the Christian Church we belong to. See what is said of that in Jude 19.

But there are two passages in which fuller directions are given to Timothy as to his personal conduct in dealing with the " troublers of Israel " about whom he has written so much.   The first of these is I. iv. 6–12. After the warning in the first three verses of this chapter, which we have already studied, and the reminder that " every creature of God is good," St. Paul goes on thus :—

> Ver. 6. If thou put the brethren in mind of these things, thou shalt be a good minister of Jesus Christ, nourished in the words of the faith, and of the good doctrine which thou hast followed until now.
>
> 7. But refuse . . . fables. And exercise thyself unto godliness.
>
> 8. For bodily exercise is profitable for a little ; but godliness is profitable for all things. . . .
>
> 10. For to this end we both labour and strive. . . .
>
> 12. Let no man despise thy youth ; but be thou an ensample. . .

There could scarcely be a more significant and impressive passage for all Christian teachers and workers, especially such as have to engage in controversy. In order to oppose error and to vindicate the true doctrine, Timothy is to see to his own personal religious life. His aim is to be " a good minister of Jesus Christ."   " Minister " here is *diakonos*, but the word does not stand definitely for " deacon," but means the " service" of Christ generally. Now to be a " good *diakonos* " four things are specified as necessary :—

(*a*) He must be " nourished in the words of the faith and of the good doctrine." " Nourished," the Greek tense implying regular nourishment. With what mental and spiritual food ? With " the words of the Faith " ; not " the word " ; not the Gospel Message (which would be " the word ") ; but the vessels (so to speak) which were conveying the Gospel Message. Not, *here*, the O.T. Scriptures. Of course they would not be excluded, but I do not think they are here specifically referred to. They would include such of St. Paul's own Epistles as Timothy had copies of, particularly the Epistle to the Ephesian group of Churches—and how truly " nourishing " *that* is !—also any primitive creeds or catechisms such as furnished some of the Faithful Sayings ; also any Gospel narratives already in circulation. If these would " nourish" Timothy, and any other servant of the Lord, then, how much more thoroughly can *we* be " nourished," who have the whole New Testament !

(*b*) He must " refuse " those " old-womanish fables " which we have before seen were then so rife.[1] They would not " nourish " him. Nor will their modern antitypes nourish us !

(*c*) He must " exercise himself unto godliness." " Exercise" : in verse 7 *gumnaze* (verb) ; in verse 8 *gumnasia* (noun) ; from which words come our " gymnastic," " gymnasium," etc. The verb occurs also in Heb. v. 14, xii. 11, 2 Pet. ii. 14, and is there also rendered " exercise " ; the noun does not occur elsewhere in the N.T. They are words used in connection with the Greek games and contests in the arena, and are derived from *gumnos*, " naked," the athletes being

---

[1] See p. 224.

unclothed. The phrase as used here is most significant. There is no such thing as drifting into godliness ; the " stream of tendency " (to adopt a modern expression) is against us. To run the heavenly race there must be training ; and training, among gymnasts and athletes, includes exercise. We all know the importance of exercise for health ; we know that if our limbs are not exercised, they lose their strength. It is the same in the spiritual life. Prayer, Bible-reading, public worship, Holy Communion, and their effect upon our souls, are all influenced by the law of habit. Justly are they sometimes called " religious exercises," and we often have to discipline the body resolutely, in order to fulfil them. And this is profitable, just as all bodily exercise is, " for a little." Not (as in A.V.) " profiteth little " ; the remark is not depreciatory, but the contrary. Only, godliness is *more* profitable. St. Paul repeats the lesson in verse 10 : " we both labour and strive." It is not even mere " exercise." It is hard labour and strenuous struggle. But we can face this, joyfully, because, as he immediately adds, " we have set our hope on the living God."

(*d*) He is to be " an ensample." But on this I need say nothing, as I included it in the " personal counsels " to Timothy noticed in an early Talk.[1]

But could anything be more impressive as a word to those who have to oppose unsound teachers ? It is all summed up in the last verse of the chapter : " Take heed *to thyself*."

The other passage, II. ii. 22–26, will occupy another chapter.

---

[1] See p. 31.

39
DEALING WITH HERETICS:
2 Timothy 2:22-26

THERE is still one passage to be examined which counsels Timothy touching his dealing with the " troublers of Israel."   It is the closing verses of the second chapter.   That chapter has several references to these " troublers."   In verse 14 is one of the warnings against " striving about words to no profit." In verse 16–18 is a reference to the " profane babblings," and to the heresy of the resurrection being " past already."   In verse 20 we find the remarkable illustration of " vessels unto dishonour."   In verse 23 " foolish and ignorant questions " which " gender strifes " are again mentioned.   All these we have looked at before.[1]   But verses 25, 26 are an important passage new to us, which will call for careful examination.

First, however, we may notice that in this Epistle, as in the other, Timothy is exhorted to take heed to his own spiritual life and conduct if he is to deal successfully with the opposers.   I once before pointed out the " Flee " and " Follow " of verse 22, like the similar words in I. vi.[2]   Here let me notice how aptly the two injunctions come together.   We are to be both *the pursued* and *the pursuers*.   Evil is pursuing us, and we must " flee " ; not lazily, or caring little whether we escape or not, but resolutely determined not to be caught up.   So also as pursuers : we are to " follow " righteousness, etc., not lazily and as if we had no intention of catching them, but as determined to succeed.

---

[1] See pp. 221–223.   [2] See p. 28.

Observe also that St. Paul here varies a little his enumeration of things to be " followed," adding to them " peace," and tacking on to " peace " a description of the class of persons with whom he is to be in peaceful association : " them that call on the Lord out of a pure heart."   Now, " calling on the Lord " was an accepted phrase to indicate Christian converts.   St. Paul himself would well remember how in his unregenerate days his work had been to persecute those who " called on the Name " of the Lord Jesus (Acts ix. 14, 21), and how the divine message brought to him as he lay blind at Damascus was " Arise and be baptized . . . calling on His Name " (Acts xxii. 16).   In Rom. x. 12–14, this " calling on the Lord " occurs three times ; and there we see that the phrase is borrowed from the Prophet Joel (ii. 32), " Whosoever shall call on the Name of the Lord shall be delivered," the passage prophetic of Pentecost, and quoted also in St. Peter's speech on that memorable day.   It is a good description of a true Christian ; and if the " calling on the Lord " is really " out of a pure heart," then the " peace " with all such which St. Paul enjoins, the fellowship and harmony with them, will be a great strength to those that " flee " and " follow " and " fight " in their conflict with the opposers of the Gospel.

We now come to the important closing verses of the chapter.   Let us read them, omitting the last words for the present :—

The Lord's servant must not strive, but be gentle towards all, apt to teach, forbearing, in meekness correcting them that oppose themselves ; if peradventure God may give them repentance unto the knowledge of the truth, and they may recover themselves out of the snare of the devil. . . .

We have here the sixth appellation of the Christian worker in this chapter. He has been likened to a soldier (verse 3), an athlete (5), a husbandman (6), a workman (15), a vessel (21) ; now he is " the Lord's servant," bond-servant, slave, *doulos*. We have before seen that St. Paul in writing to Titus calls himself the *doulos* of God [1] ; but he does not do so in the letters to Timothy, and only here does he in them give the title to the Christian minister or worker, and thus indirectly to Timothy himself. We saw when we examined the words for " servant " and " service " the beauty of this term *doulos* [2] ; and in this place it is particularly appropriate. St. Paul is describing what Timothy or any other worker must or must not be, and in doing so draws a picture which might stand for the Lord Jesus Himself ; and He, at the very climax of His lowly and even menial " service," when washing His disciples' feet, called on them to follow His example (John xiii. 14–16). So " the Lord's Servant,"—

(1) " Must not strive." Like his Divine Master, of whom it was prophesied that He should " not strive nor cry " (Matt. xii. 19, quoting Isa. xlii. 2). But is not this a strange injunction for the man who is to meet opposing heretics and profane babblers ? Well, the Lord had to " endure the contradiction of sinners " (Heb. xii. 3) ; but did He ever indulge in bitter controversial recriminations ? Nay, did He ever *argue* at all ? Look at the succession of questions put to Him on the Tuesday before His death (Matt.

---

[1] See p. 35.   [2] See p. 36.

xxii., Mark xii., Luke xx.) : do they not exactly answer to St. Paul's description here in verse 23 ? " Foolish and ignorant questionings " ; they are to be " refused," because they " gender strifes " ; " and," he goes on, " the Lord's servant must not strive." Was not Jesus the ideal " Lord's Servant " that day ? No one needs more to imitate Christ than the Christian controversialist.

(2) Must be " gentle towards all, apt to teach, forbearing."   " Gentle," not only to some who may seem to need what we call " gentle handling," but " towards all "—a hard thing indeed, yet St. Paul says " must ! "   " Apt to teach," *didaktikos*, a word we have looked at before ; [1] not merely skilful, but ready at any moment to teach even the unteachable. " Forbearing," *anexikakos*, a word not elsewhere in the N.T., rendered by Bishop Bernard " patient of wrong."   Again, how like Christ Himself !

(3) Must " correct them that oppose themselves," but " in meekness." Should we not have rather written " in sternness " ?   But " opposers " here do not seem to be the wanton and wicked opponents of the truth ; rather they are those who have been misled, who have fallen into " the snare of the devil," and whose case calls more for pity than for reproach. Anyway, both the meekness and the correction have a definite object in view, that such victims may " recover themselves " out of that snare, literally " awake to soberness " (*ananēphō*), like a drunkard waking up in the morning after a night's carouse ; God having " given them repentance."

And now we come to one of the most difficult, and

____

[1] See p. 186.

most interesting, passages in these Epistles. Let us read the words first in the A.V. :—

" And that they may recover themselves out of the snare of the devil, who are taken captive by him at his will."

The last words are literally " taken captive by him unto the will of him," *ezōgrēmenoi hup' autou eis to ekeinou thelēma*. Who are " him " and " him " ? Looking at the A.V., all seems clear : " him " would be the devil, and " his will " would be the devil's will. But the Greek pronouns for " him " and " him " are different, *autou* and *ekeinou*, which almost certainly indicates that two persons are referred to. The natural interpretation would be " taken captive by him (the devil) unto the will of *that other one* " ; and when we look back to see who " that other one " must be, it seems clearly to be " God," who had " given them repentance."   But then, how can we say " taken captive by the devil unto the will of God " ?   So the R.V., to avoid this difficulty, boldly assumes (following Bengel) that the " taking captive " cannot be by the devil, and must refer to the rescue of the man *from* the devil by the Lord's servant ; and renders the passage thus :—

" And they may recover themselves out of the snare of the devil, having been taken captive by the Lord's servant unto the will of God."

Thus the first " him " is the Lord's servant, and the second " him " is God. This is a most attractive rendering, and it has the advantage of giving a welcome significance to the word *ezōgrēmenoi*, which is the verb *zōgrein*, " to catch alive" (as in Luke v. 10).   And yet it does seem rather a strain to refer the first " him" back so far as to the opening of ver. 24 for its antecedent.

But there is a simpler solution, which I confess commends itself to me. The R.V. margin has what seemed just now the objectionable rendering " Of the devil, unto the will of God." Suppose we treat " taken captive by him " (the devil) as a parenthesis, and read the verse thus,—

" May recover themselves out of the snare of the devil (having been taken captive by him), unto the will of God."

So Bishop Bernard renders it ; and Dr. Newport White takes the same line, but alters the order of the words,—

" May recover themselves unto His will out of the snare of the devil, having been taken captive by him."

Even without the capital H to " His," the reference would, with this order, be clearly back to " God " in the preceding verse. Ellicott also gives this interpretation, in nearly the same words. Bishop Moule and Dr. Horton prefer the R.V. rendering. The former suggests this paraphrase : " That they may wake up and escape out of the devil's trap, held willing captives henceforth by him Who sets them free to do His will, the will of God."   Alford and Bishop Hervey cleave to the A.V. rendering, arguing that the two pronouns need not always indicate two persons. Dr. Plummer does not comment on this verse at all. Upon the whole there seems to be real force in the idea, " *out of* the snare of the devil " " *unto* (or *into*) the will of God " ; and both the R.V. and its margin allow of this. Personally I incline to the margin, with the parenthesis, as suggested by Bishop Bernard. Anyway, here is a task for the Christian worker. There are captives of the great enemy. They may be rescued " unto the will of God," unto the accomplishment of His purpose of grace, unto a life ordered by His will. What greater happiness can " the Lord's servant " have, however humble or however great he may be, than to be the instrument of rescuing such captives out of their captivity ?

40

ETHICAL TEACHING:
GOOD WORKS

WE now turn to our last group of topics, the Ethical Teaching of our Epistles. Nothing in them is more striking than the care which St Paul takes to exclude the possibility of our laying undue stress on mere orthodoxy. We have seen how strongly he insists on the importance of sound doctrine, and how much doctrinal teaching is incidentally given. But still more emphatically does he dwell upon practical religion in daily life.

There has been a great deal of needless controversy about the place of " good works " in the Christian system. St James's " justification by works " has been set up as correcting St Paul's " justification by faith " ; whereas there is good reason for thinking that St James wrote first, and anyway, what he opposed was not St Paul's " faith " but the barren orthodoxy of the Pharisaism that had infected some of the

Jewish Christians to whom he wrote. He would have been as much opposed as St Paul to the teaching of Pope's famous couplet—

> For modes of faith let graceless zealots fight ;
> His can't be wrong whose life is in the right.

But the fact is that nowhere in the N.T. are " good works" more strongly insisted on than in St Paul's Epistles, and particularly in the Pastorals. Not that they have any share in procuring " salvation." Very emphatic is the declaration in Tit. iii. 5, " Not by works done in righteousness, which we did ourselves, but according to His mercy He saved us." He fully acknowledges that the Christian does " do works in righteousness." The R.V. rendering makes this clear. But however good such works may be, they are imperfect and inadequate. They " fall short," as Rom. iii. 23 so picturesquely puts it. As Dr. Newport White felicitously remarks, they are " not current coin in the Kingdom of God."

> Not the labours of my hands
> Can fulfil Thy law's demands.

Now let us look at the verses in which " good works " are mentioned in our Epistles. Both the Greek words for " good," *agathos* and *kalos*, are used. The former means intrinsically good, one might perhaps say severely good ; the latter means fair, beautiful, honourable, noble, attractively good. In the following the word is *agathos* :—

l. ii. 9, 10. That women adorn themselves . . . .
through good works.
v. 10. If she hath diligently followed every good
work.

II. ii. 21.   Prepared unto every good work.
  iii. 17.   Furnished completely unto every good
             work.
Tit. i. 16.   Unto every good work reprobate.
  iii. 1.   Ready unto every good work.

And in the following the word is *kalos* :—

I. iii. 1.   If a man seeketh the office of a bishop, he
             desireth a good work.
   v. 10.   Well-reported of for good works.
     25.   There are good works that are evident.
  vi. 18.   That they be rich in good works.
Tit. ii. 7.   An example of good works.
    14.   Zealous of good works.
  iii. 8.   That they which have believed in God may
             be careful to maintain good works.
    14.   To maintain good works for necessary
             uses.

I have thought it right to print the two groups separately, but I confess I fail to see any clear distinction between the two words in these verses. The very first case of *agathos* would seem rather to require *kalos*. It will be noticed that in the first list, in every case but one, it is the singular, " work," while in the second list, in every case but one, it is the plural " works," but this must be purely accidental, as the general N.T. usage in no way suggests any such difference. In these Epistles, *kalos* is by far the more frequent : " good conscience " is *agathos*, and " good fidelity " ; but *kalos* is applied to the law, warfare, prayer, report, standing, creature, minister, doctrine, fight, soldier, confession, foundation, thing committed (deposit). This point, however, needs no further attention.

The two passages which are especially important as shewing St Paul's ethical teaching are the very two which are also the most important doctrinally ; both of them in Titus, ii. 11-14 and iii. 4-8. At these let us look.

I. " Who gave Himself for us, that He might redeem us from all iniquity, and purify unto Himself a people for His own possession, zealous of good works." Here is the purpose of the Son of God in giving Himself for us. Not merely to save us from the guilt and penalty of sin. We have before noticed the force of " redeeming from all iniquity." [1] Let us now look at the concluding words.

" A people for His own possession," or, as the A.V. has it, " a peculiar people." This idea is first revealed in Exodus and Deuteronomy. Israel were the Chosen People, the " peculiar people," the " people for God's own possession." But owing to their failure, a new choice had to be made. St Paul, in Rom. ix. 25 and 2 Cor. vi. 16, applies the old prophecies, originally meant for Israel, to the Christian Church : " I will call that My people which was not My people " ; " I will be their God, and they shall be My people " ; where the context shows that the redeemed of the new dispensation, both Jews and Gentiles, are referred to. And here he actually includes the Cretan Christians, with all their defects,—yes, even the slaves among them (ver. 9),—among the " people " redeemed that they might be purified for God's " own possession," His very own. It is a wonderful phrase. The same Greek words, *laos periousios*, are found in the Septuagint Version of Exod. xix. 5, where the English is " peculiar treasure," and in Deut. vii. 6, xiv. 2, xxvi. 18, where we have " peculiar people." A similar

---

[1] See p. 141.

expression, *eis peripoiēsin*, is used in Mal. iii. 17, where the familiar " my jewels " is altered in the R.V. to " a peculiar treasure " ; and in 1 Pet. ii. 9, where the A.V. " a peculiar people " is altered to " a people for God's own possession." Our word " peculiar " was taken by Tindale from the Latin *peculium*, a man's own special possession.

But what kind of people does God want as His *peculium* ? Orthodox people ? Evangelical people ? It does not say so. The words are " zealous of good works." For *that* we are redeemed ; for *that* we are purified. Could there be a stronger motive for being " rich in good works " (I. vi. 18), " ready unto every good work " (Tit. iii. 1) ?

But our passage has other words in it equally significant. " The grace of God hath appeared," to do two things : (1) " bringing salvation" ; (2) " instructing us, to the intent that. . . ." The verb " instruct" is *paideuō*, which means primarily training a child (*pais, paidion*), and includes discipline and correction. " Chastening," in Heb. xii., is the same or a similar word. So, in our Epistles, are " taught " (I. i. 20), " correcting " (II. ii. 25), " instruction" (II. iii. 16). " The grace of God came," *putting us to school*. And this with an object : " to the intent that . . ." It is not, as in the A.V., " teaching us that . . ." ; it is not merely giving us a lesson ; it is educating, training, *schooling* us with an end in view—so the Greek preposition *hina* implies. And what is the end in view ? That " denying ungodliness and worldly lusts, we should live soberly and righteously and godly in this present world."

In this sentence we have the negative and the posi-

tive. " Ungodliness " and " godly " are contrasted ;
but these important words we must leave for another
Talk. "Worldly lusts"—what St John (1st Ep. ii. 16)
calls " all that is in the world, the lust of the flesh, and
the lust of the eyes, and the vainglory of life," are
contrasted with " soberly" and " righteously," our
duty to ourselves and to others. They are to be
" denied " ; to be met by a never-failing and persistent
No. Very solemn is the question in the service for the
Consecration of Bishops, taken from this verse, " Will
you deny all ungodliness and worldly lusts, and live
soberly, righteously, and godly in this present world ?"

This contrast of negative and positive suggests
another lesson, which I learned years ago from the
late H. B. Macartney, the devoted Australian clergyman who was a valued speaker at Keswick. He told
this story at the Gleaners' Union Anniversary in 1893 :
—A man who was tempted to a certain sin overcame
the temptation, and reporting this to a friend said
" Is not this holiness ? " " No," was the reply : " it
is victory." " And is not victory over sin holiness ? "
" No ; victory implies struggle ; holiness takes away
the want to." So in this verse : " denying worldly
lusts" is victory ; living " soberly, righteously, godly," is holiness.

There is one other purpose of the "schooling" which
Divine grace gives us : that we should be " looking for
the blessed hope and appearing of our great God **and**
Saviour Jesus Christ " ; but this sentence we have
twice looked at before. [1]

II. The other passage, in Tit. iii. 8, follows the
most comprehensive doctrinal statement in these

----

[1] See pp. 89, 98.

Epistles. That statement, as we have before seen,[1] is very likely a part of a short catechism or creed learned by the early Christians ; and St. Paul, after quoting it, exclaims " Faithful is the saying ! " and then goes on to exhort Titus to " affirm confidently " the truths just stated. But with what object ? " To the end that "—the same strong Greek preposition *hina*—" they which have believed God may be careful to maintain good works." Incidentally we may truly gather that the way to promote good works in the Church is to be " confidently affirming " those doctrines, the glorious doctrines of grace ; but the direct lesson is that the doctrines themselves fail in their influence if they do not produce good works.

Then, so strongly does St. Paul feel the importance of this, that at the very end of the Letter, after the personal directions, he " harks back again "—if I may indulge in a colloquial phrase—and gives Titus another reminder, for fear he should forget it. Verse 14, " And let our people also learn to maintain good works for necessary uses, that they be not unfruitful." And this is no mere general language. " For necessary uses "—what does that mean ? Bishop Hervey suggests " such as the wants of the missionaries." Is this a vague guess ? Look at the preceding verse : " Set forward Zenas the lawyer and Apollos on their journey diligently, that nothing be wanting unto them." Whether Zenas was a missionary we know not ; but Apollos certainly was. Titus was to make arrangements for their journey, to provide them with whatever was " wanted " ; but he need not be solely responsible :

---

[1] See p. 57.

" Let our people *also* learn " to supply the wants
of God's messengers. Thus the great doctrines are
to bear fruit in the smallest practical acts and services ;
and such would be " *good* works " in the sense of
what is graceful and attractive—for here the word
is significantly *kalos*. An excellent missionary text !

41

ETHICAL TEACHING: GODLY, RIGHTEOUS AND SOBER

WE have seen the importance attached in these
Epistles to " good works." We have seen
that the design of the redemption of Christ is that
we might " live soberly and righteously and godly
in this present world." We must now look more
closely at these three words.

I. GODLINESS.—In our English Versions this
word occurs in the Pastorals eleven times, and cognate words six times. Here are the eleven :—

I.	ii.	2.	That we may lead a tranquil and quiet life in all godliness and gravity.
		10.	Women professing godliness.
	iii.	16.	Great is the mystery of godliness.
	iv.	7.	Exercise thyself unto godliness.
		8.	Godliness is profitable for all things.
	vi.	3.	The doctrine which is according to godli - ness.
		5.	Supposing that godliness is a way of gain.
		6.	Godliness with contentment is great gain.
		11.	Follow after . . . godliness.
II.	iii.	5.	Holding a form of godliness, but having denied the power thereof.
Tit.	i.	1.	The knowledge of the truth which is according to godliness.

In ten of these passages the Greek word is *eusebeia*. It is remarkable that St. Paul uses this word in none of his other Epistles. In the one other case (I. ii. 10) it is *theosebeia*, which occurs nowhere else in the N.T. Both words are formed from the verb *sebomai*, to worship or to reverence, a word much used by St. Luke in the Acts of the " devout " Gentiles who had learned of the true God from the Jews living in their midst. *Theosebeia* means the worship or service of God, and *eusebeia* in the N.T. is always used in the same sense, though it properly includes esteem and reverence for any superiors, human or divine. Its occurrences in the N.T. outside our Pastorals are Acts iii. 12 (A.V. holiness, R.V. godliness), and four times in 2nd Peter. Our word " godly " is of course an adjective, but it is used in an adverbial sense to render the adverb *eusebōs* in the passage from Titus (ii. 12) quoted above, " soberly and righteously and godly," and also in II. iii. 12, " All that would live godly in Christ Jesus shall suffer persecution." The phrase " show piety " in I. v. 4 represents the verb *eusebeō* ; and the negatives *asebeia* and *asebēs*, " ungodliness " and " ungodly," occur in I. i. 9, II. ii. 16, Tit. ii. 12. It is remarkable that St. Paul uses both these in the Epistle to the Romans (i. 18, iv. 5, v. 6, xi. 26), and yet never once has *eusebeia* outside the Pastorals.

Some have made this fact a reason for doubting St. Paul's authorship of these Epistles. Sir. W. M. Ramsay well replies to this.[1] He says that *eusebeia* is " one of the most characteristic words of pagan religious thought " ; and that it would be strange

---

[1] *Expositor*, April 1911, p. 362.

indeed if St. Paul had never used " a word so close to the heart of the Greco-Roman world." What he did was to explain to them what real " godliness " meant, just as he explained *sōtēria* (salvation)—as we have before seen. Why, then, is it not found in the other Epistles ? Simply, says Ramsay, because " it was not in keeping with the special message which at the moment had to be emphasised." " The Pastorals," he adds, " here, as in so many other cases, intervene to complete the picture of Paul, and to show him as in every respect the Apostle to the Gentiles."

Now observe the passages quoted above. The key text is I. iii. 16, " Great is the mystery of godliness," which we have before put in other words thus, " the secret of true religion " ;[1] and we saw that the hymn-fragment which follows shows that the secret lies in full acceptance of the historic Christ and His redeeming work.[2] And the use of the word " godliness " in itself indicates that a religion which confines itself to doing one's duty towards our fellow-men is no true religion at all. The first commandment is " Thou shalt love the Lord thy God " ; " Thou shalt love thy neighbour " is the second.

But godliness is not the mere belief in God and acknowledgment of Him. It is practical religion, only with a God-ward devotion. In I. vi. 3 St. Paul makes it the test of true doctrine, contrasting " the doctrine which is according to godliness " with the teaching that leads to envy and strife. The same test is alluded to in Tit. i. 1, " the knowledge of the truth which is according to godliness." There is

---

[1] See p. 63.   [2] See p. 65.

such a thing as having " a form of godliness " without " the power thereof " (II. iii. 5) ; taken up, in fact, with ulterior motives, " supposing that godliness is a way of gain." We have looked at that passage before, and at the passage (I. iv. 8) which shows the real sense in which godliness is a profitable investment.[1] Also at the exhortations to " follow after godliness," and to " exercise oneself unto godliness " ;[2] but perhaps these exhortations may be the more impressive now that we have examined the word itself.

II. RIGHTEOUSNESS.—This also is emphatically one of St. Paul's words, *dikaiosunē*. He uses it 60 times, against 30 times in all the rest of the N.T. And the connected words, *dikaios*, " righteous," and others, he uses 54 times ; 114 in all. Their occurrences in the Pastorals are as follows :—

I.	i.	9.	Law is not made for a righteous man.
	iii.	16.	Justified in the spirit.
	vi.	11.	Follow after righteousness. . . .
II.	ii.	22.	Follow after righteousness. . . .
	iii.	16.	Scripture . . . profitable . . . for instruction which is righteousness.
	iv.	8.	There is laid up for me the crown of righteousness.
		8.	Which the Lord, the righteous Judge, shall give me.
Tit.	i.	7, 8.	The bishop must be . . . just.
	ii.	12.	We should live soberly and righteously and godly.
	iii.	5.	Not by works done in righteousness.
		7.	Being justified by His grace.

I have included in this list the two occurrences of the verb *dikaioō*, " justify," in order to be com-

---

[1] See p. 29.   [2] See p. 57.

plete. But " justify," as explained before,[1] means not " make righteous " but " reckon (or declare) righteous." And at present we have to do with actual personal righteousness. Why, in Tit. i. 8, *dikaios* is rendered " just " rather than " righteous," it is hard to say, for the word comes in between " sober-minded " and " holy," and completes the three-fold character.

Righteousness is the fulfilment of the Second Table of the Law, as godliness may be taken as the fulfilment of the First. It represents our duty to our neighbour. In our ears the word has a lofty tone about it, by which I do not mean a vaunting tone, but one indicative of a loyal living up to a high standard. The righteous man will do *right*, even if it be to his own hindrance. And, as Tennyson says,

> Because Right is right, to follow Right
> Were wisdom—in the scorn of consequence !

And Lowell—

> They are slaves, who dare not be
> In the right with two or three !

And he will rejoice to observe the Golden Rule ; to act towards other men just as he would like them to act towards him. Suppose we all acted so in political or ecclesiastical controversy, for instance ! We should seem to have arrived at the millennium ! But righteousness is really twice put first among those things which St. Paul calls upon Timothy to " follow," to pursue ; yes, to *pursue* with the full resolve to catch it up ! " Follow after righteousness " : it stands *first* in both the places where " Follow "

---

[1] See p. 139.

comes just after " Flee " (I. vi. 11, II. ii. 22). And what at the end of the race ? What is the goal ? " The crown of righteousness " which the " Righteous Judge " will give (II. iv. 8). The " crown," *stephanos*, for the Grecian athlete was a simple wreath, but it meant achievement, victory, honour and glory. But spiritually, what is it ? what does it stand for ? Is the " crown of righteousness " something extraneous, given as a reward for righteousness ? Not if the phrase is parallel with the " crown of life " (Jas. i. 12, Rev. ii. 10) and " crown of glory " (1 Pet. v. 4). In those phrases the " crown " *is* " life " and " glory." Is not then the " crown " here " righteousness " itself, followed, pursued, gained at last ? And what more glorious crown could there be ?

III. SOBERNESS.—We now come to a remarkable group of six words, four of which appear in the N.T. only in our Epistles. There are (1) *sōphrōn*, an adjective which is a compound of two words signifying " sound mind," and which is rendered by the R.V. " sober-minded," the A.V. having " sober," and in one place " discreet " (I. iii. 2, Tit. i. 8, ii. 2, 5). (2) The adverb *sōphronōs*, " soberly " (Tit. ii. 12). (3) The noun *sōphronismos*, " sound mind " in A.V., " discipline " in R.V. (II. i. 7). (4) The verb *sōphronizo*, " teach to be sober " in A.V., " train " in R.V. (Tit. ii. 4).[1] (5) The noun *sōphrosunē*, " so-

---

[1] The literal rendering of this passage would be " make sober-minded the young women . . . to be . . . sober-minded." The A.V. has " teach the young women to be sober . . . to be discreet." The R.V. renders the verb simply " train," to avoid the repetition, and has " train the young women . . . to be sober-minded."

briety " (I. ii. 9, 15) ; also in Acts xxvi. 25, " soberness."   (6) The verb *sōphroneō*, " be sober-minded "
(Tit. ii. 6) ; also " think soberly " (Rom. xii. 3), " be
of sober mind " (2 Cor. v. 13 ; A.V. " be sober "),
" be of sound mind " (1 Pet. iv. 7 ; A.V. " be sober "),[1]
" be in right mind " (Mk. v. 15, Lu. viii. 35).

On this group of words Bishop Bernard has a very
interesting note, in which he refers to the Platonic
philosophy, which reckoned *sōphrosunē* one of the
four cardinal virtues, the others being prudence,
justice, and courage. The Greeks generally used
the word to express self-restraint, and in Aristotle
it signifies mastery over bodily passions. " But,"
observes Dr. Plummer, " when this virtue becomes
illuminated by the Gospel, its meaning is intensified."
In the N.T. it stands rather for sobriety *of mind*.
The cognate verb is used (as indicated above) of the
Gergesene demoniac when he was " in his right mind."
Twice does St. Paul use it of himself. When Festus
declares that " much learning " has made him
" mad," he replies, " I am not mad . . . but speak
forth the words of truth and soberness " ; and to
certain at Corinth who hinted the same thing he
replies, " Whether we are beside ourselves, it is unto
God ; or whether we are of sober mind, it is unto
you." Other references given above are equally
interesting.

There are no English words that exactly translate

___

[1] The A.V. here is " Be ye sober and watch unto prayer " ;
the R.V., " Be ye of sound mind, and be sober unto prayer."
The first verb is σωφρονέω, and the second νήφω. The latter
word also occurs in our Epistles, in II. iv. 5, " Be thou sober,"
A.V. " watch thou " ; and its cognate adjective is " temperate " in I. iii. 2, 11, Tit. ii. 2.

this group of Greek words. Nor are there in Latin. Trench (*Synonyms*) tells us that Cicero had sometimes to use *temperantia*, sometimes *moderatio*, and sometimes *modestia*. Several commentators adopt " self-restraint," but Alford, while accepting this, considers that it is too indicative of effort ; and he adds, " A better word would be a valuable discovery." Ellicott, in adopting " sober-mindedness," describes it as " the well-balanced state of mind arising from habitual self-restraint."

If we take godliness as our duty towards God, and righteousness as our duty towards our neighbour, what is the point of " soberness," of *sōphrosunē* ? Is it not our duty to our own souls and bodies ? In one aspect, yes ; but surely it is more than that. Is it not the inner principle which issues in both godliness and righteousness ? Think of some of the Commandments, say the third, the seventh, the tenth : is not the sound and sober mind just that which will inspire the whole-hearted fulfilment of them ?

Well may we all fervently join in the concluding words of our General Confession, " That we may hereafter live a godly, righteous, and sober life " !

42

ETHICAL TEACHING: LOVE AND PURITY

PURSUING our study of the ethical teaching of the Pastoral Epistles, we pass on from " godliness," " righteousness," and " soberness," to some of those virtues and qualities which we are wont to call " graces." In my Talk on " Grace " I rather deprecated this use of the word ;[1] but I must use it for convenience nevertheless. We find in our Epistles the following additional " graces " enjoined : faith, hope, love, goodness, loyalty, obedience, purity, gravity, shamefastness, contentment, tranquillity, peacefulness, gentleness, meekness, submissiveness, patience, long-suffering, temperance, fairness, liberality, perseverance, zeal, diligence, readiness, courage, faithfulness. Several of these have already come under our notice in various connections, but others have still to be studied.

Let us begin with that which St. Paul, at the opening of the First Epistle (i. 5), declares to be " the end of the charge," the aim and object of all his exhortations to practical goodness—Love. " Love," he had written to the Romans (xiii. 10), " is the fulfilling of the law " ; and so here he goes on to say (verse 9), " Law is not made for a righteous man, but for the lawless," etc. Dr. Goudge well observes that in dealing with Christians St. Paul never appeals to the law : " They are to be pure, not because the 7th commandment forbids impurity, but because their bodies are the members of Christ (1 Cor. vi. 15, 19) . . . ; they are not to lie one to another, because they

---

[1] See p. 128.

are members one of another (Eph. iv. 25) ; they are
to forgive because God in Christ has forgiven them
(Eph. iv. 32)."[1]   The real power for good is what the
great Scottish preacher Chalmers so happily called
" the expulsive power of a new affection."   And so
our Lord's two great commandments were " Thou
shalt love the Lord thy God," " and thy neighbour as
thyself."

The Greek word for " love," *agapē*, is called by
Trench " a word born within the bosom of revealed
religion."   It occurs in the Septuagint Version, but,
adds Trench, " there is no example of its use in any
heathen writer whatsoever."[2]   It is true that, since
he wrote, it has been found in the domestic letters
dug up from the sands of Egypt, but the instances
given by Deissmann belong to the second century A.D.,
so it does not yet appear that Trench was wrong.
The classical Greek word for love was *erōs*, but this
had a sensual note (our " erotic " is from it), and it
is nowhere used in the N.T.   *Agapē* is translated
both " love " and " charity " in the A.V., but in the
R.V. always " love."   The change in I Cor. xiii. is
familiar to us all.   *Agapē* occurs 115 times in the
N.T., 72 of which are in St. Paul's Epistles, and 30
in St. John's writings.   The following are the occurrences in our Epistles :—

I.	i.	5.	The end of the charge is love.
		14.	Love, which is in Christ Jesus.
	ii.	15.	Faith and love and sanctification.
	iv.	12.	Be thou an example . . . in love.
	vi.	11.	Follow after . . . love.

---

[1] *Pastoral Teaching of St. Paul*, p. 33.
[2] *Synonyms of the N.T.*, § 12.

<pre>
II.   i.   7.   God gave us . . . a spirit . . . of love.
          13.   Faith and love which is in Christ Jesus.
     ii.   22.   Follow after . . . love.
    iii.   10.   Thou didst follow my teaching . . . love.
Tit. ii.   2.   That aged men be . . . sound in . . .
                  love.
</pre>

There are two Greek words for the verb " to love," *agapān* and *philein*; but the latter has no cognate noun quite corresponding with *agapē*, though *philia*, " friendship," occurs once in Jas. iv. 4, and there are *philos*, a friend or lover, which is often used, and *philē*, a female friend, in Lu. xv. 9. The numerous and interesting compounds of *philein* we have looked at before.[1] *Philein* itself occurs 25 times in the N.T.,[2] and *agapān* 136 times. Our Epistles have the former once, in Tit. iii. 15 ; and the latter twice, in II. iv. 8, 10, used of those who " love His appearing," and of Demas, who " loved this present world." *Agapētos*, " beloved," occurs 60 times in the N.T., and twice in our Epistles (I. vi. 2, II. i. 2). The two verbs correspond to two in Latin, *agapān* to *diligere*, and *philein* to *amare*. The former is the love of esteem ; the latter the love of affection. Trench mentions that Cicero said of a friend, " He is not only esteemed by me (*diligi*), but loved (*amari*)." Yet in a sense *agapān* is the higher, implying worthiness of being loved, while *philein* is more concerned with the feelings. Men are commanded to love God, *agapān*, never *philein*; though the latter is once used of loving Christ (1 Cor. xvi. 22), and *philotheoi* is " lovers of God " in II. iii. 4, as we have before

---

[1] See p. 237.
[2] But in three of these cases it is Judas " kissing " our Lord.

seen. The love of God for men is almost always *agapān*, but once *philein* (John xvi. 27) ; and both words are used for our Lord's personal love of Lazarus and St. John.

" The *end* of the charge is love " ; but what is the " charge " itself ? In Timothy's case it was to prevent the " heterodox teachers " from spreading their heterodoxy. So we see, as we have seen before, that the aim in Christian controversy is not to be orthodoxy merely, but love. The controversialist who not only propounded " sound views," but actually converted his opponents to them, would be thought by most of us to be extraordinarily successful ; yet according to St. Paul, if he had not also produced *love*, he would be a failure ! What a lesson for us all !

Then, what produces love ? St. Paul mentions a three-fold source : " out of a pure heart and a good conscience and faith unfeigned." Liddon's analysis will help us to see what is meant[1] :—

Love must issue
- (*a*) from a pure heart, which alone is capable of true love ;
- (*b*) from a good conscience, which interposes no secret barrier between love and its object ;
- (*c*) from a faith which is what it professes to be, and so gazes really on the object of love.

Taking the last of the three first, " faith unfeigned," faith has been under our scrutiny more than once before ; but the word " unfeigned " should be noticed. It is *anupokritos*, which is " hypocritical " with the Greek negative *a* (or *an*) before it. We find

------

[1] *Expl. Anal.* 1st *Tim.,* p. 4.

the word also used where the " unfeigned faith "
of Timothy himself and his mother and grandmother
is mentioned (II. i. 5) ; where " love unfeigned " is
spoken of (2 Cor. vi. 6, 1 Pet. i. 22) ; where St. Paul
exhorts to " love without hypocrisy " (Rom. xii. 9 ;
A.V. dissimulation) ; and where St. James describes
" wisdom from above " as " first pure " and " without hypocrisy."

The " pure heart " and " good conscience " we
may take together. Conscience, *suneidēsis*, is emphatically a Pauline word.   Out of 32 occurrences of
it in the N.T., 21 are in St. Paul's Epistles, and two
in his speeches (Acts xxiii. 1, xxiv. 16). In the
Pastorals we have " a good conscience " twice (I. i. 5,
19), and " a pure conscience " twice (I. iii. 9, II. i. 3) ;
while the conscience of the heterodox teachers is
described as " defiled " (Tit. i. 15), and " branded
as with a hot iron " (I. iv. 2). Now the " pure " or
" good conscience " indicates a conscience that does
not reproach us, a " conscience void of offence "
such as St. Paul told Felix he " exercised himself "
to have " alway," a conscience which (in Liddon's
words quoted above) " interposes no secret barrier
between love and its object."   But the " pure heart "
suggests more than this, more than a mere negative,
and seems to describe the transparent singleness of
the affections, not only without intermixture of
anything doubtful, but as what we often mean by
" whole-hearted." We have the phrase " pure
heart " twice in our Epistles, here and in II. ii. 22,
and elsewhere in the N.T. only in our Lord's great
beatitude, " Blessed are the pure in heart, for they
shall see God " ; but we have " pure religion " in

Jas. i. 27. In the Psalms we find the " pure heart " twice mentioned (xxiv. 4, lxxiii. 1).

The Greek word for " pure " in the N.T. passages just quoted is *katharos,* and also in the much misused maxim in Tit. i. 15, " To the pure all things are pure," which we have looked at before.[1] There is another word, *agnos,* in I. v. 22 and Tit. ii. 5, which sometimes means more definitely " chaste," and is connected with *agneia,* " purity," the word used in I. iv. 12, v. 2. *Agneia* occurs nowhere else in the N.T., neither, by the way, does our word " purity " in the English Versions. One of the occurrences of *agneia* significantly illustrates our present subject. In the first two verses of I. v. Timothy is instructed as to his behaviour towards both sexes and different ages : " Rebuke not an elder, but exhort him as a father ; the younger men as brethren [better, as brothers] ; the elder women as mothers, the younger as sisters, in all purity " (*agneia*). Is there anything in all the Bible more perfect than this counsel ? The meaning is, Treat them all as if you were in your own home. What can be more delightful than the purity, the unselfishness, the love, of a well-ordered Christian home ? With regard to the younger women, Dr. Goudge, whose comments on the passage [2] are admirable, writes, " How do we deal with our sisters ? Quite differently from the way in which we deal with other girls. Plenty of chivalry and consideration, but no nonsense of any kind. It is not that we bar it out ; it is simply that it never enters in." That is *agneia.*

---

[1] See p. 233.
[2] *Pastoral Teaching of St. Paul,* pp. 120–128.

So we see St. Paul's meaning. No true love apart from a pure heart, a clear conscience, a faith that is genuine and without alloy. But where these are combined, love is awakened naturally; love that is free from the intrusion of self, of mixed motives, of hypocrisy; love that is single-eyed, sincere, transparent, in which the closest inspection may find no flaw; love that is like the love of God; the *agapē* to which Trench's expression above quoted may be justly applied, "born within the bosom of revealed religion." That is "the end of the charge." Where else can we find any Ethics like it?

43
PASSIVE GRACES

WE continue our study of the Christian virtues and graces inculcated in our Epistles, taking first some of what we are wont to call a passive character.

One of the most important of these, *sophrosunē*, "sober-mindedness," we have already examined.[1] With it might well be coupled *semnotēs*, which the R.V. renders "gravity," as also does the A.V. except in one place where it has "honesty"—that is, in the old sense of honourableness. The cognate adjective, *semnos*, is in these Epistles rendered "grave" in both versions. The noun occurs only in the Pastorals;

---

[1] See p. 266.

the adjective in one other place, Phil. iv. 8, where
the A.V. translates " whatsoever things are honest,"
the R.V. having " honourable," and the R.V. margin
" reverend."   Here are the passages in our Epistles :—

I. ii.   2.   That we may lead a tranquil and quiet life
             in all godliness and gravity (A.V.
             honesty).
   iii.   4.   Having his children in subjection with all
             gravity.
         8.   Deacons in like manner must be grave.
        11.   Women in like manner must be grave.
Tit. ii.   2.   That aged men be . . . grave.
         7.   In thy doctrine shewing . . . gravity.

In five of these passages " gravity " is enjoined on
particular classes, but the first one applies the need
of it to us all.   As in the case of " sober-mindedness,"
our word " gravity " is an inadequate rendering of
the Greek.   Bishop Bernard explains the word as
" an intense conviction of the seriousness of life,"
and he cites from Liddon's *Life of Pusey* that the
great Tractarian's " penitential rule " included daily
prayer for *semnotēs*.   Liddon himself calls it " seriousness of deportment."   Bishop A. Hervey describes
it as " the respectable, venerable, and dignified
sobriety of a truly godly man."   Dr. Horton says,
" The German *Würde* is better than the English
gravity.   It is not the solemnity of an official that
is meant, but the sweet dignity of a child of God."
Dean Spence-Jones suggests " decorum, propriety
of demeanour, reverence," and quotes the Latin
maxim about the treatment of children, *Maxima
debetur pueris reverentia*.   Dr. Goudge cites Matthew
Arnold's   rendering,   " noble   seriousness."   Shall
we not all, like Pusey, pray for *semnotēs* ?

In the first of the six passages quoted above occur the two words " tranquil " and " quiet," *ēremos* and *hēsukios*, which the A.V. renders " quiet and peaceable." The former word occurs nowhere else in the N.T. ; the latter is in 1 Pet. iii. 4, the " meek and *quiet* spirit." The noun *hēsukia* is the " quietness " enjoined on women in I. ii. 11, 12 (A.V. silence), and upon men also in 2 Thess. iii. 12 ; and it is illustrated by the effect on the Jewish mob of St. Paul addressing them in Hebrew (Acts xxii. 2) : " they were the more quiet " (A.V., kept the more silence). It is the quality which, for instance, enables a man to " hold his peace " under provocation, as our Lord Himself " held His peace " before Caiaphas. That phrase is a very common one in Scripture ; and in two cases in the N.T. the Greek is the cognate verb *hēsuchazō*, one of them being where the Jewish Christians who complained of Peter visiting and baptizing Cornelius were convinced by his explanation, and had the grace to " hold their peace " so far as grumbling went, and to " glorify God " (Acts xi. 18)—a really bright example for imitation, and not at all an easy one !

With this " quiet " spirit we may naturally connect " meekness," *praotēs*, which is enjoined once in each of our three Epistles :—

I. vi. 11. Follow after . . . meekness.
II. ii. 25. In meekness instructing them that oppose themselves.
Tit. iii. 2. Showing all meekness unto all men.

This is a grace frequently urged upon Christians in the N.T., see Gal. v. 23, vi. 1, Eph. iv. 2, Col. iii. 12,

Jas. i. 21, iii. 13, 1 Pet. iii. 4, 15 ; perhaps because it is so unwelcome to our natural tendencies. Our Lord Himself gives one of His beatitudes to the meek, and very striking is its form. A meek man is one who "seeketh not his own," who does not even "stand up" for what really are his "rights"; and yet Christ says "they shall inherit the earth." Moreover, He set us an example in His own person—"I am meek and lowly in heart."

Allied to meekness, but with a larger range and far from being a merely passive virtue, is that remarkable quality called in Greek *epieikeia*. When St. Paul entreats the Corinthians "by the meekness and gentleness of Christ" (2 Cor. x. 1), "gentleness" is this word. In the oration of Tertullus before Felix it is "clemency" (Acts xxiv. 4). These are its only occurrences in the N.T. But the cognate adjective *epieikēs* is found twice in our Epistles, in I. iii. 3 and Tit. iii. 2, where it is rendered "gentle" (A.V. patient and gentle), as also in Jas. iii. 17 and 1 Pet. ii. 18 ; while in Phil. iv. 5 it is (used substantively) "moderation" in the A.V. and "forbearance" in the R.V. Trench and Bishop Bernard refer to the chapter in Aristotle's Ethics in which it is discussed, and where the word is used of "the equitable man who does not press for the last farthing of his rights." But does it not go further than that, and include the spontaneous and unsought consideration of other people's rights ? Bishop Moule (on Phil. iv. 5) suggests "yieldingness," which might be *too* yielding ; but he also says, "It means, in effect, considerateness, the attitude of thought and will which in remembrance of others forgets self." I have always thought "considerateness" the best English equivalent ; but Matthew Arnold's "sweet reasonableness" happily hits it off.

"Gentle," in II. ii. 24, is a different word, *ēpios*, not found again in the N.T. Bishop Bernard says "it seems to have special reference to that kindliness of outward demeanour, so important in one who was, as bishop, the *persona ecclesiæ*, the representative of the Church to the world."

Then we have "long-suffering," *makrothumia*. Here also we have our Lord's example, not indeed in His human character, but in His divine dealing with St. Paul : "I obtained mercy that in me as chief might Jesus Christ shew forth all His long-suffering." No wonder the Apostle pleads that such a pattern should be followed by those who have to "reprove, rebuke, exhort" (II. iv. 2) ; and he cites his own example too, while acknowledging that Timothy had imitated it : "thou didst follow my . . . long-suffering, love, patience," etc. (II. iii. 10). It is truly a God-like quality, revealed in both the O.T. (Exod. xxxiv. 6, Num. xiv. 18, Ps. lxxxvi. 15), and in the New (Rom. ii. 4, ix. 22, 1 Pet. iii. 20, 2 Pet. iii. 9, 15) ; and in the great poem of Love, 1 Cor. xiii., St. Paul puts it first among the characteristics of *agapē* : "Love suffereth long, and is kind," etc. But an English Concordance will not give us all the references to long-suffering ; for in some places the A.V. translates *makrothumia* "patience," and the R.V. (quite rightly) has not altered it. Thus in the familiar words of Heb. vi. 12, "who through faith and patience inherit the promises" ; and in Jas. v. 7, 8, where the husbandman's "patience" is set forth as a pattern for us. "Long-suffering," meaning *bearing with* some person or thing, would not do in these cases. But in 1 Thess. v. 14, "Support the weak, be patient toward all" (A.V.), the R.V. rightly substitutes "be long-suffering towards all."

But the regular word for "patience" is an especially interesting one, *hupomonē*. It means not merely a passive patience, but rather endurance and perseverance. It occurs thirty-one times in the N.T., and is always rendered "patience" in the R.V., except in 2 Cor. i. 6, where "patient enduring" is substituted for the "enduring" of the A.V. The R.V. also alters the A.V. of Rom. ii. 7, "patient continuance," and of 2 Thess. iii. 5, "patient waiting," to the simple "patience." The cognate verb *hupomenō* is usually rendered "endure," but it is the "take patiently" of 1 Pet. ii. 20. The two words occur in our Epistles as follows :—

I.	vi.	11.	Follow after . . . faith, love, patience . . .
II.	ii.	10.	I endure all for the elect's sake.
		12.	If we endure, we shall also reign with Him.
	iii.	10.	Thou didst follow my . . . faith, . . . love, patience . . .
Tit.	ii.	2.	That aged men be . . . sound in faith, in love, in patience.

It will be noticed that faith, love, patience, stand close together in the three texts, and so they do in that striking verse, 1 Thess. i. 3, "your work of faith and labour of love and patience of hope"; while in the catalogue of virtues in 2 Pet. i. 5–7, *pistis* stands at the beginning, *hupomonē* in the middle, and *agapē* at the end. Bishop Bernard cites Ignatius as calling *pistis* the Christian's helmet, *agapē* his spear, and *hupomonē* his armour. The difference between *makrothumia* and *hupomonē* is well illustrated in St. James's Epistle. While, as we saw just now, he gives the husbandman's quiet passive patience the former word, he gives Job's enduring patience the latter ; and *hupomonē* also is the patience that is to " have its perfect work " (i. 3, 4). And while the first thing said of love in I Cor. xiii. is that it " suffereth long," the last item in the same list is " endureth all things," the verb *hupomenō*. Trench's *Synonyms* is very interesting on *hupomonē*. He cites Chrysostom as calling it " the king of virtues." Ellicott, on I Thess. i. 3, speaks of " this noble word," and notes that in the N.T. there is always in it " a background of *andreia* " (manly courage). Dr. Plummer (on 2nd Corinthians) says it is " endurance without rebellion or reproach." In our next Talk we shall look at the more active virtues, and *hupomonē* may well mark the transition from passive to active.

Meanwhile, how significant is the stress laid on these softer graces, gravity, tranquillity, quietness, meekness, forbearance, gentleness, long-suffering, patience ! Especially significant for us English folk ! We naturally think much more of courage, fortitude, vigour, and the like. We call them " manly " qualities. Our missionaries in India tell us that the Hindus, with whom the more passive virtues count for most, are puzzled by the contrast between the precepts of the N.T. and the character of the average Englishman, who is seldom distinguished for gentleness, and indeed would actually resent being called " a meek man " ! Yet St. Paul, a true " man " if ever there was one, was a pattern of most of these passive

qualities ; and what shall we say of " the man Moses " ?
—who was " very meek, above all the men which were
upon the face of the earth " (Num. xii. 3).

Finally, notice the word " all " applied to the
various graces. We find " all godliness," " all
gravity," " all purity," " all meekness," " all long-
suffering," " all good fidelity," " all good works."
Could anything be more significant ?

44

ACTIVE GRACES

UNLIKE the passive virtues, the active ones are
scarcely named in the Pastoral Epistles. But
they are indicated by a series of vivid illustrations.
We have the soldier, the athlete, the husbandman, the
artisan ; and in his brief references to them St. Paul
gives significant hints of the importance of what we
call manly qualities in the Christian life.

We finished our review of the more passive graces
with *hupomonē*, " patience " ; and we perceived
that the brave endurance implied in the word gave it
a note of manliness which made it the right tran-
sition-word between the groups. Certainly the soldier,
the athlete, the husbandman, the artizan, all need
hupomenē, and for the most part are good examples
of it.

(1) We take the sketch of the soldier first. These
are the words, in II. ii. 3, 4 : " Suffer hardship with

me, as a good soldier of Jesus Christ. No soldier on service entangleth himself in the affairs of this life ; that he may please him who enrolled him as a soldier." "A good soldier," *kalos*, that significant word again, indicating something more than ordinary " good character," a life that men can see and admire, the life of a soldier *sans peur et sans reproche*, as Bishop Bernard happily expresses it. And it is a "soldier on service" (A.V. " man that warreth ") that St. Paul is thinking of ; not one marching in a royal procession amid the plaudits of the crowd, but in the fighting line, in the labours and privations of a campaign. The same thought is expressed in I. i. 18, " war the good warfare." " Good " is again *kalos* there ; " war " is the verb *strateuomai*, and " warfare " is *strateia*, which means a campaign. " Soldier," in the passage before us, is *stratiotēs* ; " soldier on service " is *strateuomenos* ; and " enrolled him as a soldier " is the verb *stratologeō*. " No soldier on service," says St. Paul, " entangleth himself in the affairs of this life." Not that he is to shirk other duties ; but he is not to be " entangled." And then, " that he may please him who enrolled him " ; he looks for his general's smile, and strives to be worthy of it. So will the " good soldier of Jesus Christ " seek to walk worthy of his high calling and to please the Captain of his salvation.

So also will the Christian be content to " suffer hardship " in his Captain's service, as the " soldier on service " willingly bears the hardship of the bivouac, the hardship of rough fare, the hardship of cruel wounds. The Christian life is not to be one of ease and comfort. St. Paul's illustration points to hard and painful experiences. Dr. Plummer[1] quotes a striking passage from Tertullian's address to martyrs, expressing "with characteristic incisiveness the stern parallel between the severity of the soldier's life and that of the Christian." That phrase "suffer hardship" occurs three times in this Second Epistle. In i. 8 Timothy is exhorted to "suffer hardship with the Gospel"; in ii. 3 to "suffer hardship with *me,*" with St. Paul; in iv. 5, simply "suffer hardship." The A.V. renders the same Greek differently every time; but these R.V. renderings are faulty in one respect. In ii. 3 there is no "me" in the Greek, and the "with" is included in the verb, *sun-kakopathēson,* "suffer hardship *with,*" *sun* being "with"; so it would be better translated "Take thy share of hardship," without any "me." So also in i. 8, and instead of "with the Gospel" read "for the Gospel's sake." This is the view of Bishop Bernard and Dr. Newport White. Bishop Moule gives the same rendering, though he thinks the "suffering Gospel" may be understood in i. 8, and the "suffering Apostle" in ii. 3; and he enlarges beautifully on both the duty and the comfort of *sharing* hardships with fellow-workers.[2]

(2) From the example of the soldier St. Paul turns to that of the athlete. Verse 5, "And if also a man contend in the games, he is not crowned except he have contended lawfully." "Contend in the games" is one word in the Greek, the verb *athleō,* which again appears in "have contended." We see at once whence our "athlete" and "athletic" come; and if we could make a verb of them, we might translate

---

1 *Pastoral Epistles,* p. 346.   2 *Second Timothy,* p. 72.

the verse, " A man who *athletes* is not crowned except he have *athleted* lawfully." The A.V. has " strive for masteries " and " strive." *Athleō* does not occur again in the N.T. ; but the same figure appears in other language. " Fight the good fight of faith," in I. vi. 12, and " I have fought the good fight," in II. iv. 7, refer, not to the soldier, but to the athlete ; and we must remember that the sports of the arena were not only races, etc., but also wrestling, boxing, and sometimes gladiatorial fights ; so the word " fight " is quite legitimate. The Greek words are the noun *agōn* and the verb *agōnizomai*, so the phrase is literally " agonize the good agony," the English words being the Greek ones anglicised. Or we might say " strive the good strife," or " con*test* the good con-test." Bishop Bernard quotes a line from the *Alcestis* of Euripides which is almost verbatim identical. *Agōn* is " conflict " in Phil. i. 30 and I Thess. ii. 2, and " race " in Heb. xii. 1. The verb is " strive in the games " in I Cor. ix. 25, and simply " strive " in Lu. xiii. 24 and Col. i. 29, iv. 12. The idea of intense and one may say agonising struggle is always in them ; but it is remarkable that the " agony " of our Lord in Gethsemane is a slightly different word, *agōnia*, which occurs nowhere else.

But St. Paul has a particular point to urge in his use of this figure here. The athlete, he says, does not win the prize " except he have contended law-fully." There were strict rules in all the games, and the winner was disqualified if he disregarded them. What does that stand for spiritually ? Dr. Plummer replies, " No cross, no crown " ; and Bishop Moule says the Christian athlete must have " trained " in earnest, " keeping under his body," " enduring hardness for the Lord."

In I. iv. 7, 8, St. Paul likens the Christian worker to a gymnast, which is much the same thing ; but this figure we examined in a previous Talk.[1] But what a picture these similitudes taken together present to us : the valiant soldier, the successful athlete, the alert gymnast, all enduring hardness in their respective callings—in them we see the likeness of the Christian who wins his Captain's smile !

(3) Then there is the husbandman, in verse 6. We noticed his " patience " under the more passive virtues ; but that is not the point here. " The husbandman that laboureth must be the first to partake of the fruits." The emphatic word is " laboureth," *kopiōnta*, which means strenuous and persistent toil. The man who throws energy into his work is to receive his share of the produce—shall we say his " living wage " ?—*first*, before his lazy fellow-worker. Bishop Moule sums up the two sides of agriculturist character thus :—" The strenuous and prosaic toil of the tiller, his patience under uncertain seasons, his quiet waiting through pains for gains, this all is to enter deep into the life of the Lord's servant : ploughing, sowing, tending, and then reaping at last."

We may note in passing that St. Paul has the same three illustrations in 1 Cor. ix., a chapter to be read alongside this one. We see the soldier in verse 7, the husbandman in verses 7 and 10, the athlete in verses 24–27. But reverting to the passage before us, observe

---

[1] See p. 246.

how St. Paul adds to his illustrations living examples, verses. 7–10. First, " Remember Jesus Christ "—was He not the true pattern of the soldier, the athlete, the husbandman ? He won His battle, He gained His prize ; He gathered, and is still gathering, His fruit ! And secondly, St. Paul adds his own example. He, too, " suffers hardship," " unto bonds " (*i.e.* chained), " as a malefactor," a *kakourgos*, the word used of the two robbers crucified with our Lord, and which Professor Ramsay suggests may have been the very word adopted in the official indictment of St. Paul. He " endures all things for the elect's sake " ; but why should he mind ? he is not really defeated ; for " the word of God is not bound " ! And then follows that touching " Faithful Saying " which we have examined before.[1]

(4) This passage is immediately followed by a fourth illustration of Christian qualities—the workman or artisan. Verse 15, " Give diligence to present thyself approved unto God, a workman that needeth not to be ashamed, handling aright the word of truth." The A.V. " rightly dividing " is a familiar phrase to us. Commentators differ as to the exact meaning of the Greek verb *orthotomein* ; but we may take the phrase " handling aright " as covering several possible interpretations. The phrase " needeth not to be ashamed " seems plain enough, but Bishop Bernard follows Chrysostom in reading " who is not to be put to shame," that is, by the badness of the work.

But the phrase I would dwell upon is " give diligence." The A.V. has " study to shew thyself,"

---

[1] See p. 61.

but the Greek word, *spoudason*, is the same as is used three times to hasten Titus and Timothy to come to St. Paul (Titus iii. 12, II. iv. 9, 21) ; and a cognate word indicates the " diligence " with which Onesiphorus sought and found the Apostle at Rome (II. i. 17) and with which Titus is instructed to " set forward " Zenas and Apollos on their journey (Tit. iii. 13). This group of words is represented by several English expressions in the N.T., indicating zeal, earnestness, endeavour, labour, haste ; and " diligence " is the best equivalent. It is Mary's " haste " to go to Elisabeth ; and Salome's " haste " to get John the Baptist's head. It is the " earnestness " and " earnest care " of the Corinthian Church in 2 Cor. vii. and viii. It is the " business " in the A.V. of Rom. xii. 11, where the R.V. alters " not slothful in business " to " in diligence not slothful." Perhaps the most vivid rendering is in the A.V. of Lu. vii. 4, where the centurion's Jewish friends beseech Jesus " instantly," which suggests both that they lost no time in hastening to our Lord, and that they appealed to Him " earnestly " (as the R.V. has it). But it also suggests care and thought. It does not mean reckless haste. When Onesiphorus was searching for the imprisoned Apostle,[1] we may be sure that he lost no time about it ; but he did not rush and tear about with frantic inquiries. He gave his mind to it, and used tact.

Here we may refer in passing to II. iv. 2, where the same vivid English word " instant " is used, though the Greek is different : " Be instant in season, out of season " ; and this verse inculcates the same

---

[1] See p. 315.

duty of diligent and watchful and ready zeal. It is
by such diligence that the Christian worker, like the
workman of our passage, " presents himself approved
unto God."

45

CHRISTIAN SERVANTS

STILL further examining the ethical teaching of
our Epistles, we find in two places counsels to
" servants," that is, bond-servants or slaves, who
formed a large part of the early Church :—

> I. vi. 1, 2. Let as many as are servants under the
> yoke count their own masters worthy of
> all honour, that the name of God and the
> doctrine be not blasphemed. And they
> that have believing masters, let them
> not despise them because they are
> brethren ; but let them serve them the
> rather, because they that partake of the
> benefit are believing and beloved.
>
> Tit. ii. 9, 10. Exhort servants to be in subjection to
> their own masters, and to be well-
> pleasing to them in all things ; not gain-
> saying ; not purloining, but shewing all
> good fidelity ; that they may adorn the
> doctrine of God our Saviour in all things.

We have come in the course of centuries to regard
slavery as one of the greatest crimes and greatest
curses that have afflicted mankind. But it was not
always so. From Queen Elizabeth's time, for nearly

250 years, England was the leading slave-trading country, and Negro slaves were publicly sold in London as late as 1772. It was the Evangelical Revival that at last awoke the national conscience ; and the names of Clarkson and Wilberforce and Buxton, once despised and detested, are now universally honoured ; Lincoln also, for abolishing, still more recently, slavery in America ; and Livingstone, for arousing Britain to care for Africa. Now slavery was one of the great institutions of the Roman Empire, and its brutal and brutalising character is revealed in classical literature. Dr. Plummer, whose chapters on the subject (xvi. and xxii.) are among the best in his book on the Pastoral Epistles (to which I have so often referred), shows in detail how disastrous the system was to (*a*) the belief in the dignity of labour, (*b*) the personal character of the master, (*c*) the personal character of the slave, (*d*) family life. He says :—

"It has been estimated that in the Roman world of St. Paul's day the proportion of slaves to free men was in the ratio of two, or even three, to one. It was the immense number of slaves which led to some of the cruel customs and laws respecting them. In the country they often worked, and sometimes slept, in chains. Even in Rome under Augustus the house-porter was sometimes chained. And by a decree of the Senate, if the master was murdered by a slave, all the slaves of the household were put to death. The 400 slaves of Pedanius Secundus were executed under this enactment in A.D. 61, in which year St. Paul was probably in Rome."

How did St. Paul, how did the Christian Church, treat this terrible system ? It was simply accepted as a fact. It was not denounced as unchristian, or as un-moral.

There was no insistence on the " rights of man." St. Paul never called on men to assert their rights. It was duties, not rights, on which Christianity laid stress. The great fundamental principle was affirmed that in Christ all were " one," that all Christians, " whether bond or free," were " baptized into one body " (1 Cor. xii. 13) ; but the application of the principle was left to be worked out in after years, when the Christian spirit was more widely diffused ; and it is a humiliating thought that the after years have meant eighteen centuries. So St. Paul did not tell the slave converts that they might claim their freedom ; nor did he tell the masters to set them free. That would have involved a social revolution which would have filled the civilised world with bloodshed ; and probably, as Sir W. M. Ramsay says, " slavery would now be universal, and there would be no Christianity."[1]

What then did St. Paul do ? He told the masters to remember that they also had a " Master in heaven," and to " render unto their slaves that which was just and equal " ; and he told the slaves to obey their masters, " not with eye-service, as men-pleasers, but in singleness of heart, fearing the Lord " ; " working heartily, as unto the Lord, and not unto man " (Col. iii. 22–25, iv. 1 ; Eph. vi. 5–9 ; cf. 1 Pet. ii. 18–21).

More than one commentator cites Chrysostom as saying, " It is a surprising thing that there should be a good slave " ; and *he* knew what the slavery of those days was. Yet St. Paul contemplates no low level of good conduct for them. Let us now look

---

[1] *Expositor*, Nov. 1909, p. 414.

at the two passages in our Epistles, above quoted.

(1) I. vi. 1, 2. The slaves are to count their masters " worthy of all honour." Does that mean all the masters, whatever their character and treatment ? Let St. Peter answer : " Not only the good and gentle, but also the froward " (1 Pet. ii. 18). And what is the motive for this ? St. Paul uses almost the same words as he does about the younger women : " that the name of God and the doctrine be not blasphemed " —as it would have been had the social revolution ensued, whether as regards the position of women or the position of slaves.

(2) But some slaves would have " believing masters," members of the Christian Church. What was to be their attitude in that case ? " Let them [the slaves] not despise them [the masters] because they are brethren "—possibly even newer and less instructed converts ; " but let them serve them *the rather*," just because they *are* " brethren " ; not presuming on their equality in Christ, but rendering to them *the more* obedience and fidelity, because they were " believing and beloved." The best commentary on this is St. Paul's most touching Epistle to Philemon. We can guess how Philemon received Onesimus, and how Onesimus served Philemon. It was just such a case as St. Paul is thinking of, in saying here that the masters " partake of the benefit " derived from the Christian slave's more conscientious work. Alford cites a striking parallel from the Roman philosopher Seneca, who was contemporary with St. Paul. The question having arisen whether a slave could do his master any " benefit " (having only done his duty), Seneca replied that whatever the

slave might do, not by order, but *ex voluntate*, of his own free will, was *beneficium*, " benefit."

(3) Tit. ii. 9, 10. Slaves were not only to be " in subjection," but well pleasing," *euarestos*. This word, and the cognate verb and adverb, occur eight times in St. Paul's Epistles, and five times in the Epistle to the Hebrews, and it is always rendered, both in A.V. and R.V., either " well-pleasing " or " acceptable." [1] But note particularly that in every case, except the one before us, it is " well-pleasing " or " acceptable " to God ; see Rom. xii. 1, 2, xiv. 18, 2 Cor. v. 9, Eph. v. 10, Phil. iv. 18, Col. iii. 20, Heb. xi. 5, 6, xii. 28, xiii. 16, 21. To the Cretan slaves alone does St. Paul speak of their being " well-pleasing " to men, to their masters. What a dignity is thus given to the life he calls on them to lead !

(4) Then, just as St. Peter appends to his general exhortation to slaves a small hint about taking " buffetings " patiently (1 Pet. ii. 20), so here St. Paul descends to particulars : " not gainsaying," " not purloining." The A.V. " not answering again " is Tindale's graphic rendering of *antilegontas* ; and the Latin Vulgate has *contradicentes*, an exact translation. But our English word " contradict," though also verbally exact, is not quite wide enough, if it refers only to contradiction by word of mouth. The Greek word means more than that, and the R.V. " gainsaying " is better. Tindale has for " not purloining " " neither be pickers," or as we should now say " pilferers." The verb, *nosphizomai*, is used of Ananias and Sapphira " *keeping back* " part of the price of their land.

---

[1] The more common words for " please," " well-pleased," " good pleasure," etc., are different, εὐδοκέω, εὐδοκία.

(5) Then observe the motive St. Paul appeals to.
Not to gain a good character, or to be proud of it ;
but " that they may adorn the doctrine of God our
Saviour in all things." We have become so used
to this phrase that we scarcely see the wonder of it.
Suppose we find another word instead of " adorn," in
order to impart freshness to the expression.   Suppose
we say " decorate," which means the same thing :
" that they may *decorate* the doctrine of God our
Saviour in all things." At once we see what an
astonishing thing we are called upon to do. We look
at the doctrine, the message of redemption, the
Gospel, the Christian religion. We see its beauty,
its splendour, its perfection. And *that*, by our daily
conduct in daily life, we can *decorate* ! We can *add*
to its beauty, its splendour, its perfection ! I say
" we," because the words are constantly used for
Christians generally. But St. Paul here uses it for
slaves—for Cretan slaves—for slaves of that race
branded by their own poet as " always liars, evil
beasts, idle gluttons " ! And yet it was just such
people as these who, being truly converted, really
could " decorate " the Gospel.   Dr. Plummer gives us
Chrysostom's comments on the verse :—

" The passionate man, who found his slave always
gentle and submissive ; the inhuman and ferocious man,
who found his slave always meek and respectful ; the
fraudulent man of business, who noticed that his slave
never pilfered or told lies ; the sensualist, who observed
that his slave was never intemperate and always shocked
at immodesty ;—all these, even if they were not induced
to become converts to the new faith, or even to take
much trouble to understand it, would at least at times
feel something of respect, if not of awe and reverence,

for a creed which produced such results. Where did their slaves learn these lofty principles ? Whence did they derive the power to live up to them ? ''

In point of fact, it was no uncommon thing for families to be converted through the instrumentality of the slaves.   Female slaves won their mistresses, and taught the children of '' God our Saviour '' ; and they furnished a contingent to the noble army of martyrs, as the beautiful story of the slave Blandina of Lyons (A.D. 177) reminds us. Dr. Horton mentions Epictetus, the Stoic philosopher, who was by birth a slave, but '' by power of brain broke his birth's invidious bar.'' But '' it was reserved for the Gospel to teach that in the lowly duties of a slave as such, it was possible to bring lustre to the sublimest truth of revelation, the truth that God is Himself our Saviour.'' [1]

A similar '' decorating '' of Christianity is going on to-day in India. The mass movements of the non-caste or out-caste people are not wholly, perhaps not mainly, spiritual. They see that by becoming Christians they may improve their status. Their case is totally different from that of the Brahmins, who often suffer the loss of all things by embracing Christ. But the fear has been expressed that if the Church became filled with the despised '' untouchables,'' as they are called, the high castes would not join. In reality, the effect is exactly the reverse. The higher castes are astonished at the improvement morally and socially of the people they have so long despised, and are being drawn in consequence to look

---

[1] *Century Bible :* Pastoral Epistles, p. 184.

more favourably on Christianity. The Gospel has been " decorated " !

It would be good for each one of us to ask himself, What am I doing to make the religion of my Lord and Master more beautiful in other men's eyes ?

46
OTHER ETHICAL TEACHINGS

THERE are still a few fragments of the ethical teaching of our Epistles to be gathered up, and we will now take them together.

I. In Tit. ii. we find significant counsels for old men and young men, old women and young women.

(a) Aged men are to be " temperate, grave, sober-minded, sound in faith, in love, in patience." All these words we have examined before, except " temperate," *nēphalios*. This word is peculiar to the Pastoral Epistles, occurring only here and in I. iii. 2, 11 ; but we must not therefore conclude that the only persons exhorted to be temperate are aged men, bishops, and female deacons. The verb *nēphein* is also in II. iv. 5, and in 1 Thess. v. 6, 8, 1 Pet. i. 13, iv. 7, v. 8, and is always rendered " be sober." And in our Epistles, temperance in regard to strong drink is sometimes put in other words, see I. iii. 3, 8, Tit. i. 7, 8, ii. 3. But *nēphalios* does specially refer to wine, etc. ; while *egkratēs* indicates bodily self-control generally, and *sōphrōn* is sober-minded, as we have before seen. The

R.V. is more careful to distinguish them than the A.V.

(*b*) Aged women are to be " reverent in demeanour, not slanderers nor enslaved to much wine, teachers of that which is good, that they may train [1] the young women to be . . ." " Slanderers " is *diaboloi*, " devils," as in I. iii. 11, II. iii. 3. " Enslaved to much wine " is one of the R.V.'s happiest renderings, the word being *dedoulōmenas*, from *doulos*, a slave. " Reverent " scarcely expresses the force of *hieroprepēs*, which literally means " becoming " or " suitable " for what is " sacred," and refers not so much to the woman's reverent feelings as to the influence of her demeanour upon others. Bishop Bernard suggests " reverend," and if this word might be taken as meaning " to be revered," it would do ; but does not its technical use disqualify it ? Dr. Horton suggests " priest-like," the first half of the word being connected with *hiereus*, " priest " ; and he quaintly remarks that this is one of the few places where *hiereus* is used in a Christian sense, " and here it is applied to old women " ! The A.V. has a paraphrase, " in behaviour as becometh holiness," only *hieros* does not mean personally " holy," but rather " for sacred use," as we saw when we were considering the " sacred writings " of II. iii. 15. But although we cannot find an exact English equivalent for the word, we can quite see that it calls upon us all—not " aged women " only—to seek that our behaviour and demeanour shall be *becoming* for those who have the *sacred calling* of being the Lord's servants in the

---

[1] The curious choice of Greek words here has been noticed before (see p. 266), in connexion with " soberness."

world. Perhaps it is especially appropriate to Christian women of advancing age, as giving them influence for the very duty St. Paul here lays upon them, of training the younger women ; in the exercise of which duty the old maxim is emphatically true, that " example is better than precept." " Teachers of that which is good " is one word, found only here, *kalodidaskalos*, compounded of that notable word *kalos* and the ordinary word for teacher. Dean Spence-Jones quotes what he calls the " singular and expressive " rendering of this word in Latin by the French Reformer Beza, *honestatis magistræ*, " mistresses of honour."

(c) The " young women " in verses 4, 5, are assumed to be married ; and the older women are to train them " to love their husbands, to love their children " (literally " husband-lovers," " child-lovers," two of the compounds from *phileō* noticed in a former Talk [1]) ; to be sober-minded, chaste, workers at home, kind, being in subjection to their own husbands, that the word of God be not blasphemed." " Workers at home " is the R.V. alteration of the A.V. " keepers at home." It is a question of a single Greek letter. Some MSS. have *oikourous*, others *oikourgous*. The Revisers decided for the latter, but Bishop Bernard gives good reasons for preferring the A.V. Either way, it is certainly a home-loving woman that St. Paul is picturing. Note the grand motive for even such simple domestic virtues, " that the word of God "— *i.e.* here, as we have before seen, the Gospel, the Christian religion—" be not blasphemed." Christi-

---

[1] See p. 236.

anity was doing much for women, but was not intended to effect a premature social revolution.

(*d*) Young men have only one word of counsel applied to them, but it is introduced by that notable word " likewise," which helped us in a former matter. " Likewise exhort to be sober-minded," as if that really splendid word *sōphrōn*, which we examined before, summed up the whole of Pauline ethics. But again, example is better than precept ; and St. Paul goes on to exhort Titus to be " an ensample of good works " in his own person. What should a young man be ?—a Cretan might inquire. " Be a Titus ! " is the reply, in which the Apostle would include everything.

How definite and practical all this is !—suited, no doubt, to the circumstances of Crete, but, for the most part, equally suited to Christian England in the twentieth century !

Before going on, I must quote a quaint but felicitous remark of one of the writers in the Pulpit Commentary on the word " behaviour," which the A.V. has in the 3rd verse about the older women. " Behaviour," he says, " seems a commonplace word enough, and we assign it a subordinate place in religion. It is, however, a word as large as ' character.' It is a vocabulary in itself. It is not *do-haviour*, but *be-haviour*. What I may *do* may be accidental ; what I *am* is everything." Certainly that is the ethical teaching of the Pastoral Epistles.

II. To the Letter to Crete, also, we go for the duty of citizens. In iii. 1, 2, we read, " Put them in mind to be in subjection to rulers, to authorities, to be obedient, to be ready unto every good work, to speak evil of no man, not to be contentious, to be gentle, shewing all meekness toward all men." A comprehensive standard of conduct indeed, for a small community in the midst of a hostile population largely composed of men likely to provoke the members of the little community to the very faults and failures here warned against. For the Cretans were a turbulent people, and even among the Christians there were some that were "unruly" (i. 6, 10). The loyalty and obedience to authority here enjoined is implied also in I. ii. 1–3, where "kings and all in high place" are to be prayed for in the Christian services, as we have before seen[1]; and stress is laid upon it also in Rom. xiii. and 1 Pet. ii. But note especially the phrase "meekness toward all men," not merely toward fellow-believers ; and the reason for such meekness, "For *we also* were aforetime foolish," etc. Our recollection of our own faults and failures will help us to bear with others. And mark, this is enjoined as a *civic* duty ! What of our bitter controversies, political and ecclesiastical ? " To speak evil of no man "—is our conscience clear on that point ? " Not to be contentious "—can we truthfully say, " Well, I am not that " ?

III. In I. vi. we find special counsels both for the rich and for those who desire to be rich.

(*a*) In verse 17, those who are " rich in this present world " are warned against two perils : first, against being " high-minded," as Jeremiah had said in old times (Jer. ix. 23), and St. Paul in calling on Gentile Christians not to vaunt themselves over the Jews (Rom. xi. 20) ; secondly, against " setting their hope "

---

[1] See p. 171.

on so " uncertain " a thing as money, which has
wings and flies away (Prov. xxiii. 5) ; so Ps. lxii. 10,
" If riches increase, set not your heart upon them."
But they may " enjoy " the means God has so " richly " given them ; and this they will do if they " set
their hope " on Him.   Then in verse 18 four duties are
enjoined : (1) To " do good," *agathoergein*, a word
in which are embodied the " good works," *agatha
erga*, which we have before traced out [1] ; (2) to be
" rich " in *erga kala*, good works that are bright and
beautiful ; (3) to be " ready to distribute," to be
" open-handed " (as Liddon renders it), like God who
" giveth richly " ; (4) and " willing to communicate,"
to share our means with others, showing the sympathy that doubles the value of the gift—for the word
is connected with that notable word *koinōnia*, " fellowship " or " communion," implying not merely liberal
giving, but sympathy in all that is done.

And so doing, they will " lay up in store," *apothē-
saurizontas*, as " *treasure*," what our Lord calls " treasure in heaven, where neither moth nor rust corrupt,
and where thieves do not break through and steal "
—" a good foundation," in contrast with the uncertainty of money.   A " foundation " for what ?
For their spiritual life, the real life, " the life which
is life indeed," the life not merely of " this present
world," but of " the time to come."

(*b*) In verses 9, 10, St. Paul warns those who *aim at*
being rich ; not *thelontes* but *boulomenoi*, not merely
wishing but *purposing* to be rich.   All classes are
included : the errand boy at half-a-crown a week,
betting on a horse race in hope of doubling his in-

---

[1] See p. 255.

come, needs the warning as much as the millionaire in his vast speculations. Alike they " fall into temptation and a snare and many foolish and hurtful lusts "—how literally true it is !—" such as drown men in destruction and perdition." " Drown," *buthizein*, the word used in Luke v. 7, where the boats with the great draught of fishes are beginning to " sink." " Destruction," *olethros*, either final or corrective (as in 1 Cor. v. 5) ; " perdition," *apōleia*, final ruin of the soul. Yes, and St. Paul goes on to say that this is not merely a risk : it has actually happened. " Some . . . *have* pierced themselves through with many sorrows." " Sorrow " here is the strong word *odunē*, which St. Paul uses in Rom. ix. 2 of his " unceasing pain " (A.V. continual sorrow) at the rejection of Christ by the Jews. One thinks of that piteous picture in Prov. v. 11, 12, " And thou mourn at the last, when thy flesh and thy body are consumed, and say, How have I hated instruction, and my heart despised reproof ! "

Now what is the cause of all this ? Verse 10. Not money. St. Paul never calls money " the root of all evil." It is the love of money ! But I do not like the R.V. here, " a root of all kinds of evil." It is true that " *the* root " is strictly incorrect, as the Greek has no definite article ; true also that there are other roots of evil ; but we do not always require the indefinite article in English. Suppose I exclaim, " Love of money ! Root of all evils ! "—that is English, and is both intelligible and forcible. So I think St. Paul's rhetorical and emphatic phrase is, after all, better rendered by the A.V. An interesting parallel is cited by Alford from the historian Diogenes Laertius, who

said, " The love of money is the metropolis (or home)
of all evils."

And so we come to the end of our review of the
ethical teaching of our Epistles. But there is one
passage which has not happened to come under
consideration in all our Talks ; and as it comes in
I. vi., actually between the counsels to those who
aim at making money and the counsels to those who
have made money, this is a suitable niche for it.

St. Paul, having warned against the love of money,
exhorts Timothy to " flee " from it and other evils, to
" follow " righteousness, etc., etc., and to " fight " the
good fight of the faith. He reminds him of " the
good confession " he (Timothy) had " confessed before
many witnesses," at his baptism, at the " laying on of
hands," and very likely also in some crisis of persecution ; and how Christ Himself also had witnessed
" the good confession " (identical words) before
Pontius Pilate, " bearing witness to the truth "
(John xviii. 37), " testifying " to it, becoming the
First Martyr for it. For a " witness " is *martus*, and
" testimony " is *marturia*, and " witnesses " in the
verse before us is *marturēsantos*. And Timothy is to
keep " the commandment," the threefold charge of
renunciation, faith, and obedience, (*a*) unstained, (*b*)
irreproachable, until the Appearing, the Epiphany, of
Christ. *That*, after all, is for the Christian the True
Ethics.

47

THE LAST LETTER

WE are now approaching the end of our studies. We have glanced at the evidence afforded by the three Pastoral Letters that the writer of them was St. Paul, and concerning the time when, and the circumstances in which, they were respectively written. We have inquired what is known of the two men to whom they were written, and of the positions which they occupied at the time ; and we have noticed the instructions given to them. We have seen what the writer tells us of himself, as the converted persecutor, the servant of God, the Apostle of Christ, the trustee of the sacred " deposit." We have looked at the " faithful sayings " which he refers to and endorses, and at the fragments of hymns which he quotes. We have studied in detail the doctrinal teaching of the Letters, concerning the Gospel as the Faith and the Truth, concerning the Father, the Son, and the Holy Ghost, concerning the Holy Scriptures, the Grace of God, the Way of Salvation, the one Faith and the one Baptism. We have sought to understand the teaching of the Letters on the Church, its Worship and its Ministry, and the position in it of Women. We have inquired concerning the heterodox teachers of the period, and examined the Apostle's warnings against their doctrines and practices, and his instructions how to deal with them. We have traced out what the Letters say of Christian Ethics, of Good Works, of various virtues and graces, and of the duties of Church members, old and young, rich and poor, citizens and slaves.

These studies will have shown us St. Paul's objects in writing the Letter to Titus and the First to Timothy ; and both these Letters must by this time be familiar to us. But while we have frequently referred to the Second Epistle to Timothy, and drawn from it its teachings on the various matters above enumerated, we have not yet done it justice as a Letter quite different from the two others, written in circumstances of peculiar interest and solemnity ; and there are many passages in it which have not yet come under our notice. Upon it, therefore, we shall concentrate our attention in these last Talks.

I have already, in the very first Talk, stated briefly the reasons for believing that, after the imprisonment at Rome mentioned in Acts xxviii., St. Paul was released, and spent three or four years in further travels ; that he was then again arrested, again taken to Rome, and again imprisoned ; not this time dwelling under guard in his own " hired house," but confined, as a " malefactor " (II. ii. 9)—so it is commonly believed—in the Mamertine Prison. From his miserable and unhealthy dungeon he writes this Letter. He has been before his judge, but has been remanded (iv. 16, 17) ; he is expecting his further trial, and that the result will be his condemnation, and execution (iv. 6) ; and he writes to entreat Timothy to come to him, as he is almost alone (iv. 9–11), and winter is approaching (verse 21).

This is the ordinary account given by commentators. But there are obvious difficulties. The first three chapters, and iv. 1–8, are full of directions to Timothy touching his work at Ephesus, and the whole tone is that of a farewell letter to one whom St. Paul is not likely to see again. He does " long " to see Timothy (i. 4), but if he is " already being offered," and " the time of his departure is come " (iv. 6), it does not seem likely that the letter would reach Timothy, and he be able to leave Ephesus and to travel to Rome, within the time yet to elapse before the end. If condemnation and death seem so imminent, why does St. Paul write of Timothy coming " before winter " ?

On this account I am much impressed by a suggestion kindly sent to me since these Talks began to appear in a serial form. I received a letter from a Devonshire clergyman, Prebendary Buckingham, Rector of Doddiscombsleigh, sending me an unpublished MS. by the late Dr. G. A. Jacob, Headmaster of Christ's Hospital, on the question what was the special purpose of this Epistle. The MS. is dated 1878. Dr. Jacob suggests that the Epistle was written, as indicated above, as a farewell letter to a dear friend whom St. Paul was extremely unlikely ever to see again ; but that at iv. 8 the Apostle stopped, perhaps to add something presently, perhaps because there was no immediate chance of sending the letter. Then came his first trial, which resulted, not, as he expected, in his condemnation and sentence, but in a remand. Therefore there would be an interval, possibly a long one, and Timothy might be sent for. St. Paul then resumes the letter, at iv. 9, telling what had happened, and begging his dear friend to come quickly " before winter," and bring Mark with him.

Perhaps Tychicus is just starting (iv. 12), and can take the letter.

I wonder what Bishops Bernard and Moule, Dr. Plummer, and Sir W. M. Ramsay would say to this suggestion. I presume it had not occurred to them, as I have not found any reference to such a view in their writings, nor in any others that I have had an opportunity of consulting. Conybeare notices the difficulty, but thinks that St. Paul's apparent expectation of imminent death should not be taken too literally, and I suppose this may be the general view ; but Bishop Bernard does not seem to share it, as he emphasises the R.V. rendering of verse 6 (above) ; as also does Dr. Horton. But I confess that to me Dr. Jacob's suggestion adds greatly to the interest of the Letter. Even without it, this Epistle is the most touchingly personal, and the most strongly stamped with reality in the reader's eyes, of all the books of the Bible ; yet its personal character and impress of reality are certainly enhanced by this interpretation of the position. I do not wish, in the absence of further authority, to assume its truth in these concluding Talks ; but I cannot help being to some extent influenced by it.

Let us now just look at the plan and contents of the Epistle. Some of the remarks of the commentators are very interesting. Dr. Lock, in Hastings' Dictionary, views the Letter as presenting two pictures, (1) the ideal Christian minister, (2) the Christian minister in the face of death ; which works out very well. Dr. Plummer points out that " in the first chapter St. Paul looks back over the past ; in the second, he gives directions about the present ; in the third he looks forward into the future "; though he adds that " these divisions are not observed with rigidity throughout." He also remarks that, in stirring up Timothy to greater energy, St. Paul urges five considerations : the traditions of his family, the character of the Gospel, the teaching of the Apostle himself, the example of Onesiphorus, and the sure hope of salvation. Dr. Horton divides the Letter thus : (1) an exhortation to a true and fearless contention for the Gospel, i. 3–ii. 13 ; (2) the warfare against error and apostasy, ii. 14–iv. 8 ; (3) news, greetings, etc. Bishop Bernard and Dean Spence-Jones give more detailed analyses in their Introductions.

We may certainly group the contents of the Letter under two heads, viz. what St. Paul says (1) about Timothy, (2) about himself. Almost everything under the first head we have already studied. We have noticed Timothy's tears when the Apostle was torn from him (i. 4), his faith, and that of his mother and grandmother (5), the " gift " bestowed on him at his " confirmation " (?) or " ordination " (?) (6) ; the exhortations to " take a share in suffering " (8), to " guard the deposit " (13, 14), to act as a good soldier, athlete, husbandman, artisan (ii.), to cleave to and make full use of the Holy Scriptures (iii. 14–17) ; the oppositions and heresies he will meet with (ii. 14, 16–18, 23–26, iii. 1–9, 13).

As we read these passages, we feel that St. Paul, in view of his own approaching departure, is deeply solicitous touching the position and prospects of his dear young colleague. He sees the difficulties of Timothy's circumstances and the weaknesses of his character, and he feels how grievous will be the loss of his own counsels and words of cheer to such an one in such an environment. He warns him not to be downcast because the Church is not perfect (ii. 19, 20), or because persecution is sure to come (iii. 12). He encourages him by the " fact of Christ " (to use a modern phrase) (ii. 8) ; by a familiar " faithful saying " (ii. 11–13) ; by his own example (i. 11, 12, ii. 9, 10, iii. 10, 11, iv. 6–8). He winds up with a most solemn charge to " preach the word," to " be instant in season, out of season," to " reprove, rebuke, exhort," to be sober-minded and enduring, to do evangelistic work, to " fulfil his ministry " (iv. 1–5). We note the solemn yet hopeful " *buts* " of the Apostle : " But suffer hardship " (i. 8) ; " But shun profane babblings " (ii. 16) ; " But flee youthful lusts " (ii. 22) ; " But be gentle towards all " (ii. 24) ; " But know this " (iii. 1) ; " But thou didst follow " (iii. 10) ; " But abide thou " (iii. 14) ; " But be thou sober " (iv. 5). And we may be sure that those " night and day supplications " (i. 3) were specially fervent as he wrote all this, and would continue so to the end. It was a dark hour : not for the Apostle himself, but for his young colleague at Ephesus ; and his whole heart goes out in sympathy, in earnest pleading both with him and for him. If Dr. Jacob's suggestion is right, what a joy must that remand have been to St. Paul, giving him a chance, after all, of once more seeing his beloved " child " ; and how eagerly would he look for his arrival !

48

SEVENTEEN NAMES

IN the course of this short farewell Letter, St. Paul mentions twenty-three individuals by name. It has justly been remarked that such a fact is a striking evidence of the genuineness of the Epistle. What imitator in the next century would have ventured to risk detection by naming twenty-three persons? Six of these, Lois and Eunice, Phygelus and Hermogenes, Hymenæus and Philetus, have been noticed in previous Talks. The remaining seventeen are all named in the last chapter. Let us see what is said of them.

1. There are six who were, or had been, St. Paul's fellow-workers, and had been with him at Rome: Demas, Luke, Mark, Tychicus, Titus, Crescens. The first four of these are also mentioned in Col. iv. as having been with him there during his former imprisonment; and the first three are likewise named in the Epistle to Philemon, written at the same time.

(*a*) Luke is called in Col. iv. " the beloved physician." He is only *named* in that chapter, in Philemon, and here; but we all know and honour him as undoubtedly the writer of the Third Gospel and the Acts. Here the reference to him is particularly touching: ver. 11, " Only Luke is with me." The companion of St. Paul on so many journeys, his fellow-sufferer in so many trials, particularly the shipwreck at Melita, was with him to the last; not, so far as we can see, as a fellow-prisoner, but as a devoted friend who spent much of his time in visits to the dungeon, and most likely the actual writer of this Epistle at the Apostle's dictation.

(*b*) Demas, in both Colossians and Philemon, is coupled with Luke, as if both were equally faithful friends. How different now ! " Demas forsook me." Perhaps we have been wont to wrong Demas in a sense, as if " loving this present world " meant covetousness, or as if he were an apostate from the faith. Bunyan describes him as a son of Judas and a great-grandson of Gehazi, and pictures him standing by the silver mine at the hill Lucre to tempt pilgrims to their destruction. But more probably Demas feared martyrdom, and fled to Thessalonica, which some think may have been his home, as the name Demetrius (of which Demas is short) appears twice in an inscription giving a list of the city council—(but the name is a common one). Still, to " forsake " St. Paul at such a time !—a forsaking which evidently caused the Apostle deep pain—surely that alone is justification for the universal judgment of Christendom upon Demas. The remark that he " loved this present world," or rather " age," comes pathetically just after the reference to those who " love " (same verb, *agapan*) the Lord's " appearing." Bishop Bernard quotes Polycarp, who says of St. Paul, Ignatius, and other martyrs, that they " loved not this present world."

(*c*) Of Crescens we know nothing, not even whither he had gone ; for " Galatia" here may mean either the familiar province in Asia Minor, or Gaul (France), as the latter country was also called Galatia by Greek writers, and some MSS. have " Gallia " here. There is no reason to think that the departure of Crescens was in any sense a " forsaking " of St. Paul. More probably he was sent by him.

(*d*) Titus certainly is above suspicion in this respect.

We who have been studying these Epistles know him too well. He had been on the Adriatic coast before, at Nicopolis (Tit. iii. 12), or at least had been instructed to go there. He had probably come from there to Rome to report to the Apostle, and was now sent back to Dalmatia.

(*e*) Tychicus also was a tried and faithful fellow-worker; and it is possible that St. Paul was sending him to Ephesus (verse 12) to take Timothy's place while the latter hastened to Rome.[1]

(*f*) Mark was not nowwith St. Paul, though (as we have seen) he had been with him at Rome before. He was now somewhere on the route which Timothy would take to reach Rome, and Timothy was to " pick him up " (same Greek word as in Acts xx. 13) on the way and bring him on with him. Remembering St. Paul's former disappointment about Mark (Acts xii. 25, xiii. 5, 13, xv. 37–40), it is pleasant to see how differently he had turned out. " He is useful to me for ministering," says St. Paul (A.V. " profitable for the ministry "). *Diakonia* here is probably not " the ministry," but rather attendance on the Apostle personally; and " useful " is *euchrēstos*, the word applied to Onesimus in Phile. 11, and rendered " meet for use " in II. ii. 21, " meet for the Master's use." But whatever Mark was to do for St. Paul, we honour him, as we honour Luke, as the author of one of our precious four Gospels. It has been suggested that perhaps he knew Latin, while St. Paul did not ; and certainly his Gospel is peculiar for its Latin allusions.

2. Then there are three men who do not appear to

---

[1] " I sent," ἀπέστειλα, is the " epistolary aorist " ; so he may have been only just starting, and taking the letter.

have been with St. Paul at Rome, or to have had any connection with the Eternal City. These are (*a*) Carpus, who was at Troas, with whom the Apostle had left his cloak (verse 13), and whom we meet with nowhere else ; (*b*) Erastus, who is mentioned as " abiding " at Corinth (verse 20). He may possibly be the treasurer (A.V. chamberlain) of Corinth referred to in Rom. xvi. 23, or the Erastus mentioned along with Timothy in Acts xix. 22 ; or they may all three be the same person. (*c*) Trophimus, the Ephesian, who had been with St. Paul at Jerusalem, and whose supposed admission (though a Gentile) to the Temple had aroused the fury of the Jewish mob(Acts xx. 4, xxi. 29). He had again been with the Apostle lately, but had been left at Miletus ill (verse 20).

3. Among the " brethren " at Rome who, though not close friends or fellow-workers of St. Paul (for " only Luke " was with him), yet send greetings to Timothy through him, four are named : Eubulus, Pudens, Linus, Claudia (verse 21). Of Eubulus nothing is known. Pudens and Claudia have been supposed to be husband and wife, whose marriage is mentioned by the Roman writer Martial, Claudia being a British maiden ; and as an inscription discovered at Chichester records that a Pudens built a temple there when the British king was named Claudius, it has been further suggested that this was the Pudens named by St. Paul, and that his wife Claudia was the king's daughter. It is now agreed by the best commentators that these identifications are hopeless, and I only mention them because they are not infrequently referred to in popular books. For one thing, if Pudens and Claudia were husband

and wife, why are their names separated by the name of Linus ? This Linus is really the one who can be fairly identified. It is highly probable that he is the Linus whom Irenæus mentions as the first bishop of Rome.

4. There are two familiar names in verse 19, where St. Paul sends greetings to Ephesus. Prisca (or Priscilla) and Aquila are well known to us. They are also mentioned in Acts xviii. 2, 18, 26, Rom. xvi. 3, 4, 1 Cor. xvi. 19. In five out of the seven places, Priscilla's name is put first, which suggests that she was the more important of the two ; particularly in Acts xviii. 26 (R.V.), where they "expound" to Apollos "the way of God more perfectly." It is clear from Rom. xvi. 4 that on some occasion they had undergone great danger for St. Paul's sake.

5. Alexander the coppersmith (verse 14) we can leave over for the next Talk.

6. There remains one true friend who is mentioned twice in this Epistle, and whose name occurs nowhere else. Let us read the passages carefully :—

Chap. i. 16–18. The Lord grant mercy unto the house of Onesiphorus : for he oft refreshed me, and was not ashamed of my chain ; but when he was in Rome, he sought me diligently, and found me (the Lord grant unto him to find mercy of the Lord in that day) ; and in how many things he ministered at Ephesus, thou knowest very well.

Chap. iv. 19. Salute . . . the house of Onesiphorus.

Onesiphorus seems to have been a citizen of Ephesus, and is supposed to have been a church worker, on the strength of the word "ministered," which is the verb *diakonein.* His " ministry," whatever it may have been, was well known to Timothy.[1] But he had visited Rome, perhaps during both St. Paul's imprisonments. In the " two years " of the " hired house "—as I read the passage—he " oft refreshed " the Apostle, and was " not ashamed " of the " chain "—the " chain " specially mentioned in Acts xxviii. 20 and Eph. vi. 20 (same word, *alusis* ; " bonds " elsewhere is another word) ; which suggests that there were other friends of St. Paul who *were* " ashamed of the chain," and did not care to be identified with a man in custody, even though it was the Apostle himself. Then, when the second imprisonment ensued, Onesiphorus, on another visit to Rome, had to take trouble to find St. Paul. " He sought me diligently, and found me "—on which phrase I commented in a former Talk. [2]

Why, then, is no greeting sent to this good man, but only to his household ? Either he was on his travels and away from Ephesus, or he was dead. The question is regarded as important, because, if he was dead, then the words of i. 18 are the nearest approach to a prayer for a departed spirit to be found in the N.T. ; and, naturally, the answer to the question is apt to be governed by the writer's opinion on that disputed matter. I confess that I cannot help believing that were it not for the unwillingness to find any warrant in Scripture for a practice otherwise without authority, no one would ever have doubted that the verses mean that Onesiphorus was dead ; although it is quite true that they do not necessarily imply it. The words

---

[1] " Thou knowest " in verse 15 is οἶδας ; in verse 18 it is γινώσκεις. The former is ordinary knowledge, it might be " hearsay " ; the latter, personal and detailed knowledge.

[2] See p. 288.

themselves on which the advocates of the disputed practice rest their case, " The Lord grant unto him to find mercy of the Lord in that day," seem to me quite unlike anything St. Paul would say of a living man. Why " in that day " ? Why not now ? It is perhaps impertinent in me to offer what, so far as I know, is an original suggestion ; but I will venture. Suppose Onesiphorus was not a Christian at all, but a God-fearing man, perhaps an earnest inquirer, though not baptized ; although some of his slaves, perhaps of his family, had already been admitted to the Church.   In the present day there are many such men in India and other mission-fields who would act towards an imprisoned missionary whom they esteemed just as Onesiphorus did towards St. Paul. Suppose such an one died : would not the missionary be very likely to utter an aspiration about him, " Oh that he may have found mercy in Christ ! " ?—not knowing whether to count him as a real believer or not, but humbly leaving him to the mercy of God. For the words, after all, are not really a prayer, but a humble aspiration.

Expositors have from early days differed on this question. Alford quotes Theodoret and Chrysostom as thinking that Onesiphorus was actually with St. Paul at the time of writing. Among modern English writers, Conybeare, Dean Spence-Jones, Bishop Bernard, Dr. Milligan, Dr. Newport White, Bishop Hervey, Dr. Plummer, Dr. Horton, all consider that Onesiphorus was dead ; but some of these deny that the passage warrants prayers for the dead, while others regard the practice as, under certain conditions, right, whether this passage sanctions it or not.   Bishop Moule thinks that Onesiphorus was not dead, but " either then present at Rome or recently there " ; but on the further question he says, " Such prayers were undoubtedly used fairly early in the history of the Christian Church, certainly before A.D. 200, although for many generations they took only the simplest and vaguest forms. . . . Yet for even such guarded and reserved prayers, or aspirations, I for one cannot see *distinct* Scriptural warrant. . . . Let no *unloving* word be said of those Christians who feel their hearts constrained to follow their departed ones with prayer. On the other hand, let a caution, reverent and sacred, rest upon our spirits in the whole matter."

49
PAUL'S TRIAL
AND IMPRISONMENT

HAVING inquired concerning the many individuals whose names St. Paul mentions in this last chapter, let us revert to the Apostle himself. He has been before his judges, but instead of being condemned to death as he expected, he is remanded for a while. Let us see what he says of the trial :—

> Ver. 14. Alexander the coppersmith did me much evil : the Lord will render to him according to his works.
> 15. Of whom be thou ware also ; for he greatly withstood our words.

> Ver. 16.   At my first defence no one took my part,
> but all forsook me : may it not be laid to
> their account.
>
> 17.   But the Lord stood by me, and strengthened
> me ; that through me the message might
> be fully proclaimed, and that all the Gen-
> tiles might hear : and I was delivered out
> of the mouth of the lion.
>
> 18.   The Lord will deliver me from every evil
> work, and will save me unto His heavenly
> kingdom : to whom be the glory for ever
> and ever.   Amen.

Whether Alexander the coppersmith was the same Alexander as is named in I. i. 20 we cannot tell ; nor in what way he did St. Paul " much evil."   But as he is mentioned in close connection with the trial, we may fairly assume that, whether openly or secretly, he aimed at something, and in part successfully, that would prejudice the Apostle's case.   Bishop Bernard suggests that where St. Paul says " he greatly with-stood our words, the "words" may be some part of the " defence," which he contradicted.   St. Paul's solemn anticipation of God's judgment upon him implies the seriousness, and the malice, of what he did, whatever it was.   We have before noticed that the Apostle's words about him are not an imprecation, [1] as the A.V. implies.   " The Lord *will* render " (R.V.) is right, and is in fact a quotation, or rather adaptation, of Ps. lxii. 12 (as also in Rom. ii. 6).   But both A.V. and R.V. fail to show the striking parallelism between these words and those in verse 8.   " The crown of righteous-ness which the Lord . . . shall give," *apodōsei* ; " The Lord will render," *apodōsei*.

---

[1] See p. 103.

And now we will think of the Apostle standing as an accused " malefactor " (II. ii. 9) before the Roman judge ; perhaps in the Forum itself, where the Emperor Tiberius had set up a tribunal for important trials ; and perhaps before the reigning Emperor himself, the type of all wickedness, Nero.   There is a vast concourse of people : is not that implied in the phrase " all the Gentiles " ?   For this was no common prisoner.   At Cæsarea the Roman accusing counsel Tertullus had charged him with being " a mover of insurrections among all the Jews throughout the world, and a ringleader of the sect of the Nazarenes " ; and we remember the care taken of him by the governors there, and during the voyage.   Then he had been two years in custody at Rome, probably waiting for the Jewish accusers who never came ; and then released, very likely for lack of evidence. [1]   Now, after three or four years of further labours he has been again arrested ; and this time it may well be that the charge is much more serious, perhaps what we call anarchism.   For the worship of the Emperor had become the official religion of Rome ; and to the law requiring such worship the Christians were something more than " passive resisters."   As Bishop Moule says, [2] " It was very much as a nihilistic secret community that the Christian Church was actually viewed

---

[1] Farrar observes that the Jewish historian Josephus was at Rome in A.D. 64, and that his influence succeeded in releasing some Jewish prisoners whom Festus had sent for trial. He had been shipwrecked, like St. Paul, and some of the prisoners had been lost, possibly also some witnesses against them and documents of accusation.   Can, asks Farrar, the release of St. Paul be thus explained ?   (*St. Paul*, vol. ii., p. 512.)

[2] *Second Timothy*, p. 11.

by credulous and frightened pagan opinion in Rome.
. . . Allegiance to the Lord Jesus was taken to mean
high treason to the State." It is no wonder if the
trial of the chief leader of such a community excited
keen interest in the Imperial City.

Where is the counsel for the defence ? There is
none. " No one took my part " (A.V. stood with me),
oudeis moi paregeneto, literally " no one came on my
side." Every ordinary prisoner at Rome had his
patronus or *advocatus* ; St. Paul had none. No pro-
fessional man would ruin his own prospects by de-
fending an anarchist. More than that : " all forsook
me." If there were any friends who might at least
have come to cheer him by their presence, none dared
to appear that day. " Forsook " is the strong word
used also of Demas, the verb *egkataleipō*. It is the
word used by St. Matthew and St. Mark in translating
the Hebrew " *lama sabachthani*," " Why hast Thou
forsaken me ? " It signifies, says Dr. Plummer,
" leaving a person in a position, and especially in a
bad position ; leaving him in straits. It is almost the
exact counterpart of our colloquial phrase ' leave in
the lurch.'" And the tense shows that this " forsaking " was a definite act at a definite time. Perhaps
the retained counsel threw up his brief ; perhaps
friends came to the court, and then fled. What does
St. Paul say of them ? " May it not be laid to their
account ! "

But " the Lord stood by me and strengthened me."
Christ Himself is the Advocate, as His faithful servant
stands at the bar of justice. " Strengthened "—the
same word, *endunamoō*, which St. Paul had used in the
First Epistle (i. 12) of the Lord having " enabled " him

to become an apostle ; and in this Epistle also (ii. 1) when exhorting Timothy to " be strengthened " in the grace of Christ ; also in Rom. iv. 20, Eph. vi. 10, Phil. iv. 13 (" I can do all things in Him that strengtheneth me "). Strengthened—what for ? To make a skilful defence and win a verdict ? Not so ; but " that through me the message might be fully proclaimed," *to kērugma plērophorēthē*, that the proclamation (of God's love in Christ) might reach its fullest consummation. Yes, his " defence " is far more than a mere reply to personal accusations. The aged Apostle, worn out by the barbarities of the Mamertine Prison, has the opportunity of his life, and, " strengthened " by the Lord whose unseen Presence is beside him, he uses that opportunity to the uttermost. " All the Gentiles "—what a throng of distinguished Romans may be included in that simple phrase !— heard that day the Message of God to mankind ; all heard the Crucified and Exalted Jesus set forth as the one Saviour. It is an overwhelming thought ; the imagination fails to realise so tremendous a scene ; it must have been one of the great moments of history ; and what may not Eternity reveal to us of its results ?[1]

The immediate issue, at all events, was " deliverance out of the mouth of the lion," *ek stomatos leontos*, the exact phrase used of Daniel (vi. 20), and in Ps. xxii. 21, in the LXX Version. Does the lion mean Nero ? or Satan ? or the literal lions of the arena ? The absence of a definite article in the Greek is against either. Perhaps the phrase is only a figurative one,

---

[1] Farrar, in his pictures of St. Paul and Nero face to face, and of the Apostle in prison, surpasses himself in moving eloquence. (St. *Paul*, vol. ii., pp. 546–559.)

as Bishop Moule reminds us that we say " the jaws of death." Not that the Apostle was acquitted ; but the trial was adjourned ; and he could look forward to the possibility of his sending for Timothy to come to him from Ephesus. If Dr. Jacob's suggestion, before referred to, may be adopted, we may picture St. Paul calling Luke to him to finish the letter which Tychicus is waiting to start with for Ephesus, but which has been laid aside at the 8th verse. The farewells of the letter are not altered, but the postscript which begins at verse 9 is added : " Do thy diligence to come shortly." There may now yet be time for it to reach Timothy, and for him to hasten to Rome.

Let him be urged to make haste. " Before winter " if possible (verse 21), for travelling might be difficult then ; and meanwhile the dungeon is cold and miserable, so let him bring that cloak with him which was left—perhaps in fine and warm weather—with Carpus at Troas ; or perhaps it was at Troas that St. Paul was arrested, and the cloak was left behind in the scuffle. Some have thought that this " cloke " was the Roman toga, which St. Paul needed to wear in virtue of his Roman citizenship ; others that it was a case for the books ; others that it was an eucharistic vestment—for which idea, " perverse " as Bishop Bernard justly pronounces it, there is this excuse, that the same word, *phelonēs*, was actually used for a chasuble a few centuries later. But there is no reason to doubt that St. Paul wanted the cloak to keep him warm, as almost all commentators agree. I must here quote Farrar's striking sentences about it [1] :—" It was," he says, " one of those large

---

[1] *St. Paul*, vol. ii., p. 570.

sleeveless garments which we should call an overall,
Perhaps St. Paul had woven it himself of the black
goat's hair of his native province. And doubtless
it was an old companion, wetted many a time in the
water-torrents of Asia, whitened with the dust of
Roman roads, stained with the brine of shipwreck
when Euraquilo was driving the Adriatic into foam.
He may have slept in its warm shelter on the chill
Phrygian uplands, under the canopy of stars, or it
may have covered his bruised and trembling limbs
in the dungeon of Philippi. And now that the old
man sits shivering in some gloomy cell under the palace
or on the rocky floor of the Tullianum, and the winter
nights are coming on, he bethinks him of the old cloak
in the house of Carpus and asks Timothy to bring it
with him."

There is a touching parallel to this in later history.
When Tindale, the translator of the English Bible,
was in prison at Vilvorde in Belgium, in 1535, he
addressed a letter to the governor of the castle, asking
that his warm clothing, and his Hebrew Bible and
Grammar and Dictionary, might be given him. This
interesting fact is mentioned by the more recent
commentators ; but the letter was only discovered
within the last half century, and it was first published
in Demaus's Life of Tindale in 1871. That work
contains a facsimile of the actual letter, which was
written in Latin, and an English translation ; and it
seems to me worth while to print the translation here
almost in full. I take it from the revised edition of
the biography published by the R.T.S. in 1886. The
letter is addressed to the Marquis of Bergen-op-
Zoom, Governor of Vilvorde Castle :—

" I believe, right worshipful, that you are not ignorant of what has been determined concerning me ; therefore I entreat your lordship, and that by the Lord Jesus, that if I am to remain here during the winter, you will request the Procureur to be kind enough to send me, from my goods which he has in his possession, a warmer cap, for I suffer extremely from cold in the head, being afflicted with a perpetual catarrh, which is considerably increased in this cell. A warmer coat also, for that which I have is very thin ; also a piece of cloth to patch my leggings ; my overcoat is worn out ; my shirts are also worn out. . . . I wish also his permission to have a lamp in the evening, for it is wearisome to sit alone in the dark, But above all, I entreat and beseech your clemency to be urgent with the Procureur that he may kindly permit me to have my Hebrew Bible, Hebrew Grammar, and Hebrew Dictionary, that I may spend my time with that study. And in return, may you obtain your dearest wish, provided always it be consistent with the salvation of your soul. But if, before the end of the winter, a different decision be reached concerning me, I shall be patient, abiding the will of God to the glory of the grace of my Lord Jesus Christ, whose Spirit, I pray, may ever direct your heart. Amen.

W. TINDALE.

And as Tindale wished for his books, so did St. Paul. What were the books he wanted, and the parchments ? Who can say ? Perhaps the O.T. Scriptures ; possibly, with them, the documents showing his citizenship. " Books " is the regular word *biblia*, from which, through the Latin form, we derive our " bible." Of the parchments, *membranai*, Bishop Bernard says, " (It) is simply the Latin word *membranae* Græcised, and means the prepared skins of vellum, which gradually superseded papyrus for writing purposes. In the first century vellum would only be used for the more precious codices and documents, papyrus serving for ordinary books and letters, which sufficiently explains the *malista*" (especially). But how real and vivid it all is !

50
PAUL'S LAST DAYS AND CONTINUOUS INFLUENCE

BUT while St. Paul now feels that he may send for Timothy, he has no doubt of the ultimate issue of his deferred trial. He does not tell Luke to strike out the words of verse 6, " I am already being offered, and the time of my departure is come." There is only a little respite. " Offered," *spendomai*, means " poured out as a drink-offering." St. Paul had once before used the figure of the " drink-offering " or libation of wine under the Mosaic law to illustrate the " pouring out " of his life in the Lord's service. To the Philippians he wrote, during his former detention at Rome, " If I am offered, *spendomai*, . . ." But now, " I am already being offered." The word " departure," *analusis*, suggests another illustration. It is the original of our " analysis," and means, in Bishop Moule's words, " a setting free, a detachment, a separation of things or thoughts from one another." It is used in Homer's Odyssey of a ship loosing from her moorings. In Phil. i. 23 St. Paul had said he had " a desire to depart," to un-moor, *analusai*, and " be with Christ " : here, " the time of my un-mooring is come."

And note the " for " at the beginning of the verse. It marks the reason for the extreme earnestness of the appeal to Timothy just before. " I charge thee in the sight of God . . . preach the word . . . be instant . . . fulfil thy ministry "—" *for* " I can no longer help thee : I am being " poured out " ; the time of my " un-mooring " is come. Bishop Moule reminds us of God's charge to Joshua : " Moses My servant is dead ; *now therefore* arise, go over this Jordan." And the " I " of St. Paul—" For I "— the *egō*, is emphatic, following on the " thou " (*su*) of verse 5.

Now, how does St. Paul view the prospect of " out-pouring " and " un-mooring " ? At the very beginning of this Letter he has written those noble words, so often appropriated since by Christians in every age, " I know Him Whom I have believed, and I am per-suaded . . . ."—equally impressive whether he was thinking of himself or of the work committed to him, an alternative discussed in one of our early Talks.[1] Then, as he draws near the close of the Letter, he pens —or dictates—that equally familiar and truly wonder-ful retrospect, " I have fought the good fight, . . ." It is the arena that supplies him with the imagery : literally, " I have agonised the good agony," " con-tested the good contest," " striven the good strife." [2] " The *good* fight," *kalos*, a contest which the crowds round the arena would watch admiringly. " I have finished the course " : the " fight " might be a gladiatorial struggle, or a wrestling bout ; here it is definitely a race, and he has run it successfully. " I

See p. 52.   [2] See p. 285.

have kept the faith "; yes, indeed, and not only kept it with undaunted fidelity, but handed it down, as no other man has done, in those Epistles which have been among the Church's chief treasures in all ages. " Henceforth "—" the crown of righteousness "—" at that day "—" to me," yes, and " to all them that . . ."—wonderful words which we have dwelt upon before.[1]   And now, in what I have ventured to treat as a postscript, " The Lord will deliver me from every evil work, and will save me unto His heavenly Kingdom : to Whom be the glory for ever and ever. Amen." Is the Lord's Prayer in St. Paul's mind as he dictates these words ? Are they not an echo of its language ? [2]

And, ere long, the end came. Whether Timothy arrived in time we know not.   Probably the adjourned trial was resumed, the prisoner condemned, the sentence pronounced, very soon. And what was the sentence ? They could not crucify him, as they did his Lord. He was a Roman citizen, and exempt from that ignominious death, and from the horrible tortures sometimes inflicted. He could claim to be beheaded ; and beheaded he was, according to several of the Fathers. We think of Paul the aged summoned one day by his jailer to come forth out of the dungeon ; marched from the Mamertine Prison, across the Forum, past the Imperial Palace on the Palatine Hill, past the sites of the future Arch of Titus and the Coliseum ; out of the Ostian Gate, at the south end of

---

[1] See pp. 101, 266.

[2] Bishop Bernard, in a footnote, refers us to a book by Dr. Chase, now Bishop of Ely, *The Lord's Prayer in the Early Church*, in which are shown the parallelisms between the 17th and 18th verses and the language of the Lord's Prayer.

the city ; past the pyramidal mausoleum of Caius Cestus, upon which, as we look at it to-day, we remember that St. Paul's eyes may have rested ; past the site of the future English cemetery, where now lie the remains of Keats and Shelley ; out on the Ostian Road to the place of execution, now known as the *Tre Fontane*, the three fountains which the old legend affirms sprang up as the Apostle's head, falling from the block, struck the ground three times. Not far off, now stands the magnificent Basilica, *S. Paolo fuori le mura*, " St. Paul without the Walls," originally built by the Emperor Constantine, but owing its splendour to later times.

A few years earlier, during his former imprisonment, St. Paul had expressed himself, in writing to the Church at Philippi, as " in a strait betwixt two," between " living," which was " Christ," and " dying," which was " gain." He had " the desire to depart and be with Christ, for," said he, " it is very far better." How much more keenly would he feel this after these days of toil and suffering ! What a glorious day for him, the day of execution ! What a triumphant march out of the Ostian Gate to the " three springs " bubbling up from the wide-spreading Campagna ! Yea rather, what an entrance into the manifested Presence of the Lord Whose Name he had, for so many years and in so many lands, faithfully proclaimed !

But there is another side. In that very passage in the Philippian Epistle, he had added, to illustrate the " strait betwixt two," " yet to abide in the flesh is more needful for you." And this, too, he would now feel still more keenly. But I think he had learned a fresh lesson in the meantime. When he writes, in this last Letter, " I know Him Whom I have believed," etc., if " my deposit " may be taken as that which the Lord had committed *to him*,[1] the beautiful verse is an expression of his perfect confidence that the work entrusted to him should not suffer by his death. And in the very next chapter (ii. 9) we read, " I suffer hardship unto bonds, as a malefactor ; *but the word of God is not bound.*" The Glad Tidings of Redemption were not dependent for their promulgation on the life of any one man. The Apostles were all dead, or soon to die ; but the Lord Himself was now " the Living One," " alive for evermore " (Rev. i. 18). As the 102nd Psalm has it (as quoted in Heb. i. and there rendered in the A.V.), " *But Thou remainest.*" *That* was now St. Paul's comfort, as he thought of the Churches bereft of his presence.

Truly he needed the comfort. " Looked at with human eyes," says Dr. Plummer, " the Apostle's life at that moment was a failure, a tragic and dismal failure." As regards himself : " From the world's point of view he had given up much, and gained little beyond trouble and disgrace. He had given up a distinguished position in the Jewish Church, in order to become the best hated man among that people of passionate hatreds. While his efforts on behalf of the Gentiles had ended for a third time in confinement in a Gentile prison, from which, as he saw clearly, nothing but death was likely to release him." As regards his work : it is true that, in Farrar's picturesque

---

[1] See p. 52.

language,[1] " during the short space of twenty years he had proclaimed Christ crucified to the simple Pagans of Lystra, the fickle fanatics of Galatia, the dreamy mystics of Phrygia, the vigorous colonists of Macedonia, the superficial dilettanti of Athens, the sensual and self-satisfied traders of Corinth, the semi-barbarous natives of Dalmatia, the ill-reputed islanders of Crete, the slaves and soldiers and seething multitudes of Rome." But, as Dr. Plummer continues, " He had preached and argued, had entreated and rebuked, . . . and what had been the outcome of it all ? The few Churches which he had founded were but as handfuls in the cities in which he had established them ; and there were countless cities in which he had established nothing. Even the few Churches which he had succeeded in founding had in most cases soon fallen away from their first faith and enthusiasm. . . . As the results of a life of intense energy and self-devotion, all these things had the appearance of total failure."

It was indeed a dark day. We can now hardly realise how dark. Christianity is to-day one of the great powers of the world. It was then the creed of a minute and utterly despised minority. How easy, apparently, for the Imperial Power of Rome simply to wipe it out, simply to exterminate, once for all, those hateful anarchists ! And Rome did set itself to the task, over and over again, in the next two centuries and a half. How was it that Rome failed, and the Church survived ? For the same reason that

---

[1] *St. Paul*, vol. ii., p. 541. It will be noticed that Ramsay's " South Galatian theory " had not been set forth when Farrar wrote.

the bush at Horeb " burned with fire and was not consumed "—because the Lord was in it.

Eighteen centuries and a half have passed away since St. Paul laid his head on the block. What is his reputation now ? If we take only the standpoint of the world, and view him with the eyes of the secular historian, he is seen to be one of the greatest men in the annals of the race. I suppose that more has been written about him than about any other of the characters of ancient and modern history. There were many voyages of distinguished men across the Mediterranean in the first century A.D. ; but what voyage can be compared in interest with the one detailed in Acts xxvii., or has been studied with equal minuteness ? Whose writings, in any age of the world, have absorbed the attention of scholars and commentators like the writings of St. Paul ? Can Dante, or Milton, or even Shakespeare, be compared with him in this respect ? As for translations, his Letters must no doubt take a second place after the Four Gospels in regard to the number of languages in which versions of them have been made ; yet who in St. Paul's day could have conceived—how could he himself have conceived—that they would be eagerly read to-day in some two hundred and fifty tongues in all parts of the world ?

And turning from the man himself to the results of his labours, think of Christendom to-day. With all its imperfections and failures, it is the greatest fact in the visible world. And if we could rise above the things of time and sense, and see the mighty invisible world, what should we say of the multitudes that lived and died in the faith of Christ, and who now experience the fulness of joy in His immediate presence ? Now of all the instruments used of God to accomplish these triumphs of Divine Grace, St. Paul, indisputably, stands first.

In these plain and unpretending Talks we have just taken the three latest of the Letters written by him which have come down to us. They are stamped with the endorsement of the whole Church of Christ, guided by the Spirit of God, as parts of Holy Scripture, of God's inspired revelation to mankind. Cursorily and inadequately we have studied them ; yet has it not been worth while ?

INDEX OF TOPICS

Baptism, 150
Bishops, 2, 10, 56, 176–189

Christ, Doctrine of, 87, 91
    Second Advent of, 98
Church, The, 2, 157–216
Crete, The Environment, 24

Deacons, 196

Ephesus, The Environment, 19
Ethical Teachings, 254–289

Faith, 71, 146
Faithful Sayings, 54

God the Father, Doctrine of, 79
Grace of God, The, 125
Graces, Christian : Love and
        Purity, 269
    Passive, 275
    Active, 282

Heterodox Teachers, 217–241
    Dealing with, 242–254
Holy Scriptures, The, 112–125
Holy Spirit, The, 105
Hymn Fragments, 60

Life and Death, 144

Ministry, The, of the Church, 176–201

Paul, St., His Later Journeys, 1
    As a Servant, 34
    As an Apostle, 41
    His Retrospect, 47
    His Deposit, 51
    His Last Letter, 304
    His Imprisonment and Death, 317, 325
Presbyters, 176–195

Salvation, Doctrine of, 131–149
Slaves, Christian, 289

Timothy, Who was ? 12
    Counsels to, 27
Titus, Who was ? 6
Truth, The, 73

Widows, Care and Service of, 210
Women in the Church, 202
Works, Good, 254
Worship of the Church, 169

INDEX TO BIBLICAL NAMES

Abraham, 155, 167
Adam, 206
Agabus, 109
Ahimaaz, 69
Alexander, 103, 242, 318
Amos, 100
Ananias (Damascus), 152, 154
Ananias and Sapphira, 243, 293
Anna, 212
Apollos, 201, 260, 288
Artemas, 11, 180

Barnabas, 6, 13, 14, 46

Caesar (Nero), 6, 102, 171, 319, 321
Caiaphas, 80
Carpus, 313, 322
Claudia, 313
Crescens, 310

Daniel, 32, 80, 321
Darius, 80
David, 69, 79, 95, 111
Demas, 271, 310, 311
Diana (Artemis), 20, 80

Elijah, 108
Elisabeth, 288
Elymas, 243
Erastus, 17, 313
Esau, 225
Eubulus, 313
Eunice, 12, 310
Eve, 206

Ezekiel, 100, 111

Festus, 267
Felix, 273, 278

Hermogenes, 310
Hezekiah, 80, 145
Hymenæus, 220, 232, 242, 310

Isaiah, 69, 100, 108, 111, 132

James, St., 60, 127, 174, 180, 195, 212, 254, 273, 281
Jeremiah, 100, 300
Job, 281
Joel, 100
John Baptist, 288
John, St., 87, 95, 123, 127, 270
Judas Barsabas, 109
Jude, St., 86, 127, 171

Korah, 165

Linus, 313
Lois, 12, 310
Luke, St., 15, 18, 22, 67, 75, 127, 262, 310, 322

Mark, St., 14, 38, 104, 127, 168, 197, 310, 312, 320
Mary, 86, 126, 288
Moses, 96, 111, 141, 165–6, 240

Nahum, 69, 167
Nicodemus, 45, 153
Noah, 288

Obadiah, 100
Onesimus, 168, 292, 312
Onesiphorus, 38, 197, 288,
    314–17

Paul, St., *passim*
Peter, St., 80, 87, 100, 108,
    126–7, 136, 142, 151,
    153, 155, 189, 191, 204–5,
    212, 231, 249, 277, 292
Phebe, 200
Philemon, 292
Philetus, 220, 232, 310
Philip the Evangelist, 68,
    109, 201

Phygelus, 310
Pilate, Pontius, 72, 95
Priscilla, 201, 314
Pudens, 313

Rabshakeh, 80

Silas, 14, 15, 16, 17, 43, 109
Simon Magus, 29
Stephen, St., 141, 154

Tertullus, 278, 319
Timothy, *passim*
Titus, *passim*
Trophimus, 18, 313
Tychicus, 11, 180, 307, 310,
    312, 322

Zenas, 260, 288
Zephaniah, 100

INDEX OF WRITERS, ETC.

Alford, Dean, 30, 89, 152, 239, 253, 268, 274, 276, 292, 302, 316
Anselm, 143
Aristotle, 278
Arnold, M., 276, 278

Bartlet, V., 2
Bengel, 50, 145, 252
Bernard, Bp., 64, 73, 83, 102, 107, 120, 143, 161, 172, 185, 204, 214, 226, 231–2, 236, 239, 243, 251, 253, 267, 276, 278–9, 280, 283–4–5–7, 297–8, 307–8, 311, 316, 318, 322, 324–7
Beza, 298
Bonar, H., 128
Buckingham, Preb., 306
Bunyan, John, 49, 53, 129, 230, 238, 240, 311

Chadwick, Dr., 30, 42
Chalmers, T., 270
Chase, Bp., 327
Chrysostom, 117, 143, 172, 194, 203, 281, 287, 291, 294, 316
Cicero, 152, 268, 271
Clement of Alexandria, 111, 177
Clement of Rome, 5, 111, 174
Conybeare, 25, 316
Coverdale, 117, 212
Cowper, 77
Cranmer, 59

Deissmann, Prof., 91, 93, 138, 140, 143, 158, 270
Demaus, 323
Denney, Prof., 135

Dickens, C., 230
Didachē, 181
Ditchfield, Bp. Watts, 186
Diogenes Laertius, 302
Doddridge, 131
Duchesne, 176

Ellicott, Bp., 65, 194, 253, 268, 281
Ensor, G., 9
Epictetus, 295
Epimenides, 24, 26
Euripides, 285
Eusebius, 219

Farrar, F. W., 22, 184, 319, 321, 330
Forsyth, Principal, 135
French, Bp., 99

Gore, Bp., 139
Goudge, Dr., 269, 274, 276
Gwatkin, Prof., 197

Handel, 62, 69
Harnack, Prof., 176
Harris, Prof. Rendel, 26
Hastings, Dr., 95, 197, 200,
Havergal, F. R., 104
Headlam, Dr., 176
Heraclitus, 22
Hervey, Bp. Lord A., 89, 104, 152, 194, 253, 260, 276, 316
Hogarth, 240
Homer, 24, 127, 325
Hooker, 160
Hort, Dr., 41, 90, 128, 133, 157–8–9, 161, 194, 198
Horton, Dr., 64, 89, 194, 227, 229, 240, 253, 276, 295, 297, 307–8, 316

Ignatius, 280, 311
Irenæus, 111, 177, 239, 314

Jackson, Bp., 143, 206, 209
Jacob, Dr. G. A., 306, 308, 322
Jerome, 239
Josephus, 82, 152, 319
Justin Martyr, 111, 175
Juvenal, 21, 220

Lang, Abp., 39
Lees, H. C., 96
Liddon, Canon, 4, 30, 56, 173, 178, 194, 204, 212, 214, 226, 229, 243, 272–3, 276, 301
Lightfoot, Bp., 181, 201
Lock, Dr., 307
Lowell, 265
Luther, 30, 53, 117

Macartney, H. B., 259
Maclean, N., 183
McClure, E., 241
Madras, Bp. of (Whitehead), 176
Marcion, 1
Martial, 313
Mendelssohn, 69
Milligan, Dr., 316
Moberly, R. C., 134
Moody, D. L., 50
Moule, Bp. H. C. G., 23, 26, 28, 32, 78, 104, 123, 139, 145, 164, 169, 209, 253, 278, 284–285, 307, 316, 319, 322, 325–6

Origen, 117, 172
Oxford Dictionary, 145

Philo, 82
Pliny, 60
Plummer, Dr., 8, 26, 48, 73, 83, 89, 99, 127, 137, 163, 177, 185, 194–5, 203,
216, 219, 244, 253, 267, 281, 284–5, 290, 294, 307, 316, 320, 329, 330
Plumptre, Dean, 69
Polycarp, 172, 311
Pope, 255
Pulpit Commentary, 299 (see also Hervey)
Pusey, Dr., 276

Ramsay, Prof. Sir W. M., 2, 6, 16, 21, 133, 171, 177, 202, 207, 220, 225, 262, 287, 291, 307, 330

Sanday, Prof., 158, 176
Seneca, 292
Sheppard, W. J. L., 15
Simpson, Canon, 134
Sophocles, 212
Spence-Jones, Dean, 7, 162, 164, 212, 276, 298, 308
Spurgeon, C. H., 210
Stock, E., 35, 99

Tennyson, A., 265
Tertullian, 172, 177, 284
Theodoret, 316
Thomas, Dr. Griffith, 78
Tindale, W., 25, 117, 233, 258, 293, 323
Trench, Abp., 106, 205, 236, 268, 270–1, 275, 278, 281
Turner, C. H., 176
Twentieth Cent. N.T., 238

Wace, Dean, 116
Warington, G., 124
Westcott, Bp., 111, 134
Weymouth, Dr., 214
White, Dr. Newport, 50, 89, 145, 168, 204, 253, 255, 284, 316
Whytehead, T., 100
Wiclif, 10, 117, 204, 240
Wordsworth, Bp. C., 117
Wordsworth, Bp. J., 180, 201, 216

INDEX OF GREEK WORDS

ἀγαθοεργέω, 301
ἀγαθός, 255, 301
ἀγαπάω, 271, 311
ἀγάπη, 270, 279, 280
ἀγαπητός, 271
ἄγγελος, 63
ἅγιος, 81, 115
ἁγνεία, 274
ἁγνός, 274
ἀγοράζω, 141
ἀγών, 285
ἀγωνία, 285
ἀγωνίζομαι, 285
ἀδόκιμος, 234
ἀεί, 24
ἀθανασία, 62, 82
ἀθλέω, 284
αἰδώς, 204
αἵρεσις, 244
αἱρετικός, 244
αἰών, 81
αἰώνιος, 81
ἀκρατής, 238
ἀλαζών, 238
ἀλήθεια, 76
ἄλλος, 218
ἅλυσις, 315
ἀμελέω, 32
ἀνακαίνωσις, 106
ἀναλαμβάνω, 63, 64
ἀναλογία, 109
ἀνάλυσις, 325
ἀναλύω, 325
ἀνανήφω, 251
ἀναστοφή, 31
ἀνδρεία, 281
ἀνεξίκακος, 251
ἀνήρ, 174, 213
ἄνθρωπος, 62, 94, 174
ἀντί, 142
ἀντιλέγω, 293
ἀντίλυτρον, 142
ἀνυπόκριτος, 272
ἀόρατος, 82

απαίδευτος, 225
ἀπέραντος, 224
ἀπιστέω, 61
ἀπιστία, 148
ἄπιστος, 211
ἀποδίδωμι, 318
ἀποθησαυρίζω, 301
ἀπολύτρωσις, 141
ἀποστέλλω, 41, 312
ἀπόστολος, 41
ἀπρόσιτος, 62, 82
ἀποτόμως, 244
ἀπώλεια, 302
ἀργός, 25, 215
ἀρνέομαι, 61
ἀσέβεια, 262
ἀσεβής, 262
αὐτάρκεια, 232
αὐτάρκης, 232
ἄφθαρτος, 82
ἀφιλάγαθος, 236–7
ἀφιλάργυρος, 237
ἀχάριστος, 238
ἀψευδής, 81

βαθμός, 199
βασιλεύς, 62
βδελυκτός, 234
βέβηλος, 225
βιβλίον, 324
βλάσφημος, 238
βούλομαι, 301
βρέφος, 112
βρῶμα, 229
βυθίζω, 302

γάγγραινα, 223
γαστήρ, 25
γενεαλογία, 224
γένεσις, 15
γινώσκω, 165, 315
γνῶσις, 23, 76, 219
γόης, 239
γράμμα, 114
γραύς, 224

γραφή, 113, 116, 118
γραώδης, 224
γυμνάζω, 57, 246
γυμνασία, 246
γυμνός, 246
γυναικάριον, 239
γυνή, 213, 239

δέησις, 172
δεῖ, 184, 233
δειλία, 30
διά, 15, 208
διάβολος, 200, 238, 297
διακονία, 35–40, 197–201, 312
διακονέω, 35–40, 197–201, 315
διάκονος, 35–40, 197–201, 245
διδακτικός, 45, 186, 251
διδασκαλία, 10, 45, 73
διδάσκαλος, 45
διδάσκω, 45, 73
διδαχή, 73, 74
δίκαιος, 139, 264
δικαιοσύνη, 139, 264
δικαιόω, 63, 139, 264
διώκω, 30
δόξα, 63, 218
δουλεία, 30, 36
δοῦλος, 35–40, 250, 297
δουλόω, 297
δύναμαι, 62, 120
δύναμις, 51, 83, 129
δυνάστης, 62, 82

ἐγκαταλείπω, 320
ἐγκράτεια, 238
ἐγκρατής, 187, 238, 296
ἑδραίωμα, 161
ἔθνος, 63
ἔκγονος, 211
ἐκεῖνος, 61, 252
ἐκκλησία, 157–160
ἐνοικέω, 106

ἐνδυναμόω, 51, 129, 320
ἔντευξις, 172
ἐξαγοράζω, 141
ἔξωθεν, 187
ἐπαγγέλλω, 225
ἐπακολουθέω, 214
ἐπίγνωσις, 76
ἐπιείκεια, 278
ἐπιεικής, 188, 278
ἐπιμέλομαι, 189
ἐπίσκοπος, 178–189, 197
ἐπισκοπή, 56
ἐπιφαίνω, 97
ἐπιφάνεια, 97–99, 145
ἔργον, 56, 184, 189, 194, 214, 215, 301
ἔρως, 270
ἔσχατος, 235
ἔσωθεν, 187
ἑτεροδιδασκαλέω, 45, 218
ἕτερος, 218
εὐαγγελίζω, 45, 67–69
εὐαγγέλιον, 45, 67–69
εὐαγγελιστής, 68
εὐάρεστος, 293
εὐδοκέω, 293
εὐδοκία, 293
εὐλογητός, 83
εὐσέβεια, 3, 57, 232, 262
εὐσεβέω, 262
εὐσεβής, 262
εὐχαριστία, 126, 172
εὔχρηστος, 168, 312
ἔχω, 62

ζάω, 102
ζήτησις, 224
ζωγρέω, 252

ἡδονή, 236
ἡμέρα, 235
ἤπιος, 279
ἤρεμος, 277
ἡσυχάζω, 277

ἡσυχία, 205, 265, 277
ἡσύχιος, 277

θάνατος, 82
θέλημα, 252
θέλω, 301
θεμέλιος, 164
Θεός, 65, 94, 165, 229
θεόπνευστος, 111, 117
θεοσέβεια, 262
θηρίον, 24

ἴδιος, 104
ἱερεύς, 115, 179, 297
ἱερόν, 115
ἱεροπρεπής, 297
ἱερός, 115, 297
ἱερουργέω. 179
Ἰησοῦς, 94
ἵνα, 258, 260
ἴσθι, 32
καθαρός, 274
καινός, 106
καιρός, 104, 235
κακός, 24
κακοῦργος, 287
καλέω, 157
καλοδιδάσκαλος, 45, 298
καλός, 3, 56, 173, 184, 194, 214, 255, 261, 283, 298, 301, 326
καταλέγω, 213
καταργέω, 145
κελεύω, 228
κενοφωνία, 225
κήρυγμα, 44, 321
κῆρυξ, 43
κηρύσσω, 43, 63
κοινωνία, 301
κοπιάω, 191, 286
κοσμέω, 204
κόσμιος, 188, 204
κόσμος, 63, 204
κράτος, 238
Κρής, 24
κρίνω, 102
κτίσμα, 229

κυριακός, 158
κυριεύω, 62
κύριος, 62, 165
κωλύω, 228

λαός, 257
λατρεία, 40
λατρεύω, 36–39
λέων, 321
λόγιον, 75
λογομαχία, 225
λόγος, 54, 151, 171
λουτρόν, 151
λύτρον, 142
λυτρόω, 141
λύτρωσις, 141
λυτρωτής, 141

μακάριος, 62, 83, 104
μακροθυμία, 279
μαρτυρέω, 303
μαρτυρία, 303
μάρτυς, 303
ματαιολογία, 225
μελετάω, 32
μεμβράνα, 324
μένω, 61
μεσίτης, 94, 96
μετά, 315
μόνος, 62, 82
μορφή, 239
μόρφωσις, 239
μῦθος, 224

νεκρός, 102
νέος, 106
νεόφυτος, 187
νεώκορος, 21
νεώτερος, 215
νήπιος, 120
νήφω, 267, 296
νομοδιδάσκαλος, 45
νόσος, 230
νοσφίζω, 293

ὀδύνη, 302
οἰκέω, 62
οἰκία, 161

οἰκοδομία, 162
οἰκονομία, 162
οἰκονόμος, 161
οἶκος, 161
οἰκουργός, 298
ὄλεθρος, 302
ὁράω, 62, 63, 315
ὀρθοτομέω, 287
ὅς, 65
ὀστράκινος, 168

παιδεία, 120
παιδεύω, 243, 258
παῖς, 120, 258
παλινγενεσία, 152
παραγίνομαι, 320
παραδίδωμι, 243
παραθήκη, 51
παράκλησις, 175
παρουσία, 99
πᾶς, 143, 229
περίεργος, 215
περιίστημι, 244
περιούσιος, 257
περιποίησις, 258
πιστεύω, 63, 148, 149
πίστις, 71, 109, 146, 149, 280
πιστός, 54, 61, 147, 149, 211
πλεονεξία, 236
πληροφορέω, 44, 321
πνεῦμα, 30, 63
πραότης, 277
πρεσβύτερος, 178, 190
πρόγονος, 211
πρόδηλος, 194
προκόπτω, 240
πρόκριμα, 193
προπετής, 238
προσέρχομαι, 231
προσευχή, 172

πρόσκλισις, 193
ῥῆμα, 151
σάρξ, 63
σέβομαι, 262
σεμνός, 188, 200, 275
σεμνότης, 275
σοφίζω, 120
σπαταλάω, 212
σπένδω, 325
σπουδάζω, 288
στερεός, 164
στέφανος, 266
στόμα, 321
στρατεία, 283
στρατεύομαι, 283
στρατευόμενος, 283
στρατιώτης, 283
στρατολογέω, 283
συμβασιλεύω, 61
σύν, 3, 284
συναποθνήσκω, 61
συνείδησις, 273
συνζάω, 61
συνκακοπαθέω, 284
σωτήρ, 3
σωτηρία, 132, 133, 263
σωτήριος, 132
σωφρονέω, 267
σωφρονίζω, 266
σωφρονισμός, 266
σωφροσύνη, 204, 209, 266-8
σώφρων, 188, 266, 299
σωφρόνως, 266

τεκνογονία, 207
τέκνον, 7
τύπος, 11
τυφός, 230
τυφόω, 230
ὑγιαίνω, 74

ὑγιής, 74
ὑπέρ, 142-3
ὑπερήφανος, 49, 238
ὑπεροχή, 49, 171
ὑπερπλεονάζω, 49
ὑπόκρισις, 227
ὑπομένω, 61, 280
ὑπομονή, 280-282
ὕστερος, 235

φανερόω, 63, 99, 145
φελόνης, 322
φιλάγαθος, 187, 237
φιλαδελφία, 236
φίλανδρος, 237
φιλανθρωπία, 58, 137, 237
φιλαργυρία, 236-7
φιλάργυρος, 236-7
φίλαυτος, 236-7
φιλέω, 236, 271, 298
φιλήδονος, 236-7
φιλόθεος, 237, 271
φιλόξενος, 186, 237
φιλοσοφία, 236
φιλότεκνος, 237
φλύαρος, 215
φῶς, 62
φωτίζω, 145

χαλεπός, 235
χαρίς, 32, 125-131, 238
χάρισμα, 32, 110, 181
χρηστός, 137
χρηστότης, 137
Χριστός, 94
χρόνος, 81

ψευδολόγος, 227
ψεύστης, 24

ὡσαύτος, 200

BIBLIOGRAPHY

Adeney, W.F., ed., *The Century Bible*. (London: Caxton Publishing Co.). The volume on the Pastoral Epistles by Dr. Horton gives valuable suggestions.

Alford, Henry, *The Greek Testament*. (Chicago: Moody Press). Should by no means be regarded as superseded.

Chadwick, W. Edward. *Pastoral Teaching of Paul*. (Grand Rapids: Kregel Publications). I have derived important suggestions from this work.

Conybeare, W.J. and Howson, J.S., *The Life and Epistles of St. Paul*. (Grand Rapids: Wm. B. Eerdmans Publishing Co.). Well worth consulting.

Cook, F.C., *The Bible Commentary*. (Grand Rapids: Baker Book House). Has an able introduction to the Epistles by Dean Wace. The notes by Bishop Jackson are rather thin.

Deissmann, G. Adolph, *Light from the Ancient East*. (Grand Rapids: Baker Book House).

———, *Paul: A Study in Social and Religious History*. (New York: Harper and Row).

Ellicott, Charles J., *Ellicott's Commentary on the Whole Bible*. (Grand Rapids: Zondervan Publishing House). Dean Spence - Jones's commentary in this set is excellent in practical application.

Farrar, F.W., *Life of St. Paul*.

Goudge, H.L., *Pastoral Teaching of St. Paul*.

Hastings, James, ed., *Dictionary of the Bible*. (Edinburgh: T. & T. Clark). The articles on Timothy and Titus are particularly interesting.

Hort, Fenton J.A., *Christian Ecclesia*. (London: Macmillan Co.).

Liddon, Henry P., *Explanatory Analysis of St. Paul's First Epistle to Timothy.* Has given me great help. (London: Longmans, Green & Co.).

Moule, H.C.G., *Studies in 2 Timothy.* (Grand Rapids: Kregel Publications). Is delightful in its spiritual character.

Nicoll, Wm. R., ed., *The Expositor's Greek Testament.* (Grand Rapids: Wm. B. Eerdmans Publishing Co.). Newton White's commentary is frequently very suggestive.

Plummer, Alfred, *The Expositor's Bible.* (New York: A.C. Armstrong & Son). In every way excellent. It is not a commentary but a series of chapters.

Ramsay, Wm. M., *A Historical Commentary on St. Paul's Epistle to the Galatians.* (Grand Rapids: Baker Book House). Are as important as any of his highly-esteemed writings. Formerly appeared as articles in *The Expositor* (1909-11).

Smith, William, *Smith's Dictionary of the Bible.* (Grand Rapids: Baker Book House). Nothing that Dean Plumptre writes in this volume is ever out-of-date.

Spence, H.D. and Exell, Joseph S., eds., *The Pulpit Commentary.* A very full and excellent commentary, by the late Lord Arthur Hervey, appears in this set.

Stewart, J.J. ed., *Cambridge Greek Testament for Schools and Colleges.* (Cambridge: University Press). The Pastoral Epistles by J.H. Bernard are full of instructive notes.

Trench, Richard C., *Synonyms of the New Testament* (Grand Rapids: Wm. B. Eerdmans Publishing Co.).

Westcott, Brooke F., *An Introduction to the Study of the Gospels.* (London: Macmillan Co.).